D0604741

ley 7—

Horton Foote

Volume II: Collected Plays

Horton Foote

Volume II: Collected Plays

Contemporary Playwrights Series

SK
A Smith and Kraus Book

A Smith and Kraus Book
Published by Smith and Kraus, Inc.
One Main Street, PO Box 127, Lyme, NH 03768

ISBN 1-56865-454-5

Contents

Introduction
by Robert Ellermann
page vi

The Trip to Bountiful
page 1

The Chase
page 61

The Traveling Lady
page 113

The Roads to Home
page 173

Introduction

As an actor and director, it has taken nearly twenty years for me to grasp the creative nature and structure of Horton Foote's beautiful plays. I am a slow study but I hope in this case the time was essential because of the depth of the material. Horton Foote is an artist of the rarest form of theatre. He is a dramatic poet: each play *is* the experience which formed it.

I discovered these plays while looking for information on America's great tragic actor, Kim Stanley. At the time, Kim Stanley was already a legend within the acting community but she had retired from the theatre and very few examples of her art existed on film. I had seen her genius only once, as Masha, in a video recording of Lee Strasberg's profoundly humane production of *The Three Sisters*. I had to know more. A friend mentioned that he had seen Kim Stanley in a play of Horton Foote's on television in the late 1950s. The play was *The Traveling Lady*. To the library I went.

Growing up in Texas, I was bombarded with the comic strip mentality of the Lone Star State. In elementary school we laughed at our state's silliness when our teacher entertained us with selections from a popular satirical book entitled *Texas Brags*. When I first read Horton Foote's plays, my university acting class was devoted to scene study based on the commercial cliches of Preston Jones' *A Texas Trilogy*. Imagine my joy upon experiencing the truth of Horton Foote's dramatic world. His Texas was not the marketable image found in movies, television and popular fiction. Horton Foote created the soul of his home on a piece of paper.

I was also thrilled to find out that the forgotten legacy of the First Studio of the Moscow Art Theatre, where Konstantin Stanislavsky and Leopold Sulerzhitsky practiced the spiritual aesthetic of the original Stanislavsky "system," formed the basis of Horton Foote's theatrical training. As a young actor in Depression era New York, Horton Foote had studied acting with two former members of the First Studio: Andrius Jilinsky and Vera Soloviova. I came to New York in the late 1970s as a young actor and I went straight to Vera Soloviova. I wanted to learn from the last surviving member of the First Studio. Here was an experience Horton Foote and I shared.

Jilinsky and Soloviova spent many years in the First Studio working along side Stanislavsky, Sulerzhitsky, Mikhail Chekhov, Richard Boleslavsky, Yevgeny Vahktangov and Maria Ouspenskaya. Andrius Jilinsky became an extraordinary teacher of Stanislavsky's principles, as can be seen in his book *The Joy of Acting*.

Vera Soloviova's art was emblematic of the spiritual truth of the First Studio. She was one of the Stanislavsky's favorite actors. She once told me, "Even after I had sinned and sinned and sinned, Stanislavsky still loved me." Of all the gifted teachers of the "system," these two artists are unmatched in their ability to communicate the deep spiritual consciousness which is the origin of Stanislavsky's great work.

Over the years, Horton Foote has testified to the seminal influence of these two individuals and the "system," they taught on the development of his art. I urge anyone who is involved in recreating one of Horton Foote's plays on stage to immerse themselves in the artistic ideals and process of the First Studio and its members. Be forewarned: The work of the First Studio bares little resemblance to the crude materialism, naturalistic cliches and meaningless "professional craft" which is Stanislavsky's "system" today. Although its life was short, the spiritual theatre Stanislavsky and Sulerzhitsky sought to create with the actors of the First Studio was, in many ways, the true artistic home of Horton Foote.

Like the First Studio, Horton Foote is an artist of spiritual transcendence. His characters are the conflicts of the soul struggling for inner peace. At the center of his plays is loneliness, loss, grief, fear, courage and love: the existential state of our common humanity. The elemental through-action of Horton Foote's world is Beckett's "I can't go on…I will go on." The conflicts between characters in a Foote play are rarely motivated by the egotism we label "success" and "failure." His creations are on a path of action which inspires all of the world's great religions. These men and women are seeking the experience we call God. *To be enlightened, they are willing to face the divine nothingness of reality and the "infinite within" of the human spirit.* If life has not rewarded the actors cast in a Foote play with a deeply experiential consciousness formed in the wisdom and pain of silence, loneliness, oppression and love, then there is little chance that the actors—as human beings—will become one with their author's truth.

Like all good playwrights, Horton Foote gives his art to the actors. Watch Geraldine Page in the film of *The Trip To Bountiful.* She is a master of what Horton Foote asks of the actor. Her acting of Mrs. Watts is an acting class no one can afford to miss. She simply talks. She truly listens. She concentrates *in* her senses. Through the oceanic flow of affective memory, she experiences the world of the play's given circumstances. She never plays "objectives" but she is always *in* action. Like Horton Foote, himself, Geraldine Page brings a lifetime of observed human behavior to the "body" of her acting. She is constantly improvising. She never stops to "remember to remember" some element of her process or performance. She is a fearless juggler of all she has memorized and then so wisely forgets as she abandons herself to the truth of the moment—knowing her endless preparation will always be there to guide her. She acts. She feels. She thinks. She waits. She imagines. She does. Most of all, taking Stanislavsky's advice to heart, Geraldine Page feels an identical spine in herself, the character and the play as a whole. Each moment is an aspect of the experiential doing of one action: to struggle within and without to be at peace. A singular *experienced* through-action is a constant in all great acting. Allow the Stanislavskian acting of Geraldine Page, Robert Duvall, Steven Hill, Kim Stanley and Hallie Foote to teach this truth through the plays of Horton Foote.

Stanislavsky's quest for a theatre of "the life of the human spirit" was inspired by a simple insight: "There can be no aesthetic without the ethic." Sadly, the emptiness of our postmodern theatre of technology and greed is hardly the foundation for Stanislavsky's truth. Hopefully, one day, America will create and support theatrical organizations worthy of the gifts of our vanishing artists have to give. Maybe, the audience who needs the theatre will come home. Until then, the theatre of the soul's imagination is the place to experience Horton Foote's transcendental art. To borrow from Eva LeGallienne's tribute to Eleonora Duse, Horton Foote is our "mystic in the theatre."

ROBERT ELLERMANN studied theatre with Bobby Lewis, Frank Corsaro, David Garfield, Kim Stanley and the Mikhail Chekhov Studio. He taught acting at the Bobby Lewis Theatre Workshop in Los Angeles. Mr. Ellermann has taught acting in private classes in New York, Los Angeles, Chicago and Houston. He was a founding member and artistic director of the Cactus Theatre Company. During the seven years he led the theatre, it produced the plays of Clifford Odets, Horton Foote, Michael Weller, Tennessee Williams, Liudmila Petrushevskaya and David Rabe. In 1988, Mr. Ellermann was invited to teach and lecture at the National Conservatory of Dramatic Art in Paris as part of an international conference on the life and work of Konstantin Stanislavsky. In 1990, he was invited to Moscow to conduct research on the origins of Stanislavsky's "system." In recent years, Mr. Ellermann has published several essays on the "system" and worked as an acting coach in feature films.

The Trip to Bountiful

*dedicated to Lillian Gish
with love and deep gratitude*

TRIP TO BOUNTIFUL
by Michael Blumenthal

It is good to have someone to sit beside
late at night, at the movies
when the lights have dimmed
and the previews are over
and you have pigged out over a large order of popcorn,
and the old woman who has lived unhappily
for twenty-one years with her failed son
and her miserable daughter-in-law takes off
to return to that beautiful small town
where she has always remembered herself
as perfectly happy, only to find
that her one friend, the town's last citizen,
has died that very morning, and that when she returns
to the beautiful house that has remained unaltered
in the scrapbook of her wishfulness,
it is a mere ghost of what it once was,
the curtains rotted against the sashes,
the wood frame sagging like an old scarecrow,
the neighbors' houses all abandoned
by death, ice storms, the vicissitudes
of profit; yes, it is good not to be alone
at times like these, when the woman
sitting beside you (who this very morning
seemed merely a burden) sends small sobs
wafting like pollen into the theater
and squeezes your hand, and says "It's
so sad, this movie," and you agree, yes,
it is very sad, this movie, and this life
in which so much we imagine as inalterable
will be taken from us, in which
there are so many towns where someone
will die, this very day, alone and unclaimed
by any of their loved ones (who have all left
to marry in another country or find their fortunes
in some greed-stricken Houston)
which is why it is good to be here,
even just tonight, in this dimly lit theater,
with a good woman and the scent of popcorn
and a wide bed you can climb into again together,
as if it were the town you originally came from
and you could always go back to it,
as if no one could ever die in the dark alone,
not even you.

PRODUCTION

The Trip to Bountiful was first produced by The Theatre Guild and Fred Coe on November 3, 1953, at Henry Miller's Theatre, New York City. It was Directed by Vincent J. Donehue and the settings were designed by Otis Riggs. The cast was as follows:

Mrs. Carrie Watts	Lillian Gish
Ludie Watts	Gene Lyons
Jessie Mae Watts	Jo Van Fleet
Thelma	Eva Marie Saint
Houston Ticket Man	Will Hare
A Traveler	Salem Ludwig
Second Houston Ticket Man	David Clive
Harrison Ticket Man	Frederick Downs
Sheriff	Frank Overton
Travelers	Patricia MacDonald, Neil Laurence, Helen Cordes

SYNOPSIS OF SCENES
ACT I: A Houston Apartment
ACT II: The Trip
ACT III: A Country Place

PRODUCTION NOTES

ACT I: The bedroom and living room of a Houston Apartment. The walls of these two rooms can be defined by the placement of furniture and by the use of certain necessary fragments of flats needed to contain a door or a window frame.

ACT II: The Houston bus station, a seat on a bus, the Harrison bus station. The Houston and Harrison bus stations require no more than a bench each and cut outs to represent ticket windows. Two chairs are all that are required for the bus seats.

ACT III: The house at Bountiful. Since this house is seen through the eyes and heart of Mrs. Watts the actual house can be as symbolic or as realistic as the individual designer chooses. An atmospheric description of this set is included in the text for groups wanting to make use of it.

THE TRIP TO BOUNTIFUL

ACT I
Scene 1

The curtain rises. The stage is dark. The lights are slowly brought up and we see the living room and bedroom of a small three room apartment. The two rooms have been furnished on very little money. The living room is R. D. R. In the living room is a sofa that at night has to serve as a bed. It has been made up for the night. U. L. of the room is a door leading out to the hallway, kitchen and bathroom. At the opposite end of this hallway is a door leading to the bedroom. To get back and forth, then, between these two rooms it is necessary to go out into the hallway. C. R., in the living room, is a window looking out on the street. Above the window is a wardrobe in which Mrs. Watts's clothes and other belongings are kept. On top of the wardrobe are a suitcase and Mrs. Watts's purse. A rocking chair is beside the window, and about the room are an easy chair and another straight chair. C., in the living room, is a drop leaf table with two straight chairs at either end. On the table are a small radio and a book. U. C. is a door leading to the outside stairs. Against the rear wall, R., is a desk and on the desk are a phone, a newspaper and a movie magazine.

A full moon shines in the window. The two rooms are kept immaculately. The bedroom is smaller than the living room. There is a bed with its headboard against U. S. C. A small table with a bed light stands by the bed. R. C. is a vanity with its back against the imaginary wall separating living room from bedroom. There are two straight chairs in the room, one in front of the vanity. U. L. is a closet with dresses hanging in it.

In the living room a woman of sixty is sitting in the rocking chair, rocking back and forth. She is small and thin and fragile. The woman is Mrs. Watts. She lives in the apartment with her son, Ludie, and her daughter-in-law, Jessie Mae.

The lights are out in the bedroom and we can't see much. Ludie and Jessie Mae are both in bed. Jessie Mae is asleep and Ludie isn't.

Ludie slips out of his bed, in the bedroom. He starts tiptoeing out the door that leads to the hallway.

Mrs. Watts continues to rock back and forth in the chair. She doesn't hear Ludie. She hums a hymn to herself, "There's not a friend like the lowly Jesus." Then she hears Ludie.

Ludie is in his early forties. He has on pajamas and a robe. Ludie has had a difficult life. He had been employed as an accountant until his health broke down. He was unable to work for two years. His mother and his wife are both dependent on him and their small savings were depleted during his illness. Now he has started working again, but at a very small salary.

MRS. WATTS: Don't be afraid of makin' noise, Sonny. I'm awake.

LUDIE: Yes, Ma'm. (*He comes into the living room. He comes over to the window. Mrs. Watts is looking back out the window, rocking and singing her hymn. He stands behind his mother's chair looking out the window at moonlight. We can clearly see his face now. It is a sensitive face. After a moment Mrs. Watts looks up at Ludie. The rocking ceases for a second.*)

MRS. WATTS: Pretty night.

LUDIE: Sure is.

MRS. WATTS: Couldn't you sleep?

LUDIE: No, Ma'm.

MRS. WATTS: Why couldn't you sleep?

LUDIE: I just couldn't.

(*Mrs. Watts turns away from Ludie to look out the window again. She starts her rocking once more, and hums her hymn to herself. She is opening and closing her hands nervously.*)

Couldn't you sleep?

MRS. WATTS: No. I haven't been to bed at all. (*Outside the window in the street we hear a car's brakes grind to a sudden stop.*)

LUDIE: There's going to be a bad accident at that corner one of these days.

MRS. WATTS: I wouldn't be surprised. I think the whole state of Texas is going to meet its death on the highways. (*Pause.*) I don't see what pleasure they get drivin' these cars as fast as they do. Do you?

LUDIE: No, Ma'm. (*A pause. Mrs. Watts goes back to her humming and her rocking.*) But there's a lot of things I don't understand. Never did and never will, I guess. (*A pause.*)

MRS. WATTS: Is Jessie Mae asleep?

LUDIE: Yes, Ma'm. That's why I thought I'd better come out here. I got to tossin' an' turnin' so I was afraid I was gonna wake up Jessie Mae. *(A pause.)*

MRS. WATTS: You're not worryin' about your job, are you, Sonny?

LUDIE: No, Ma'm. I don't think so. Everybody seems to like me there. I'm thinking about askin' for a raise.

MRS. WATTS: You should, hard as you work.

LUDIE: Why couldn't you sleep, Mama?

MRS. WATTS: Because there's a full moon. *(She rocks back and forth opening and closing her hands.)* I never could sleep when there was a full moon. Even back in Bountiful when I'd been working out in the fields all day, and I'd be so tired I'd think my legs would give out on me, let there be a full moon and I'd just toss the night through. I've given up trying to sleep on nights like this. I just sit and watch out the window and think my thoughts. *(She looks out the window smiling to herself.)* I used to love to look out the window back at Bountiful. Once when you were little and there was a full moon, I woke you up and dressed you and took you for a walk with me. Do you remember?

LUDIE: No, Ma'm.

MRS. WATTS: You don't?

LUDIE: No, Ma'm.

MRS. WATTS: I do. I remember just like it was yesterday. I dressed you and took you outside and there was an old dog howlin' away off somewhere and you got scared an' started cryin' an' I said, "Son, why are you cryin'?" You said someone had told you that when a dog howled a person was dyin' some place. I held you close to me, because you were tremblin' with fear. An' then you asked me to explain to you about dyin', an' I said you were too young to worry about things like that for a long time to come. *(A pause.)* I was just sittin' here thinkin', Sonny. *(She looks up at Ludie. She sees he is lost in his own thoughts.)* A penny for your thoughts.

LUDIE: Ma'm?

MRS. WATTS: A penny for your thoughts.

LUDIE: I didn't have any, Mama.

(She goes back to her rocking.)

I wish we had a yard here. Part of my trouble is that I get no exercise. *(A pause.)* Funny the things you think about when you can't sleep. I was trying to think of the song I used to like to hear you sing back home. I'd always laugh when you'd sing it.

MRS. WATTS: Which song was that, Son?

LUDIE: I don't remember the name. I just remember I'd always laugh when you'd sing it. *(A pause. She thinks a moment)*

MRS. WATTS: Oh, yes. That old song. *(She thinks for another moment.)* What was the name of it?

LUDIE: I don't know. *(A pause.)*

MRS. WATTS: Less see. Oh, I hate not to be able to think of something. It's on the tip of my tongue. *(A pause. She thinks. She recites the words.)*

> Hush little baby, don't say a word.
> Mama's gonna buy you a mockin' bird.
> And if that mockin' bird don't sing,
> Mama's gonna buy you a diamond ring.

I used to think I was gonna buy you the world back in those days. I remember remarking that to my Papa. He said that world can't be bought. I didn't rightly understand what he meant then. *(She suddenly turns to him, taking his hand.)* Ludie.

(He looks down at her, almost afraid of the question she intends to ask. She sees his fear and decides not to ask it. She lets go of his hand.)

Nothin'. Nothin'. *(A pause.)* Would you like me to get you some hot milk?

LUDIE: Yes, Ma'm. If you don't mind.

MRS. WATTS: I don't mind at all. *(She gets up out of her chair and exits to kitchen. Ludie repeats the lines of the song to himself quietly.)*

LUDIE: Hush little baby, don't say a word.
> Mama's gonna buy you a mockin' bird.
> And if that mockin' bird don't sing,
> Mama's gonna buy you a diamond ring.

(Another car comes to a sudden stop out in the street, screeching its brakes. He peers out the window, his face close against the screen, trying to see the car. Jessie Mae is awakened by the screech. She gets out of bed and puts on a dressing gown.)

JESSIE MAE: *(From the bedroom.)* Ludie! Ludie!

MRS. WATTS: *(Re-enters from hallway.)* You want butter and pepper and salt in it?

LUDIE: Yes, Ma'm, if it's not too much trouble.

MRS. WATTS: No trouble at all. *(Exits to hallway.)*

JESSIE MAE: *(From the bedroom.)* Ludie.

LUDIE: Come in, Jessie Mae. Mama isn't asleep. *(Jessie Mae goes out the bedroom into the living room. She immediately turns on the lights, flooding the room with an ugly glare. Jessie Mae was probably called very cute when she was young. Now she is hard, driven, nervous and hysterical.)*

JESSIE MAE: Why don't you turn on the lights? What's the sense of sitting around in the dark? I don't know what woke me up. I was sleeping as sound as a log. All of a sudden I woke up and looked over in bed and you weren't there. Where is your mama?

LUDIE: In the kitchen.

JESSIE MAE: What's she doing out there?

LUDIE: Fixing some hot milk for me.

JESSIE MAE: *(She glances out the hallway.)* Putter, putter, putter. Honestly! Do you want a cigarette?

LUDIE: No, thanks. *(Jessie Mae takes cigarettes and lighter from her dressing gown pocket. She struggles with the cigarette lighter.)*

JESSIE MAE: Do you have a match? My lighter is out of fluid. I have to remember to get some tomorrow.

(Ludie lights her cigarette. A pause. She takes a drag off her cigarette. Ludie gives her package of matches.)

Thanks. Couldn't you sleep?

LUDIE: Uh. Uh.

JESSIE MAE: How do you expect to work tomorrow if you don't get your sleep, Ludie?

LUDIE: I'm hopin' the hot milk will make me sleepy. I slept last night. I don't know what got into me tonight.

JESSIE MAE: You didn't sleep the night before last.

LUDIE: I know. But I slept the night before that.

JESSIE MAE: I don't think your mama has even been to bed.

(Mrs. Watts comes in from hallway with the milk.)

What's the matter with you that you can't sleep, Mother Watts?

MRS. WATTS: It's a full moon, Jessie Mae.

JESSIE MAE: What's that got to do with it?

MRS. WATTS: I never could sleep when there's a full moon.

JESSIE MAE: That's just your imagination.

(Mrs. Watts doesn't answer. She hands Ludie the hot milk. He takes it and blows it to cool it off before drinking. Jessie Mae goes over to a small radio on drop leaf table and turns it on.)

I don't know what's the matter with you all. I never had trouble sleepin' in my life. I guess I have a clear conscience. The only time that I remember having had any trouble sleeping was the night I spent out at Bountiful. The mosquitoes like to have chewed me up. I never saw such mosquitoes. Regular Gallow nippers. *(The radio plays a blues. Jessie Mae picks up a movie magazine from desk and sits in chair by the radio.)* Mother Watts, where did you put that recipe that Rosella gave me on the phone today?

MRS. WATTS: What recipe was that, Jessie Mae?

JESSIE MAE: What recipe was that? She only gave me one. The one I wrote down while I was talkin' to Rosella this mornin'. You remember, I asked you to find me a pencil.

MRS. WATTS: Yes, I remember something about it.

JESSIE MAE: Then I handed it to you and asked you to put it away on the top of my dresser.

MRS. WATTS: Jessie Mae, I don't remember you havin' given me any recipe.

JESSIE MAE: Well, I did.

MRS. WATTS: I certainly have no recollection of it.

JESSIE MAE: You don't?

MRS. WATTS: No, Ma'm.

JESSIE MAE: I swear, Mother Watts, you just don't have any memory at all any more.

MRS. WATTS: Jessie Mae, I think I…

JESSIE MAE: I gave it to you this mornin' in this very room and I said to please put it on my dresser and you said I will and went out holding it in your hand.

MRS. WATTS: I did?

JESSIE MAE: Yes, you did.

MRS. WATTS: Did you look on your dresser?

JESSIE MAE: Yes, Ma'm.

MRS. WATTS: And it wasn't there?

JESSIE MAE: No, Ma'm. I looked just before I went to bed.

MRS. WATTS: Oh. Well, let me look around. *(She gets up and goes out the door L., into hallway. Jessie Mae paces around the room.)*

JESSIE MAE: I swear. Have you noticed how forgetful she's getting? I think her memory is definitely going. Honestly, it just gets on my nerves. We're just gonna have to get out a little more, Ludie. No wonder you can't sleep. You get up in the morning, you go to work, you come home, you have your supper, read the paper and then go right off to bed. Every couple I know goes out three or four times a week. I know we couldn't afford it before, so I kept quiet about it. But now you're working again I don't think a picture show once or twice a week would break us. We don't have a car. We don't go to nightclubs. We have to do something.

LUDIE: O.K. Why don't we go out one night this week?

JESSIE MAE: I mean, I think we have to. I was talkin' to Rosella about it this morning on the phone and she said she just didn't see how we stood it. Well, I said, Rosella, we have Mother Watts and it's hard for us to leave her alone.

LUDIE: When did you and Rosella get friendly again?

JESSIE MAE: This morning. She just all of a sudden called me up on the telephone. She said she would quit being mad if I would. I said shucks, I wasn't mad in the first place. She was the one that was mad. I told her I was plainspoken and said exactly what I felt and people will just have to take me as I am or leave me alone. I said furthermore, I had told her the truth when I remarked that that beauty parlor must have seen her coming a long way down the road when they charged her good money for that last permanent they gave her. She said she agreed with me now entirely and had stopped patronizing that beauty shop. *(A pause. She goes back to her movie magazine.)* Rosella found out definitely that she can't have any children...

(Mrs. Watts comes into living room at U.L. To Mrs. Watts.)

Walk, don't run.

(Mrs. Watts looks around the room for the recipe. A pause.)

You know your mother's pension check didn't come today. It's the eighteenth. I swear it was due. I just can't understand the Government. Always late. *(Looking up from her reading—then to Mrs. Watts.)* Did you find it?

MRS. WATTS: Not yet.

JESSIE MAE: Well, then forget about it. Look for it in the morning.

MRS. WATTS: No, I'm going to look for it until I find it. *(Mrs. Watts goes out of the room U.L.)*

JESSIE MAE: Honestly, Ludie, she's so stubborn. *(She goes back to her movie magazine. Turns the radio dial—radio plays a popular tune.)* I just love this song and this singer: I could just listen to him all day. *(Jessie Mae begins to sing with the singer. There is an immediate knocking upstairs. She continues singing louder than ever. The knocking continues. Finally she jumps up out of her chair. She is very angry.)* Now what are they knocking about? Do you consider this on too loud?

LUDIE: No sense in arguing with them, Jessie Mae.

JESSIE MAE: They'd like it if we didn't breathe.

LUDIE: Well, it is kinda late.

(Ludie turns radio down. Jessie Mae yawns. She goes over to the sofa with the movie magazine.)

JESSIE MAE: Who played the Captain in *Mutiny on the Bounty?*

LUDIE: Search me.

JESSIE MAE: They're running a contest in here but I never saw such hard questions. *(A pause. She looks up at Ludie.)* Rosella said Jim used to have trouble sleepin'. She said a man told him to lie in bed and count backwards and that would cure him. He tried it and she said it did. She said you start with a hundred and instead of going forward you go backwards. One hundred, ninety-nine, ninety-eight, ninety-seven, ninety-six, ninety-five.…She said it would just knock him out.

LUDIE: Jessie Mae, maybe we can take in a baseball game one night this week. The series is getting exciting. I think Houston has the best team they've had in a long time. I'd sure like to be there when they play Shreveport. *(Pause.)* I used to play baseball back at Bountiful. I used to rather play baseball than eat, when I was a kid.

JESSIE MAE: Come on, let's go to bed. *(She gets up. There is another screech of brakes.)* There goes another car smashed up. *(She runs to the window and stands looking out.)* Nope, they missed each other. Six cars smashed up on the Freeway to Galveston I read yesterday in the *Chronicle.* One right on top of another. One car was trying to pass another car and ran right smack into a third car. Then the ones behind both cars started pilin' up. A lot of them were killed. I bet they were all drunk. Been down to Galveston, gamblin', likely. I think the whole of Houston goes into Galveston gambling and drinking. Everybody but us. I don't see how some people hold down a job the way they drink and gamble. Do you?

LUDIE: No.…I don't.

JESSIE MAE: That's why I told Rosella I could hardly keep from callin' up your boss and givin' him a piece of my mind for payin' you the salary he pays you. Like I said to Rosella, you're so steady and so conscientious and they just take advantage of your good nature. Maybe you're too steady, Ludie. *(Ludie has taken a book off the drop leaf table. He goes to the chair, reading it. A pause. Mrs. Watts goes into the bedroom. She turns on the lights in the bedroom and begins a systematic search for the recipe. To Ludie.)* Rosella was glad to hear you're workin' again. She said she was cleanin' out some drawers night before last and had come across some pictures of you and me she'd taken when we started goin' together. I said I don't care to see them. No, thank you. *(Mrs. Watts is looking, now, in Jessie Mae's vanity drawer. She finds the recipe.)* The passin's of time makes me sad. That's why I never want a house with the room to keep a lot of junk in to remind you of things you're better off forgetting. If we ever get any money you wouldn't catch me buying a house. I'd move into a hotel and have me room service. *(Mrs. Watts comes in to living room, holding the recipe.)*

MRS. WATTS: Here's your recipe, Jessie Mae.

JESSIE MAE: Thank you but I told you not to bother. Where did you find it? *(She takes the recipe.)*

MRS. WATTS: In your room.

JESSIE MAE: In my room?

MRS. WATTS: Yes, Ma'm.

JESSIE MAE: Where in my room?

MRS. WATTS: In your dresser drawer. Right-hand side.

JESSIE MAE: In my dresser drawer?

MRS. WATTS: Yes, Ma'm. I looked on top of the dresser and it wasn't there an' something said to me…

(Jessie Mae rises and angrily throws her package of matches down on table.)

JESSIE MAE: Mother Watts.

MRS. WATTS: Ma'm.

JESSIE MAE: Ludie, how many times have I asked her never to go into my dresser drawer?

MRS. WATTS: I thought you wanted me to find your recipe?

JESSIE MAE: Well, I don't want you to go into my dresser drawers. I'd like a little privacy if you don't mind.

MRS. WATTS: Yes, Ma'm. *(She turns away. She is trying to avoid a fight.)*

JESSIE MAE: *(She is very angry now. She takes Mrs. Watts by the shoulder and shakes her.)* And just let me never catch you looking in them again. For anything. I can't stand people snoopin' in my dresser drawers.

(Mrs. Watts grabs the paper from Jessie Mae and throws it on the floor. She is hurt and angry.)

MRS. WATTS: All right. Then the next time you find it yourself.

JESSIE MAE: Pick that recipe up, if you please.

MRS. WATTS: Pick it up yourself. I have no intention of picking it up.

JESSIE MAE: *(Shouting.)* You pick that up!

MRS. WATTS: *(Shouting back.)* I won't!

LUDIE: Mama.

JESSIE MAE: *(Shouting even louder.)* You will!

LUDIE: Jessie Mae. For God sakes! You're both acting like children. It's one-thirty in the morning.

JESSIE MAE: You tell her to pick that up.

MRS. WATTS: I won't. *(Mrs. Watts stubbornly goes to her rocking chair and sits.)*

JESSIE MAE: *(Screaming.)* You will! This is my house and you'll do as you're told.

(Ludie walks out of the room. He goes into his bedroom. Jessie Mae crosses to Mrs. Watts.)

Now. I hope you're satisfied. You've got Ludie good and upset. He won't sleep for the rest of the night. What do you want to do? Get him sick again?

(There is a knocking on the floor. Jessie Mae screams up at them.)

Shut up. *(To Mrs. Watts.)* You're going too far with me one of these days, old lady. *(Jessie Mae walks out of the room at U. L. Mrs. Watts is ready to scream back at her, but she controls the impulse. She takes her anger out in rocking violently back and forth. Jessie Mae throws open the door to the bedroom and comes in. Ludie is sitting on the edge of the bed. She marches over to the vanity and sits. She starts to throw things around on top of the vanity. After a moment, Ludie gets up and starts toward her.)*

LUDIE: Jessie Mae.

JESSIE MAE: I just can't stand this, Ludie. I'm at the end of my rope. I won't take being insulted by your mother or anyone else. You hear that?

Ludie rises and stands uncomfortably for a moment. He turns and goes out the bedroom door and into the living room. He stands by the living room door looking at his mother. She stops her rocking. She goes and picks up the recipe. Ludie sees what she is doing and tries to get there first. He is not able to. She hands the recipe to him. He stands there for a moment looking at it. He turns to his mother and speaks with great gentleness.)

LUDIE: Mama. Will you give this recipe to Jessie Mae?

MRS. WATTS: All right, Ludie.

(She takes the recipe. She starts out of the living room and Ludie stops her. He obviously hates asking the next question.)

LUDIE: Mama, will you please tell Jessie Mae you're sorry?

MRS. WATTS: Ludie…

LUDIE: Please, Mama.

MRS. WATTS: All right, Ludie.

LUDIE: Jessie Mae.

(Mrs. Watts goes out of the room to the bedroom.)

JESSIE MAE: What do you want, Ludie?

LUDIE: Mama has something to say to you.

JESSIE MAE: What is it?

(Mrs. Watts hands her the recipe.)

MRS. WATTS: I'm sorry, Jessie Mae, for throwing the recipe on the floor.

JESSIE MAE: I accept your apology.

(Mrs. Watts goes out, reappears in living room. Calling.)

Come on, Ludie. Let's all go to bed.

LUDIE: All right. *(He starts for the living room door U.L.)*

JESSIE MAE: *(Calling.)* And you'd better go to bed, too, Mother Watts. A woman your age ought to have better sense than to sit up half the night.

MRS. WATTS: Yes, Ma'm. Good night, Ludie.

LUDIE: Good night, Mama.

(He waits until his mother sits in the rocking chair and then he turns the lights off in the living room and goes into the bedroom, taking his book with him. Mrs. Watts buries her face in her hands. She is crying. Ludie, now in bedroom.)
Jessie Mae. I know it's hard and all, but for your own sake, I just think sometimes if you'd try to ignore certain things.

JESSIE MAE: Ignore? How can you ignore something when it's done right under your very nose?

LUDIE: Look, Jessie Mae.

JESSIE MAE: I know her, Ludie. She does things just to aggravate me. Well, I hope she's happy now. She aggravated me. Now you take her hymn singin'. She never starts until I come into a room. And her poutin'! Why sometimes she goes a whole day just sittin' and starin' out that window. How would you like to spend twenty-four hours a day shut up with a woman that either sang hymns or looked out the window and pouted? You couldn't ignore it and don't tell me you could. No. There's only one thing to do and that's to say quit it, every time she does something like that until she stops for good and all.

LUDIE: I'm not sayin' it's easy, Jessie Mae. I'm only sayin'…

JESSIE MAE: Well, let's change the subject. I don't want to get mad all over again. She keeps me so nervous never knowing when I leave whether she is going to try to run off to that old town or not.

LUDIE: Well, she's not going to run off again, Jessie Mae. She promised me she wouldn't.

JESSIE MAE: What she promised and…

LUDIE: Now, she can't run off. Her pension check hasn't come. You said yourself…

(Mrs. Watts hears them. She goes to the edge of the rug, lifts it up, and takes the pension check. She stands there for a moment, looking at it, trying to decide whether to take this in to Jessie Mae.)

JESSIE MAE: Well, I am not too sure that that check hasn't come. Sometimes I think she hides that check and I tell you right now if it is not here tomorrow I am going to search this house from top to bottom.

LUDIE: Well, I know the check will come tomorrow.

JESSIE MAE: I hope so. Rosella says she thinks it's terrible how close I have to stay here. Well, I told Rosella ever since your mother started that running off business I don't feel easygoing. I used to love it when I could get up from the breakfast table with an easy mind and go downtown and shop all morning, then get a sandwich and a coke, or a salad at the cafeteria, see

a picture show in the afternoon and then come home. That was fun.
Shhh. I think I hear your mother still up.

(Mrs. Watts has decided not to give them the check. She is now sitting in her rocking chair, rocking and looking out the window. Ludie comes into the living room. She puts the check inside her nightgown.)

LUDIE: Mama. Are you still up?

MRS. WATTS: Yes. I don't feel like sleeping, Ludie. You go on back to bed and don't worry about me.

LUDIE: All right, Mama. *(He goes back to bedroom.)*

JESSIE MAE: Was she still up?

LUDIE: Yes.

JESSIE MAE: I knew it. I never get to go out of the house except for the beauty parlor. I'm not giving that up for anyone. I told Rosella that. I said no one was more faithful to a husband than I was to Ludie, when he was sick, but even then I went out to the beauty parlor once a week. I mean, I had to.

LUDIE: I wanted you to.

JESSIE MAE: I know you did. *(Jessie Mae sings absentmindedly. She is sitting at the vanity, brushing her hair, putting on face lotion, etc. A pause.)* Next time I see one of those little portable radios on sale, I'm going to get one. It would be nice to have by our bed. It would be so much company for us. *(A pause.)* That was a good supper we had tonight, wasn't it?

LUDIE: Uh. Huh. Mama is a good cook.

JESSIE MAE: Yes. She is. I'll have to hand that to her. And an economical one. Well, she enjoys cooking. I guess you're born to enjoy it. I could never see how anyone could get any pleasure standing over a hot stove, but she seems to. *(A pause.)* Rosella asked me if I realized that it would be fifteen years this August since we were married. I hadn't realized it. Had you? *(Ludie thinks for a moment. He counts back over the years.)*

LUDIE: That's right, Jessie Mae. It'll be fifteen years this August.

JESSIE MAE: I hate to think of time going that fast. *(A pause.)* I never will forget the night I came home and told Rosella you had proposed. I thought you were the handsomest man alive.

LUDIE: And I thought you were the prettiest girl.

JESSIE MAE: Did you, Ludie? I guess I did have my good features. People used to tell me I looked like a cross between Joan Crawford and Clara Bow. And I thought you were the smartest man in the world. I still do. The thing that burns me up is that you don't let other people know it. Do you remember Sue Carol in the movies?

LUDIE: Sure.

JESSIE MAE: I loved her. She was my ideal when I was growing up. She was always so cute in whatever she did. I always tried to act like her, be good company and a sport. *(A pause.)* Sue Carol's married to Alan Ladd now. They've got a bunch of kids. Well, she can afford them. They've got servants and I don't know what all.

(Ludie has his book in his hand. He is walking around the room.)

LUDIE: Jessie Mae, I've just got to start makin' some more money. I'm thinkin' about askin' for a raise. I'm entitled to it. I've been there six months now. I haven't been late or sick once. I've got to do it. I've got to ask for a raise tomorrow. *(He continues to walk around the room.)* I'm gonna walk into Mr. Douglas's office the first thing in the mornin' and I'm gonna take the bull by the horns and I'm gonna say, Mr. Douglas, I've got to have a raise starting as of now. We can't live on what you pay us. We have my mother's pension check to help us out and if we didn't have that I don't know what we'd do.

JESSIE MAE: Well, I would.

LUDIE: I don't understand it, Jessie Mae. I try not to be bitter. I try not to…. Oh, I don't know. All I know is that a man works eight years with a company. He saves a little money. He gets sick and has to spend two years in bed watching his savings all go. Then start all over again with a new company. *(A pause. He sits on the bed, placing his book on it.)* Of course, the doctor says I shouldn't worry about it. He says I've got to take things like they come. Every day, and that's what I try to do. But how can you help worryin' when you end up every month holding your breath to see if you're gonna make ends meet.

(Jessie Mae gets up from the vanity. She crosses to bed.)

JESSIE MAE: You can't help being nervous. A lot of people get nervous. *(She sits on the bed and picks up the book.)* What's this book?

LUDIE: It's mine. I bought it at the drug store coming home from the office.

JESSIE MAE: *How to become an Executive.* What's that about?

LUDIE: It tells you how to prepare yourself for an executive position. It looks like there might be some helpful things in it. *(Ludie takes the book and leans back against the headboard of the bed, reading. Jessie Mae restlessly looks around the room.)*

JESSIE MAE: You sleepy, Ludie?

LUDIE: No, not yet.

JESSIE MAE: I'm not either. I wish I had something good to eat. I wish the drug store was open. We could get us some ice cream. I wish I had my movie magazine.

LUDIE: Where is it?

JESSIE MAE: In the living room.

> *(Ludie starts off bed.)*

LUDIE: I'll get it.

JESSIE MAE: No, honey, I don't want to get your mother awake. *(Jessie Mae lies across the foot of the bed. She hums and gets off bed.)* I think I'll get me a cigarette. Want me to get you one?

LUDIE: Thanks. I think I will have one. I can get them.

JESSIE MAE: No. You rest. *(She goes to the vanity and gets a package of cigarettes.)* Rosella cried like her heart would break when she told me she couldn't have children. *(She lights a cigarette and gives one to Ludie.)*

LUDIE: Thanks.

JESSIE MAE: She wanted to know how I stood it not havin' children. I said I don't know about Ludie 'cause you can't always tell what he feels, but I stand it by never thinking about it. *(She walks back to foot of bed and sits.)* I have my own philosophy about those things, anyway. I feel things like that are in the hands of the Lord. Don't you, Ludie?

LUDIE: I guess so

JESSIE MAE: I've been as good a wife to you as I know how. But if the Lord doesn't want to give us children, all the worryin' in the world won't help. Do you think?

LUDIE: No. It won't.

JESSIE MAE: Anyway, like I told Rosella, I don't have the money to be runnin' around the doctors about it, even if I wanted to. *(A pause.)* Do you have an ashtray?

LUDIE: Right here. *(Ludie get ashtray from vanity and brings it to her.)* Jessie Mae, if I get a raise the first thing I want you to do is buy yourself a new dress.

JESSIE MAE: Well, thank you, Ludie. *(She goes back to vanity and puts pin curlers in her hair. She puts a hair net on and is finished by end of speech.)* Besides, when you were sick what would I have done if I'd had a bunch of kids to worry me? Your mother said to me the other day, Jessie Mae, I don't know how you and Ludie stand livin' in the city. What are you talkin' about, I said. I didn't start livin' until I moved to the city. Who but a fool would want to live in the country? She wouldn't even listen to my arguments. Honestly, she's so stubborn. I declare, I believe your mother's about the stubbornest woman in forty-eight states. *(She looks at herself in vanity mirror and then gets up laughing.)* Well, I don't look like Joan Crawford now. But who cares? I don't. What are you thinking about?

LUDIE: Oh, I was just thinking about this book. *(A pause.... Ludie gets into bed.)*

JESSIE MAE: Ludie, do you ever think back over the past?

LUDIE: No.

JESSIE MAE: I don't either. I started today a little when Rosella brought up that fifteen year business. But I think it's morbid. Your mother does that all the time.

LUDIE: I know.

JESSIE MAE: Turn your head the other way.

(He does so. She takes her dressing gown off and slips into bed.)

LUDIE: My boss likes me. Billy Davidson told me today he was positive he did. Billy has been there ten years now, you know. He said he thought he liked my work a lot. *(A pause.)* Feelin' sleepy now?

JESSIE MAE: Uh. Huh. Are you?

LUDIE: Yes, I am. Good night.

JESSIE MAE: Good night.

(Ludie turns off the bed light by the side of the bed. Mrs. Watts is rocking back and forth in her rocker now, working her hands nervously, humming quietly to herself. Ludie hears her and sits up in bed. He gets out of bed and goes into the living room.)

LUDIE: Mama.

MRS. WATTS: I'm all right, Ludie. I'm just still not sleepy.

LUDIE: You're sure you're feelin' all right?

MRS. WATTS: Yes, I am.

LUDIE: Good night.

(He starts out of the room. She turns to him.)

MRS. WATTS: Ludie, please, I want to go home.

LUDIE: Mama, you know I can't make a living there. We have to live in Houston.

MRS. WATTS: Ludie, son, I can't stay here any longer. I want to go home.

LUDIE: I beg you not to ask me that again. There's nothing I can do about it.

(Ludie goes back to the bedroom. He gets into bed.)

JESSIE MAE: Was she still up?

LUDIE: Uh. Huh. Good night.

JESSIE MAE: Good night.

(Mrs. Watts is standing at the back of the rocking chair. She paces around the room thinking what to do. She listens for a moment to see if they are asleep. She decides they are and quietly takes a suitcase down from the top of the wardrobe. She waits a moment then takes some clothing from the drawer of the cupboard and puts them in the suitcase, then she quietly closes it and hides the suitcase under the sofa. She then goes back to her chair, sits and is rocking back and forth violently as the lights fade.)

ACT I
Scene 2

At Rise of Curtain, Mrs. Watts is discovered sleeping in the rocker. Jessie Mae is in bed. Ludie is offstage in the bathroom, washing. Mrs. Watts awakens, looks for check, finds it inside her nightgown and hides it under mattress. She looks out the window to see the time, runs over to Ludie's bedroom to see if he's awake, and runs into the kitchen to put some water on for coffee, calling as she goes.

MRS. WATTS: Ludie, it's eight-fifteen by the drugstore clock....

LUDIE: *(Calling back, offstage.)* Yes'm.

(Mrs. Watts is back in living room with breakfast tray and dishes. Jessie Mae has gotten out of bed and is at vanity. Ludie sticks his head in living room door.)

Good morning, Mama.

MRS. WATTS: Good morning, son.

LUDIE: Did you get any sleep at all last night?

MRS. WATTS: Yes. Don't worry about me.

(Mrs. Watts goes back into the kitchen, takes the tray out with her. Mrs. Watts comes back with tray and finishes setting table, humming to herself, absentmindedly. Jessie Mae hollers from next room.)

JESSIE MAE: It's too early for hymn singing. *(Jessie Mae comes into living room.)*

MRS. WATTS: Good morning, Jessie Mae.

JESSIE MAE: Good morning, Mother Watts.

(Mrs. Watts goes out to kitchen. Jessie Mae turns on radio and we hear a popular song. She goes out to bathroom. Ludie enters living room from hallway, puts his jacket on chair, C. Jessie Mae, calling.)

Ludie, turn that radio down, please, before they start knocking again.

(Mrs. Watts enters from the kitchen with coffee, which she sets on table.)

LUDIE: *(At the radio.)* Would you like me to turn it off?

JESSIE MAE: *(Calling.)* Oh, you might as well.

MRS. WATTS: I'll have your toast ready for you in a minute.

(Crosses into the kitchen. Jessie Mae enters living room from hallway as Mrs. Watts is rushing out.)

JESSIE MAE: Walk, don't run. I've just got to get me out of this house today, if no more than to ride downtown and back on the bus.

LUDIE: *(Sits at table, drinking coffee.)* Why don't you?

JESSIE MAE: If Mother Watts's pension check comes I'll go to the beauty parlor. I'm just as tense. I think I've got a trip to the beauty parlor comin' to me.

LUDIE: You ought to go if the check comes or not. It doesn't cost that much.
  (Mrs. Watts comes in with toast.)

JESSIE MAE: Mother Watts, will you skip down and see if the mail has come yet? Your pension check ought to be here and I want to get me to that beauty parlor.

MRS. WATTS: Yes, Ma'm. *(Mrs. Watts goes out for the mail at outside door, U. C. Jessie Mae looks after her suspiciously.)*

JESSIE MAE: Ludie, she's actin' silent again. Don't you think she's actin' silent again?

LUDIE: I hadn't noticed. *(He takes a last swig out of his coffee.)*

JESSIE MAE: Well, she definitely is. You can say what you please, but to me it's always a sure sign she's gonna try and run off when she starts actin' silent.

LUDIE: She's not going to run off again, Jessie Mae. She promised me last time she wouldn't. *(He starts up from the table.)*

JESSIE MAE: She just better not. What do you want, Ludie?

LUDIE: I want more coffee.

JESSIE MAE: Well, keep your seat. I'll get it.

LUDIE: No, I'll get it.

JESSIE MAE: No. I want to get it. You'll have a tiring day ahead of you. Now rest while you can. *(She goes out to hallway for coffee. Mrs. Watts enters U. C.)*

MRS. WATTS: Where's Jessie Mae?

LUDIE: In the kitchen.

MRS. WATTS: There was no mail, Jessie Mae.
  (Jessie Mae comes in U. L. with coffee.)

JESSIE MAE: Had it been delivered yet?

MRS. WATTS: I don't know.

JESSIE MAE: Did you look in the other boxes to see if there was mail?

MRS. WATTS: No Ma'm. I didn't think to. *(Mrs. Watts goes to the bedroom.)*

LUDIE: I'll look on my way out. Why don't we have an early supper tonight? Six-thirty if that's all right with you and Mama. After supper I'll take you both to the picture show.

JESSIE MAE: That's fine. What would you like to see, Ludie?

LUDIE: Whatever you want to see, Jessie Mae. You know best about picture shows.

JESSIE MAE: Do you want to go downtown or to one of the neighborhood movies? *(She picks up paper from desk.)*

LUDIE: Whatever you want to do, Jessie Mae.

JESSIE MAE: Maybe it would do us good to go downtown. There's something about walkin' into the Majestic or the Metropolitan, or the Loew's State that just picks me up. People dress so much nicer when they're going to see a movie downtown. Of course, on the other hand, I could stand a good double bill myself.

LUDIE: *(Half to himself.)* I want to get to the office a little early this morning. Mr. Douglas is usually in by nine. I'd like a chance to talk to him before the others get there. I think I'm doin' the right thing, askin' for a raise. Don't you?

JESSIE MAE: Sure. I think I'll phone the beauty parlor for an appointment. I hope I can still get one.

(She goes to the phone on desk. Mrs. Watts has been making up the bed. She stops when she hears Jessie Mae dial the phone and goes to the bedroom door to listen.)

Hello, Rita. This is Jessie Mae Watts. Can I have an appointment for my hair? The usual. Uh. Huh. *(She laughs.)* Four o'clock. Nothin' earlier. All right. See you then. *(She hangs up the phone.)* Well, I can't get an appointment until four o'clock.

LUDIE: I'm ready to go. Wish me luck on my raise.

JESSIE MAE: Good luck, Ludie.

(He kisses her on the cheek. He calls into the bedroom.)

LUDIE: Good-bye, Mama.

MRS. WATTS: Good-bye, son. *(Mrs. Watts goes back to making up the bed.)*

LUDIE: Good-bye, Jessie Mae.

JESSIE MAE: So long. Holler if there's any mail down there so we won't be runnin' up and down lookin' for mail that won't be there.

LUDIE: *(Calling back.)* All right. *(Exits outside door, U. C.)*

JESSIE MAE: *(Calling into the bedroom.)* That pension check should have been here yesterday, shouldn't it, Mother Watts?

MRS. WATTS: *(Calling back and trying to seem unconcerned.)* I reckon so.

LUDIE: *(Calling from offstage downstairs.)* No mail for us.

JESSIE MAE: All right! I can't understand about that pension check, can you?

MRS. WATTS: No, Ma'm.

(Jessie Mae casually takes Mrs. Watts's purse off the wardrobe and looks inside. Finding nothing, she closes it and puts it back.)

JESSIE MAE: I sure hope it isn't lost. You know you're so absentminded you don't think you put it around the room some place by mistake and forgot all about it.

(Mrs. Watts comes into the living room.)

MRS. WATTS: I don't believe so.

(Jessie Mae looks around the room. Mrs. Watts watches anxiously everything she does.)

JESSIE MAE: You know you said you lost that check once before and it took us five days to find it. I came across it under this radio.

MRS. WATTS: I don't think I did that again, Jessie Mae.

(Jessie Mae begins a halfhearted search of the room, looking under a vase, a pillow on the sofa, and when she gets to the corner of the rug where the check is hidden, she stoops as if to look under it, but it is only a strand of thread that has caught her attention. She picks it up and goes over to radio, looking under that. Jessie Mae gives up the search and Mrs. Watts goes back to the bedroom. Jessie Mae calls after her.)

JESSIE MAE: What could I do 'til four o'clock? What are you gonna do today?

(Jessie Mae goes into bedroom.)

MRS. WATTS: Well, I'm going to give the kitchen a good cleaning and put fresh paper on the shelves and clean the icebox.

JESSIE MAE: Well, I have a lot of things I have to do. I got some drawers I can straighten up. Or maybe I'll put some flowers on that red dress of mine. If I wear the red dress tonight. I really don't know yet which dress I'm going to wear. Well, if I wear my red dress tonight, I'll wear this print one to the beauty parlor.

(She has taken a dress out of her closet and goes out hallway to the bathroom to try it on. Mrs. Watts decides to use this opportunity to run into the living room to get the check. Jessie Mae hears her running and calls to her from the bathroom before she can reach the rug.)

Mother Watts!

(Mrs. Watts quickly finds something to do in the living room.)

MRS. WATTS: Yes, Ma'm.

(Jessie Mae comes into the living room.)

JESSIE MAE: There you go again. You never walk when you can run.

(Jessie Mae goes back into the bathroom. Mrs. Watts quickly reaches under the rug and gets the check. She puts it inside her dress. Then she takes the dishes out to the kitchen. Jessie Mae continues to lecture her from the bathroom.)

You know it's none of my business, and I know you don't like me to suggest anything, but I don't think a woman your age should go running around a three-room apartment like a cyclone. It's really not necessary, Mother Watts. You never walk when you can run. *(Jessie Mae comes out to the living room with the dress on. She watches Mrs. Watts.)* I wish for once you'd listen to me.

MRS. WATTS: I'm listening, Jessie Mae.

JESSIE MAE: You're not listening to a word. Mother Watts, are you feeling all right? You look a little pale.

MRS. WATTS: I'm feeling fine, Jessie Mae.

(Jessie Mae zips up her dress. Straightens out the skirt and etc. during following speech.)

JESSIE MAE: That movie magazine Ludie brought me last night is running a contest. First prize is a free trip to Hollywood. I'd like to enter it if I thought I could win. I wouldn't win. I don't have that kind of luck. I want you to look at the hem of this dress for me, to see if it's straight.

MRS. WATTS: Yes, Ma'm. *(Mrs. Watts gets a tape measure from her wardrobe and measures the dress.)*

JESSIE MAE: I'm gonna make Ludie take me to Hollywood one of these days. I want to visit Hollywood as bad as you want to visit Bountiful.

MRS. WATTS: It measures straight, Jessie Mae.

(She returns tape measure to wardrobe and starts to make her own bed. Jessie Mae walks restlessly around the living room.)

JESSIE MAE: Do you need anything from the drug store?

MRS. WATTS: Just let me think a moment, Jessie Mae.

JESSIE MAE: Because if you do, I'd walk over to the drugstore and have me a fountain coke with lots of chipped ice. We don't need toothpaste. We don't need toothbrushes. I got a bottle of Listerine yesterday. Can you think of anything we need from the drugstore?

MRS. WATTS: Did you get that nail polish you mentioned?

JESSIE MAE: Oh, yes I have that. I hate to wait around here until four o'clock. I think I'm gonna call Rosella and tell her to meet me at the drugstore for a coke.

(She goes to phone and dials. Mrs. Watts is humming to herself as she finishes making up her bed.)

Will you stop that hymn singing? Do you want me to jump right out of my skin? You know what hymns do to my nerves.

(Mrs. Watts stops her humming.)

And don't pout. You know I can't stand pouting.

MRS. WATTS: I didn't mean to pout, Jessie Mae. I only meant to be silent.

JESSIE MAE: *(Hangs up phone.)* Wouldn't you know it. She's not home. I bet she's at the drugstore right now. I think I'll go on over to the drugstore and just take a chance on Rosella's being there.

(Jessie Mae begins to put her hat on. Mrs. Watts has gotten a hand sweeper from kitchen and is sweeping around the room.)

I can't make up my mind what movie I want to see tonight. Well, I'll ask Rosella. Will you stop that noise for a minute. I'm nervous.

(Mrs. Watts stops sweeping and gets a dust rag from kitchen. She begins to

dust the room. Jessie Mae continues putting on her hat and arranging her dress in front of the mirror.)

You know when I first came to Houston, I went to see three picture shows in one day. I went to the Kirby in the morning, and the Metropolitan in the afternoon, and the Majestic that night. People don't go to see picture shows the way they used to. Well, I'm ready. *(She turns to Mrs. Watts.)* I just want you to promise me one thing. That you won't put a foot out of this house and start that Bountiful business again. You'll kill Ludie if he has to chase all over Houston looking for you. And I'm warning you. The next time you run off I'm calling the police. I don't care what Ludie says. *(Jessie Mae starts out of the room U. C.)* If Rosella calls just tell her I'm at the drugstore.

(Mrs. Watts has done her best to continue dusting the furniture during the latter speech, but she has been getting physically weaker and weaker. Finally in a last desperate attempt to keep Jessie Mae from noticing her weakness she grabs hold again of the sweeper trying to support herself. She sways, drops the sweeper and reaches for the sofa to keep from falling, just as Jessie Mae is ready to leave the room.)

Mother Watts… *(Jessie Mae runs to her. She is very frightened.)*

MRS. WATTS: *(Trying desperately to control herself.)* I'm all right, Jessie Mae.

JESSIE MAE: Is it your heart?

MRS. WATTS: No. Just a sinkin' spell. Just let me lie down on the sofa for a minute and I'll be all right.

JESSIE MAE: Can I get you some water?

MRS. WATTS: Thank you.

(Jessie Mae runs into kitchen for water.)

JESSIE MAE: *(Offstage, from kitchen.)* Do you want me to call a doctor?

MRS. WATTS: No, Ma'm.

JESSIE MAE: Do you want me to call Ludie?

MRS. WATTS: No, Ma'm.

(Jessie Mae re-enters living room with a glass of water. Mrs. Watts drinks it.)

JESSIE MAE: Are you feelin' better?

MRS. WATTS: Yes, I am, Jessie Mae. *(Mrs. Watts get up off the sofa.)*

JESSIE MAE: Do you think you ought to get up so soon?

MRS. WATTS: Yes, Ma'm. I'm feeling much better already. I'll just sit here in the chair.

JESSIE MAE: All right. I'll sit here for a while and keep you company.

(Mrs. Watts sits in her rocking chair. Jessie Mae sits in her chair, restless as a cat.)

How do you feel now?

MRS. WATTS: Better.

JESSIE MAE: That's good. It always scares the daylights out of me when you get one of those sinkin' spells. Of course, like I told you this morning, you wouldn't be having these sinkin' spells if you'd stop this running around. Well, it's your heart. If you don't want to take care of it no one can make you. But I tell you right now all I need is to have an invalid on my hands. I wish you'd think of Ludie. He's got enough to worry him without your gettin' down flat on your back.

(Phone rings. She goes to it.)

Oh, hello, Rosella. I tried to call you earlier. Oh. You're at the drugstore. That's what I just figured. Well, I'd like to, Rosella, but Mother Watts has had a sinking spell again and…

MRS. WATTS: You go on, Jessie Mae. I'm gonna be all right. I'll just rest here. There's nothing you can do for me.

JESSIE MAE: Are you sure?

MRS. WATTS: Yes, Jessie Mae. I'm sure.

JESSIE MAE: Well, all right then. Rosella, Mother Watts says she won't need me here. So I think I will come over for a little while. All right. I'll see you in a few minutes. Good-bye. *(She hangs up phone.)* Now you're sure you'll be all right?

MRS. WATTS: Yes, Jessie Mae.

JESSIE MAE: Well, then I'll go on over. Now you call me at the drugstore if you need me. You hear?

MRS. WATTS: Yes, Ma'm.

(Jessie Mae goes out entrance to stairs U. C. Mrs. Watts sits for a moment, rocking and using all her will to get her strength back. After a moment she slowly and weakly gets up and goes to the door, listening. She is sure Jessie Mae has gone. She gets her suitcase from under the bed. Then remembers the check, which she takes out, and goes to the desk to endorse it. She takes writing paper and envelope from desk at the same time. While Mrs. Watts is endorsing the check, Jessie Mae comes running back in U. C. Mrs. Watts doesn't see her until she has opened the door.)

JESSIE MAE: I forgot to take any money along with me.

(Jessie Mae is in such a hurry she doesn't see Mrs. Watts. She goes into the bedroom to get her money, which she takes from vanity. Mrs. Watts has just time to get the suitcase and get it back in the wardrobe, stuffs the check inside her dress, and is back to the writing desk when Jessie Mae comes in again.)

Who are you writing to?

MRS. WATTS: I thought I'd drop a line to Callie Davis, Jessie Mae. Let her know I'm still alive.

JESSIE MAE: Why did you decide to do that all of a sudden?

MRS. WATTS: No reason. The notion just struck me.

JESSIE MAE: All right. *(She starts out.)* But just in case you're trying to put something over on me with that pension check, I've told Mr. Reynolds at the grocery store never to cash anything for you.

(She goes out the U. C. door. Mrs. Watts again stands quietly waiting. Then she goes to the door, listening. She decides Jessie Mae has really gone. She gets her hat and coat from wardrobe. She gets her suitcase and goes quietly out the U. C. door as the...)

CURTAIN FALLS

ACT II

SCENE: *The lights are brought up on part of a bus terminal in Houston, Texas. It is placed stage Right. U. C. R. of this area is a door to the street. D. R. is an exit to wash rooms, etc.*

There is a man sitting on one of the benches eating a sandwich. A pretty blond girl, carrying a suitcase and a magazine, is standing at the ticket window R. C. waiting to buy a ticket, a man is standing behind her. The girl's name is Thelma.

The Ticket Man is busy on the telephone. He puts the phone down and comes to the front of the window.

TICKET MAN: Yes?

THELMA: I want a ticket to Old Gulf, please.

TICKET MAN: Yes, Ma'm. *(He reaches for a ticket.)* Here you are. You change busses at Harrison.

THELMA: I know. How much, please?

TICKET MAN: Four eighty.

THELMA: Yessir. *(She gives him the money and steps out of line. Goes to bench and sits, reading a magazine. The Man steps up to the window.)*

MAN: Ticket to Leighton.

TICKET MAN: Leighton. Yes, indeed.

(Mrs. Watts, carrying a suitcase and purse, comes into the terminal from the street entrance U. C. R. She is looking all around her to see if Jessie Mae or Ludie have put in an appearance. Satisfied that they haven't, she hurries to the ticket window. She gets in line behind the Man. She is humming the

hymn to herself and keeps an eye on the doors all the time. Ticket Man hands the Man his ticket.)

Be seven sixty, please.

MAN: Yessir. *(He gets the money for the Ticket Man. Two people have come up behind Mrs. Watts. The Man gives the Ticket Man the money for the tickets, the Ticket Man reaches for change.)*

TICKET MAN: Seven sixty out of ten dollars.

MAN: Thank you. *(He takes his change and exits* D. R. *Mrs. Watts is so busy watching the doors that she doesn't notice it's her turn.)*

TICKET MAN: *(Calling.)* Lady.

(She is still so absorbed in watching, she doesn't hear him.)

Lady. It's your turn.

(Mrs. Watts turns and sees she is next in line. She moves up to the counter.)

MRS. WATTS: Oh, yes. Excuse me. I'd like a ticket to Bountiful, please.

TICKET MAN: Where?

MRS. WATTS: Bountiful.

TICKET MAN: What's it near?

MRS. WATTS: It's between Harrison and Cotton.

TICKET MAN: Just a minute.

(He takes a book from behind the window on a shelf. He looks inside it. Mrs. Watts is again watching the doors. He looks up.)

Lady.

MRS. WATTS: Oh. Yessir.

TICKET MAN: I can sell you a ticket to Harrison or to Cotton. But there's no Bountiful.

MRS. WATTS: Oh, yes there is, it's between...

TICKET MAN: I'm sorry, lady. You say there is, but the book says there isn't. And the book don't lie.

MRS. WATTS: But...I...

TICKET MAN: *(Impatiently.)* Make up your mind, lady. Cotton or Harrison. There are other people waiting.

MRS. WATTS: Well...let me see....How much is a ticket to Harrison?

TICKET MAN: Three fifty...

MRS. WATTS: Cotton?

TICKET MAN: Four twenty.

MRS. WATTS: Oh, yes. Well, I'll have the one to Harrison, please.

TICKET MAN: All right. That'll be three fifty, please.

MRS. WATTS: Yessir. *(She reaches for her pocketbook and is about to open it. She turns to the Ticket Man.)* Can you cash a pension check? You see I decided to come at the last minute and I didn't have time to stop by the grocery store.

TICKET MAN: I'm sorry, lady. I can't cash any checks.

MRS. WATTS: It's perfectly good. It's a government check.

TICKET MAN: I'm sorry. It's against the rules to cash checks.

MRS. WATTS: Oh, is that so? I understand. A rule's a rule. How much was that again?

TICKET MAN: Three fifty.

MRS. WATTS: Oh, yes. Three fifty. Just a minute, sir. I've got it all here in nickels and dimes and quarters. *(She opens her purse and takes a handkerchief out. The money is tied in the handkerchief. She unties it, places it on the counter and begins to count out the amount for the ticket. She counts half aloud as she does it. She shoves a pile of silver towards the Ticket Man.)* Here. I think this is three fifty.

TICKET MAN: Thank you. *(He rakes the money into his hand. She ties her handkerchief back up.)*

MRS. WATTS: That's quite all right. I'm sorry to have taken up so much of your time. *(She picks up her suitcase and starts off.)*

TICKET MAN: Here, lady. Don't forget your ticket.

(She comes running back.)

MRS. WATTS: Oh, my heavens. Yes. I'd forget my head if it wasn't on my neck. *(She takes the ticket and goes away. The man next in line steps up to the window. Mrs. Watts goes back to the entrance U. C. R. She peers out and then comes back into the bus station. She comes down to the bench. Thelma is seated there, reading. Looks up from her magazine. There is an empty space next to her. Mrs. Watts comes up to it.)* Good evening.

THELMA: Good evening.

MRS. WATTS: Is this seat taken?

THELMA: No, Ma'm.

MRS. WATTS: Are you expectin' anyone?

THELMA: No, Ma'm.

MRS. WATTS: May I sit here then?

THELMA: Yes, Ma'm.

(Mrs. Watts puts the suitcase down along the side of the bench. She looks nervously around the station. All of a sudden she jumps up.)

MRS. WATTS: Would you watch my suitcase, honey?

THELMA: Yes, Ma'm.

MRS. WATTS: I'll be right back.

THELMA: Yes'm.

(Mrs. Watts goes running back toward the door to the street. Thelma watches her go for a minute and then goes back to reading her magazine. The Man at the ticket window is joined by the Man who is to relieve him for the night. They greet each other and the First Ticket Man leaves the bus station. Mrs. Watts comes back to the bench. She sits down and takes a handkerchief out of her purse. She wipes her forehead.)

MRS. WATTS: Thank you so much.

THELMA: That's all right.

(Mrs. Watts wipes her brow again.)

MRS. WATTS: Little warm isn't it when you're rushing around?

THELMA: Yes'm.

MRS. WATTS: I had to get myself ready in the biggest kind of hurry.

THELMA: Are you going on a trip?

MRS. WATTS: Yes, I am. I'm trying to get to a town nobody ever heard of around here.

THELMA: What town is that?

MRS. WATTS: Bountiful.

THELMA: Oh.

MRS. WATTS: Did you ever hear of it?

THELMA: No.

MRS. WATTS: You see. Nobody has. Well, it's not much of a town now, I guess. I haven't seen it myself in thirty years. But it used to be quite prosperous. All they have left is a post office and a filling station and a general store. At least they did when I left.

THELMA: Do your people live there?

MRS. WATTS: No. My people are all dead except my son and his wife, Jessie Mae. They live here in the city. I'm hurrying to see Bountiful before I die. I had a sinking spell this morning. I had to climb up on the bed and rest. It was my heart.

THELMA: Do you have a bad heart?

MRS. WATTS: Well, it's not what you call a good one. Doctor says it would last as long as I needed it if I could just cut out worrying. But seems I can't do that lately. *(She looks around the bus station again. She gets up out of her seat.)* Excuse me. Would you keep your eye on that suitcase again?

THELMA: Yes, Ma'm.

(Mrs. Watts hurries back to the U. C. R. entrance of the bus station. Thelma picks up her magazine and goes back to reading. Mrs. Watts comes hurrying back to the seat. She doesn't sit down, but stands over by the side.)

Lady. Is there anything wrong?

MRS. WATTS: No, honey. I'm just a little nervous. That's all.

(She hurries back towards the U. C. R. door. This time she opens it and goes outside. Thelma goes back to her reading. Mrs. Watts comes running back in. She hurries over to the seat and picks up the suitcase. In her confusion, she drops her handkerchief on the floor. Neither she nor Thelma sees it fall.)

Say a prayer for me, honey. Good luck.

THELMA: Good luck to you.

(Mrs. Watts goes running out D. R. toward the rest room. Ludie comes in outside door U. C. to the bus station. He stands a moment at the entrance, looking all around. He wanders slowly down until he gets to the bench where Thelma is sitting. He pauses here, looking out in front of him and to each side. Jessie Mae comes in U. C. R. She is in a rage. She walks over to Ludie.)

LUDIE: You want to sit down, Jessie Mae?

JESSIE MAE: Yes, I do. If you want to look around, go ahead. I'll wait here.

LUDIE: You looked carefully in the coffee shop?

JESSIE MAE: Yes.

LUDIE: Want me to bring you a coke?

JESSIE MAE: No.

LUDIE: Want me to buy you a movie magazine?

JESSIE MAE: Yes.

LUDIE: All right. I'll be right back. *(He goes back out the outside U. C. R. door he came in. Looking around as he goes. Jessie Mae sits down next to Thelma. She takes out a package of cigarettes. She gets her lighter. It doesn't work. She opens her purse and starts looking for a match. She can't find one. She turns to Thelma.)*

JESSIE MAE: Excuse me. Do you have a match? My lighter's out of fluid.

(Thelma reaches in the pocket of her jacket. She finds matches and gives them to her.)

Thank you. *(She lights her cigarette and hands the matches back to Thelma. Jessie Mae takes a deep drag off her cigarette.)* I hope you're lucky enough not to have to fool with any in-laws. I've got a mother-in-law about to drive me crazy. At least twice a year we have to try and keep her from getting on a train to go back to her home town. *(She takes another drag off her cigarette.)* I swear, she always has to spoil everything. My husband was goin' to take us to a double bill tonight at the picture show for the first time in I don't know when. I had called the beauty parlor for an appointment and I couldn't get one till four o'clock, see, and I was nervous sitting around the house, and so I went to the drug store for a fountain coke and I come home and what did I find...no Mother Watts. So I had to call my husband at the office and say the picture show was off. We've got to go looking for Mother Watts. Oh, she's so stubborn. I could just wring her neck. Her son spoils her that's the whole trouble. She's just rotten spoiled. Do you live with your in-laws?

THELMA: No.

JESSIE MAE: Well, you're lucky. They're all stubborn. My husband is as stubborn as she is. We should be over at the depot right now instead of sitting here. She always tries to go by train, but no. We wait at one railroad station five minutes and the other railroad station for five minutes and because she isn't there, right then, he drags me over here. And don't ask me why she always tries to go by train. That's just how she is. *(She takes another drag off her cigarette. It has gone out.)* Could I trouble you for another match, please? My cigarette has gone out.

(Thelma gets the match for her. Jessie Mae takes it and lights her cigarette.)

Of course, there hasn't been a train to that town in I don't know when. But if you try to tell her that she just looks at you like you're makin' it up. Always before we've been there waitin' for her when she walks into the railroad station, but today I was too trustin'. I gave her all the time in the world to get away. Well, we're payin' for it now. I told Ludie at breakfast she had that silent look, and I bet she tries to run away. But no, he said she wouldn't, because she had promised she wouldn't, and Ludie believes anything she says. I'm just worn out. I've had my fourth Coca-Cola today, just to keep my spirits up. People ask me why I don't have any children. Why? I say I've got Ludie and Mother Watts. That's all the children I need.

(Ludie comes in U. C. R. with a movie magazine. He comes up to Jessie Mae.)

What did you bring me?

(He shows her the magazine.)

Oh, I've seen that one.

LUDIE: *(He puts it absentmindedly under his arm. He looks around the station.)* Have you seen Mama?

JESSIE MAE: No, you goose. Do you think I'd be sittin' here so calm if I had! Personally I think we're wastin' our time sittin' here. She always tries to go by train.

LUDIE: But she can't go by train, Jessie Mae.

JESSIE MAE: She doesn't know that.

LUDIE: She's bound to by now. What time did she leave again?

JESSIE MAE: I don't know what time she left. I told you I called from the drug store at 11:30 and she was gone, the sneaky thing.

LUDIE: Well, you see she's had the time to find out a lot of things she hasn't known before.

(Jessie Mae gets up and goes to him.)

JESSIE MAE: I don't care what you say, Ludie. My hunch is that she's at one of those train stations. We've always found her there. You know how she is. Stubborn. Why, she won't believe them at the depot if they tell her there's not a train to Bountiful. She says there is and you watch, as far as she's concerned that's how it'll have to be. Ludie, I know she's there. I'm never wrong about these things.

LUDIE: All right. Have it your way. Let's go.

JESSIE MAE: Well, now we're here we might as well inquire from someone if they've seen her wanderin' around.

LUDIE: I thought you said she wouldn't come here.

JESSIE MAE: I said I didn't think she would come here. I don't know what the crazy thing will do. I could wring her neck. I can tell you that. I ought to be sitting at the beauty parlor right this very minute.

LUDIE: All right, Jessie Mae. Let's go on back to the depot.

JESSIE MAE: Will you stop rushing me around. I'm so mad I could chew nails. I tell you again I think we ought to just turn this whole thing over to the police. That would scare her once and for all.

LUDIE: Well, we're not going to call any police. We've been through that once and we're…

JESSIE MAE: It's for her own good. She's crazy.

LUDIE: *(He is very angry with her.)* Now why do you talk like that? You know Mama isn't crazy. *(A pause.)* I just wish you wouldn't say things like that.

JESSIE MAE: *(Jessie Mae has taken off her hat and hands it to Ludie. She is combing her hair and freshening her make-up during the following speech.)* Then why does she keep runnin' off from a perfectly good home like this? To try and get to some old swamp. Don't you call that crazy? I mean, she doesn't have to turn her hand. Hardly. We only have a bedroom and a living room and a kitchen. We're all certainly very light eaters, so cooking three meals a day isn't killing her. And like I told her this morning. She wouldn't be havin' her sinkin' spells if she'd start walkin' like a normal human bein' and not go trottin' all over the place. I said, Mother Watts, please tell me why with a bad heart you insist on running.…

(Ludie is getting more and more embarrassed. He sees people looking at them.)

LUDIE: Well, let's don't stand here arguing. People are looking at us. Do you want to go to the depot or not?

(Jessie Mae turns and sees they're being watched. She lowers her voice but not her intensity.)

JESSIE MAE: It's your mother. I don't care what you do. Only you better do something. Let me tell you that, or she's gonna clonk out someplace. She'll get to Bountiful and die from the excitement and then we'll have all kinds of expenses bringing her body back here. Do you know what a thing like that could cost? Do you realize she had a sinkin' spell this mornin'?

LUDIE: I know. You've told me a hundred times. What can I do about it, Jessie Mae?

JESSIE MAE: I'm trying to tell you what you can do about it. Call the police.

LUDIE: I'm not going to call the police.

JESSIE MAE: Oh, you won't.

LUDIE: No.

JESSIE MAE: Then I think I will. That'll settle it once and for all.

(She goes outside U. C. R. Ludie looks around for a minute, then sits down dejectedly in the seat next to Thelma. Thelma has been watching the preceding scene. She has tried not to be seen by them, but the audience should know that she has taken in every single word. Ludie reaches in his back pocket and takes out a handkerchief. He mops his forehead. He notices the magazine under his arm. He takes it in his hand and turns to Thelma.)

LUDIE: Would you like this? I never read them, and my wife has seen it.

THELMA: Thank you.

(She takes the magazine and puts it in her lap. She goes back to her reading. Ludie looks on the floor and sees the handkerchief that was dropped by Mrs. Watts. He reaches down and picks it up. He recognizes it. He gets up and goes running over to the ticket window.)

LUDIE: Excuse me. Did an old lady come here and buy a ticket to a town called Bountiful?

MAN: Where?

LUDIE: Bountiful!

MAN: Not since I've been on duty.

LUDIE: How long have you been on duty?

MAN: About fifteen minutes.

LUDIE: Where is the man that was on before?

MAN: He's gone home.

LUDIE: Oh. *(He walks away thinking what to do next. He sees Thelma and goes to her.)* Excuse me, Miss.

THELMA: Yes?

LUDIE: I found this handkerchief here that belongs, I think, to my mother.

She's run off from home. She has a heart condition and it might be serious for her to be all alone. I don't think she has much money, and I'd like to find her. Do you remember having seen her?

THELMA: Well…I…

LUDIE: She'd be on her way to a town called Bountiful.

THELMA: Yes, I did see her. She was here talkin' to me. She left all of a sudden.

LUDIE: Thank you so much.

(Jessie Mae has come back in U. C. R. *Ludie goes up to her.)*

JESSIE MAE: Ludie.

LUDIE: I was right. She was here. The lady there said so.

JESSIE MAE: Well, it's too late now.

LUDIE: But this lady was talking to her.

JESSIE MAE: We're not going to wait. The police and I talked it over.

(Thelma takes advantage of their argument to slip out of the station U. C.*)*

LUDIE: *(Turning on Jessie Mae.)* You didn't really call them!

JESSIE MAE: I did and they said in their opinion she was just trying to get our attention this way and we should just go home and pay her no mind at all.

LUDIE: How can I go home with Mama…

JESSIE MAE: The police tell me they have hundreds of cases like this every day. They say such things are very common among young people and old people, and they're positive that if we just go home and show her that we don't care if she goes or stays, she'll come home of her own free will.

LUDIE: Jessie Mae…

JESSIE MAE: Now, we're going to do what the police tell us to. They say she will come home when she's tired and hungry enough and that makes a lot of sense to me. Now, Ludie, I wish you'd think of me for a change.…I'm not going to spend the rest of my life running after your mother.

LUDIE: All right, Jessie Mae. *(He stands there, thinking.)*

JESSIE MAE: Now, come on, let's go. Come on.

(She starts out. Ludie pauses for a moment, thinking. He goes after her.)

LUDIE: All right. But if Mama is not home in an hour I'm going after her. . . .

JESSIE MAE: Honestly, Ludie, you're so stubborn.

(They go out U. C. R. *as the lights are brought down. Over the loudspeaker we hear the stations being called: Bus leaving for: Newton, Sugarland, Gerard, Harrison, Cotton, Old Gulf, Don Tarle.… In the darkness we hear the sound of a bus starting, then the noise of the traffic of a downtown city. Brakes grinding, horns honking. This is brought down to almost a whisper. The lights are brought up on the Center section and we see a seat in the bus. Mrs. Watts and Thelma are sitting there. Mrs. Watts is gazing out into the night. Thelma*

is casually glancing at the movie magazine. After a moment Mrs. Watts turns to her.)

MRS. WATTS: Isn't it a small world? I didn't know we'd be on the same bus. Where do you go, honey?

THELMA: Harrison.

MRS. WATTS: Harrison!

THELMA: Yes. I change busses there.

MRS. WATTS: So do I go there. Isn't that nice? Is that a moving picture magazine?

THELMA: Yes, Ma'm. Would you like to look at it?

MRS. WATTS: No, thank you. *(She leans her head back on the seat and turns her head away.)* The bus is nice to ride, isn't it?

THELMA: Yes It is.

MRS. WATTS: I'm sorry I couldn't take a train, though.

THELMA: I tried to go by train, but you couldn't get connections tonight.

MRS. WATTS: I know. When I was a girl I used to take excursions from Bountiful to Houston to Galveston. For the day, you know. Leave at five in the morning and return at ten that night. The whole town would be down to see you get off the train. I have such fond memories of those trips. *(A pause. She looks over at Thelma.)* Excuse me for getting personal, but what's a pretty girl like you doing travelling alone?

THELMA: My husband has just been sent overseas. I'm going to stay with my family.

MRS. WATTS: Oh, I'm sorry to hear that. Just say the Ninety-first Psalm over and over to yourself. It will be a bower of strength and protection for him. *(She begins to recite with closed eyes.)* "He that dwelleth in the secret place of the most high, shall abide under the shadow of the Almighty. I will say of the Lord, He is my refuge and my fortress: My God; in Him will I trust. Surely He shall deliver thee from the fowler and the noisome pestilence. He shall cover thee with His feathers and under his wing shalt thou trust: His truth shall be thy shield and buckler."
(Thelma covers her face with her hands—she is crying. Mrs. Watts looks up and sees her.)
Oh, I'm sorry. I'm sorry, honey.

THELMA: That's all right. I'm just lonesome for him.

MRS. WATTS: Keep him under the Lord's wing, honey, and he'll be safe.

THELMA: Yes, Ma'm. *(She dries her eyes.)* I'm sorry. I don't know what gets into me.

MRS. WATTS: Nobody needs be ashamed of crying. I guess we've all dampened our pillows sometime or other. I have, goodness knows.

THELMA: If I could only learn not to worry.

MRS. WATTS: I know. I guess we all ask that. Jessie Mae, my daughter-in-law, don't worry. What for? She says. Well, like I tell her that's a fine attitude if you can cultivate it. Trouble is I can't any longer.

THELMA: It is hard

MRS. WATTS: I didn't use to worry. I was so carefree as a girl. Had lots to worry me, too. Everybody was so poor back in Bountiful. But we got along. I said to Papa once after our third crop failure in a row, whoever gave this place the name of Bountiful? His Papa did, he said, because in those days it was a land of plenty. You just had to drop seeds in the ground and the crops would spring up. Cotton and corn and sugar cane. I still think it's the prettiest place I know of. Jessie Mae says it's the ugliest. But she just says that I know to make me mad. She only saw it once, and then on a rainy day, at that. She says it's nothing but a swamp. That may be, I said, but it's a mighty pretty swamp to me. And then Sonny, that's my boy, Ludie, I call him Sonny, he said not to answer her back. He said it only caused arguments. And nobody ever won an argument with Jessie Mae, and I guess that's right. *(A pause. She looks out into space.)*

THELMA: Mrs. Watts...

MRS. WATTS: Yes?

THELMA: I think I ought to tell you this...I...I don't want you to think I'm interfering in your business...but...well...you see your son and daughter-in-law came in just after you left....

MRS. WATTS: I know. I saw them coming. That's why I left so fast.

THELMA: Your son seemed very concerned.

MRS. WATTS: Bless his heart.

THELMA: He found a handkerchief that you had dropped.

MRS. WATTS: Oh, mercy. That's right, I did.

THELMA: He asked me if I had seen you. I felt I had to say yes. I wouldn't have said anything if he hadn't asked me.

MRS. WATTS: Oh, that's all right. I would have done the same thing in your place. Did you talk to Jessie Mae?

THELMA: Yes.

MRS. WATTS: Isn't she a sight? I bet she told you I was crazy....

THELMA: Well...

MRS. WATTS: Oh, don't be afraid of hurting my feelings. Poor Jessie Mae, she thinks everybody's crazy that don't want to sit in the beauty parlor all day and drink Coca-colas. She tells me a million times a day I'm crazy. That's the only time Ludie will talk back to her. He gets real mad when she calls me crazy. I think Ludie knows how I feel about getting back to Bountiful.

Once when I was talkin' about somethin' we did back there in the old days, he just broke out cryin'. He was so overcome he had to leave the room. *(A pause. Mrs. Watts starts to hum…"There's Not a Friend Like the Lowly Jesus.")*

THELMA: That's a pretty hymn. What's the name of it?

MRS. WATTS: "There's Not a Friend Like the Lowly Jesus." Do you like hymns?

THELMA: Yes, I do.

MRS. WATTS: So do I. Jessie Mae says they've gone out of style…but I don't agree. I always sing one walking down the street or riding in the streetcar. Keeps my spirits up. What's your favorite hymn?

THELMA: Oh, I don't know.

MRS. WATTS: The one I was singin' is mine. I bet I sing it a hundred times a day. When Jessie Mae isn't home. Hymns make Jessie Mae nervous. *(A pause.)* Did Ludie mention my heart condition?

THELMA: Yes, he did.

MRS. WATTS: Poor Ludie. He worries about it so. I hated to leave him. Well, I hope he'll forgive me in time. So many people are nervous today. He wasn't nervous back in Bountiful. Neither was I. The breeze from the Gulf would always quiet your nerves. You could sit on your front gallery and smell the ocean blowing in around you. *(A pause.)* I regret the day I left. But I thought it was the best thing at the time. There were only three families left there then. Farming was so hard to make a living by, and I had to see to our farm myself; our house was old and there was no money to fix it with, nor send Ludie to school. So I sold off the land and gave him an education. Callie said I could always come back and visit her. She meant it, too. That's who I'm going to stay with now. Callie Davis. I get a card from her every Christmas. I wrote her last week and told her to expect me. Told her not to answer though on account of Jessie Mae opens all my mail. I didn't want her to know I was going. She'd try to stop me. Jessie Mae hates me. I don't know why, but she hates me. *(A pause.)* Hate me or not. I gotta get back and smell that salt air and work that dirt. I'm gonna spend the whole first month of my visit workin' in Callie's garden. I haven't had my hands in dirt in twenty years. My hands feel the need of dirt. *(A pause.)* Do you like to work the ground?

THELMA: I never have.

MRS. WATTS: Try it sometimes. It'll do wonders for you. I bet I'll live to be a hundred once I can get outside again. It was being cooped up in those two rooms that was killing me. I used to work the land like a man. Had to when papa died….I got two little babies buried there. Renee Sue and

Douglas. Diphtheria got Renee Sue. I never knew what carried Douglas away. He was just weak from the start. I know Callie's kept their graves weeded. Oh, if my heart just holds out until I get there. *(A pause.)* Where do you go from Harrison?

THELMA: Old Gulf. My family have just moved there from Louisiana. I'll stay there with them until my husband comes home again.

MRS. WATTS: That's nice.

THELMA: It'll be funny living at home again.

MRS. WATTS: How long have you been married?

THELMA: A year. My husband was anxious for me to go. He said he'd worry about my being alone. I'm the only child and my parents and I are very close.

MRS. WATTS: That's nice.

THELMA: My father being in the oil business we've always moved around a lot. I guess I went to school in fifteen different towns along the Coast. I guess moving around like that made me and my mother and father even closer. I hoped so my mother and daddy would like my husband and he'd like them. I needn't have worried. They hit it off from the very first. Mother and daddy say they feel like they have two children now. A son and a daughter.

MRS. WATTS: Isn't that nice? I've heard people say that when your son marries you lose a son, but when your daughter marries you get a son. *(A pause.)* What's your husband's name?

THELMA: Robert.

MRS. WATTS: That's a nice name.

THELMA: I think so. But I guess any name he had I would think was nice. I love my husband very much. Lots of girls I know think I'm silly about him, but I can't help it. *(A pause.)*

MRS. WATTS: I wasn't in love with my husband. *(A pause.)* Do you believe we are punished for what we do wrong? I sometimes think that's why I've had all my trouble. I've talked to many a preacher about it, all but one said they didn't think so. But I can't see any other reason. Of course, I didn't lie to my husband. I told him I didn't love him, that I admired him, which I did, but I didn't love him. That I'd never love anybody but Ray John Murray as long as I lived and I didn't, and I couldn't help it. Even after my husband died and I had to move back with Mama and Papa I used to sit on the front gallery every morning and every evening just to nod hello to Ray John Murray as he went by the house to work at the store. He went a block out of his way to pass the house. He never loved nobody but me.

THELMA: Why didn't you marry him?

MRS. WATTS: His papa and my papa didn't speak. My papa forced me to write a letter saying I never wanted to see him again and he got drunk and married out of spite. I felt sorry for his wife. She knew he never loved her. *(A pause.)* I don't think about those things any more. But they're all part of Bountiful and I guess that's why I'm starting to think of them again. You're lucky to be married to the man you love, honey.

THELMA: I know I am.

MRS. WATTS: Awfully lucky. *(A pause. She looks out the window.)* Did you see that star fall over there?

THELMA: No.

MRS. WATTS: It was the prettiest thing I ever saw. You can make a wish on a falling star, honey.

THELMA: I know. It's too bad I didn't see it.

MRS. WATTS: You take my wish.

THELMA: Oh, no.

MRS. WATTS: Go on. I've gotten mine already. I'm on my way to Bountiful.

THELMA: Thank you.

(A pause. Thelma closes her eyes. Mrs. Watts watches her for a moment.)

MRS. WATTS: Did you make your wish?

THELMA: Yes, I did.

(Mrs. Watts leans her head back on the seat. She hums to herself. Thelma leans her head back, too. They close their eyes. The lights fade. The lights on the area L. are brought up. It is the Harrison bus station. An Old Man is inside the ticket window, C. L. with his head on the ledge asleep. He wakes up. He comes out of the cage into the room, yawning and stretching. We hear a bus pull up in the distance and stop. He starts for the entrance of the bus station, U. C. L., as Thelma comes in carrying her suitcase and Mrs. Watts's suitcase.)

TICKET MAN: Want any help with those bags?

THELMA: No, thank you.

(The Ticket Man turns a light on in the Station. Thelma takes the bags and puts them down beside a bench. She goes over to the Ticket Man.)

Excuse me.

TICKET MAN: Yes?

THELMA: Is the bus to Old Gulf going to be on time?

TICKET MAN: Always is.

THELMA: Thank you. *(Thelma goes back to her seat near the suitcases. Mrs. Watts comes in U. L. C. She sees the Ticket Man. She speaks to him.)*

MRS. WATTS: Good evening. *(To Thelma.)* What time is it, honey?

THELMA: Twelve o'clock.

MRS. WATTS: Twelve o'clock. I bet Callie will be surprised to see me walk in at twelve o'clock.

THELMA: Did you tell her you were coming today?

MRS. WATTS: No. I couldn't. Because I didn't know. I had to wait until Jessie Mae went to the drugstore.

THELMA: My bus is leaving in half an hour.

MRS. WATTS: Oh, I see. I guess I'd better be finding out how I'm going to get to Bountiful.

THELMA: You sit down. I'll find the man.

MRS. WATTS: Thank you.

(She sits on the bench. Thelma goes over to the Ticket Man at the door. He is busy bringing in the morning papers left by the bus.)

THELMA: Excuse me again.

TICKET MAN: Yes?

THELMA: My friend here wants to know how she can get to Bountiful.

TICKET MAN: Bountiful?

THELMA: Yes.

TICKET MAN: What's she going there for?

(Mrs. Watts comes up to the Ticket Man.)

MRS. WATTS: I'm going to visit my girlhood friend.

TICKET MAN: I don't know who that's gonna be. The last person in Bountiful was Mrs. Callie Davis. She died day before yesterday. That is they found her day before yesterday. She lived all alone so they don't know exactly when she died.

MRS. WATTS: Callie Davis!

TICKET MAN: Yes, Ma'm. They had the funeral this morning. Was she the one you were going to visit?

MRS. WATTS: Yessir. She was the one. She was my friend. My girlhood friend.

(Mrs. Watts stands for a moment. Then she goes to the bench. She seems very old and tired and defeated. Thelma crosses to Ticket Man.)

THELMA: Is there a hotel here?

TICKET MAN: Yes'm. The Riverview.

THELMA: How far is it?

TICKET MAN: About five blocks.

THELMA: Is there a taxi around?

TICKET MAN: No, Ma'm. Not this time of night.

THELMA: Thank you.

(The Man goes back into the ticket window. Thelma goes over to Mrs. Watts at the bench. She speaks to her with great sympathy.)
What'll you do now, Mrs. Watts?

MRS. WATTS: I'm thinking, honey. I'm thinking. It's come as quite a blow.

THELMA: I'm sorry. I'm so sorry.

MRS. WATTS: I know. I know. *(A pause. Her strength and her will reviving.)* It's come to me what to do. I'll go on. That much has come to me. To go on. I feel my strength and my purpose strong within me. I'll go on to Bountiful. I'll walk those twelve miles if I have to. *(She is standing now.)*

THELMA: But if there's no one out there what'll you do this time of night?
(Thelma gets her to sit back down.)

MRS. WATTS: Oh, yes. I guess that's right.

THELMA: I think you should wait until morning.

MRS. WATTS: Yes. I guess I should. Then I can hire someone to drive me out. You know what I'll do. I'll stay at my own house, or what's left of it. Put me in a garden. I'll get along fine with the help of my government checks.

THELMA: Mrs. Watts, the man says there's a hotel not too far away. I think you'd better let me take you there.

MRS. WATTS: Oh, no thank you. I wouldn't want to waste my money on a hotel. They're high as cats' backs you know. I'll just sleep right here on this bench. Put my coat under my head, hold my purse under my arm. *(She puts the coat down on the bench like a pillow. She begins to look around for her purse. She has lost it.)* My purse! *(She begins to search frantically.)* Have you seen my purse, honey?

THELMA: Why, no.
(They begin to look around for it.)

MRS. WATTS: Oh, good heavens. I remember now. I left my purse on the bus.
(Thelma runs to the entrance and looks out.)

THELMA: You're sure you left it there?

MRS. WATTS: *(Joining her.)* Yes. I am. I remember now. I didn't have it when I got off that bus. I kept thinking something was missing, but then I decided it was my suitcase that you had brought in for me. What am I gonna do, honey? All I have in the world is in that purse.
(Thelma and Mrs. Watts go back to the ticket window. The Man is drowsing.)

THELMA: Excuse me again.

TICKET MAN: Yeah?

THELMA: This lady left her purse on the bus.

TICKET MAN: All right. I'll call ahead. How can you identify it?

MRS. WATTS: It's a plain brown purse.

TICKET MAN: How much money?

MRS. WATTS: Thirty-five cents and a pension check.

TICKET MAN: Who was the check made out to?

MRS. WATTS: To me. Mrs. Carrie Watts.

TICKET MAN: All right. I'll call up about it.

MRS. WATTS: Oh, thank. you. You're most kind.

THELMA: How long will it take to get it back?

TICKET MAN: Depends. If I can get ahead of the bus at Don Tarle, I can get them to send it back on the Victoria bus and it should be here in a couple of hours.

MRS. WATTS: That's awful kind of you.

(He goes. Thelma and Mrs. Watts go back to the bench.)

I don't know what I would have done without you.

THELMA: Try not to worry about the purse.

MRS. WATTS: I won't.

(They sit on the bench.)

I'm too tired to worry. Be time enough to start worrying when I wake up in the morning.

THELMA: Why don't you go on to sleep now if you can?

MRS. WATTS: Oh, I thought I'd stay up and see you off.

THELMA: No. You go on to sleep.

MRS. WATTS: I couldn't go right off to sleep now. I'm too wound up. You know I don't go on a trip every day of my life.

(The Ticket Man comes over to them on the bench.)

TICKET MAN: You're lucky. Bus hadn't gotten to Don Tarle yet. If they can find the purse it'll be here around five.

MRS. WATTS: Thank you. Thank you so much.

THELMA: Make you feel better?

MRS. WATTS: Yes. It does. Of course, everything has seemed to work out today. Why is it some days everything works out, and some days nothing works out. What I mean, is, I've been trying to get on that bus for Bountiful for over five years. Usually Jessie Mae and Ludie find me before I ever get inside the railroad station good. Today, I got inside both the railroad station and the bus station. Bought a ticket, seen Ludie and Jessie Mae before they saw me. Hid out. Met a pretty friend like you. Lost my purse, and now I'm having it found for me. I guess the good Lord is just with me today. *(A pause.)* I wonder why the Lord isn't with us every day? It would be so nice if He was. Well, maybe then we wouldn't appreciate so much the days when He's on our side. Or maybe He's always on our side and we don't know it. Maybe I had to wait twenty years cooped up in a city before I could appreciate getting back here.

(A pause. Thelma rests her head back on the bench. Mrs. Watts rests her head. She hums her hymn.)

It's so nice being able to sing a hymn when you want to. I'm a happy woman, young lady. A very happy woman.

THELMA: I still have a sandwich left. Will you have one?

MRS. WATTS: Sure you don't want it?

THELMA: No. I'm full.

MRS. WATTS: Then I'll have a half, thank you.

(Thelma gets the sandwich from her suitcase and unwraps it.)

THELMA: Take the whole sandwich. I'm not hungry.

MRS. WATTS: No, thank you. Just half. You know I don't eat much. Particularly if I'm excited. *(She rises and stands nibbling on the sandwich and walking around the room.)* You know, I came to my first dance in this town.

THELMA: Did you?

MRS. WATTS: Yes, Ma'm. It was the summertime. My father couldn't decide if he thought dancin' was right or not. But my mother said she had danced when she was a girl and I was gonna dance. And so I went. The girls from all over the county came for this dance. It was at the Opera House. I forget what the occasion was. Somethin' special though. *(A pause. She looks at Thelma. She goes over to her.)* Do you know something, young lady? If my daughter had lived I would have wanted her to be just like you.

THELMA: Oh, thank you.

MRS. WATTS: *(With great tenderness.)* Just like you. Sweet and considerate and thoughtful.

THELMA: Oh, no…I'm…

MRS. WATTS: Oh, yes. Sweet and considerate and thoughtful. And pretty.

THELMA: Well, thank you. *(A pause.)* Mrs. Watts…I hope you don't mind my askin' this, but I worry about your son. Are you going to let him know where you are?

MRS. WATTS: Oh, yes, Ma'm. As soon as I get that check cashed I'm going to send him a telegram.

(The Ticket Man comes by checking his watch as he passes. Mrs. Watts follows after him.)

I was tellin' my little friend here that I came to my first dance in this town.

TICKET MAN: Is that so?

MRS. WATTS: Yes. And I've been to Harrison quite a few times in my life, shopping.

TICKET MAN: *(To Thelma.)* You'd better get outside, Miss. Bus will be up the road. It won't wait this time of night unless it sees we have a passenger.

THELMA: All right. *(She gets her suitcase.)* Good-bye, Mrs. Watts.

MRS. WATTS: *(Following her to the door.)* Good-bye, honey. Good luck to you. And thank you for everything.

THELMA: That's all right. Good luck to you.

MRS. WATTS: Thank you.

> *(Thelma kisses her. Thelma goes out into the night, followed by the Ticket Man. Mrs. Watts stands at the door watching Thelma. We hear a bus pulling up. Mrs. Watts waves. We hear the bus leave. The Ticket Man comes back inside the bus station.)*

TICKET MAN: Are you gonna stay here all night?

MRS. WATTS: I have to. Everything I have is in that purse and we can't go any place without money.

TICKET MAN: I guess that's right. *(He starts away.)*

MRS. WATTS: Do they still have dances in Borden's Opera House?

TICKET MAN: No, Ma'm. It's torn down. They condemned it, you know. *(He starts on. He pauses.)* Did you ever know anybody in Harrison?

MRS. WATTS: I knew a few people when I was a girl. Priscilla Nytelle. Did you know her?

TICKET MAN: No, Ma'm.

MRS. WATTS: Nancy Lee Goodhue?

TICKET MAN: No, Ma'm.

MRS. WATTS: The Fay girls?

TICKET MAN: No, Ma'm.

MRS. WATTS: I used to trade in Mr. Ewing's store. I knew him to speak to.

TICKET MAN: Which Ewing was that?

MRS. WATTS: George White Ewing.

TICKET MAN: He's dead.

MRS. WATTS: Is that so?

TICKET MAN: Been dead for twelve years.

MRS. WATTS: Is that so?

TICKET MAN: He left quite a bit of money, but his son took over his store and lost it all. Drank.

MRS. WATTS: Is that so? One thing I can say about my boy is that he never gave me any worry that way.

TICKET MAN: Well, that's good. I've got one boy that drinks and one boy that doesn't. I can't understand it. I raised them the same way.

MRS. WATTS: I know. I've known of other cases like that. One drinks. The other doesn't.

TICKET MAN: A friend of mine has a girl that drinks. I think that's the saddest thing in the world.

MRS. WATTS: Isn't it? *(A pause.)*

TICKET MAN: Well. Good night.

MRS. WATTS: Good night.

(Ticket Man stands waiting to switch off the light while Mrs. Watts takes her suitcase and coat and makes a bed for herself on the bench. She lies down. He goes inside the ticket booth. He sticks his head out the cage.)

TICKET MAN: Good night.

MRS. WATTS: Good night.

(He turns the light inside the ticket window out. Mrs. Watts is humming quietly to herself. Her humming fades away as the lights are faded out. The lights are brought up. The Ticket Man is in his office sound asleep and snoring slightly. The door opens and a Man comes in. He is the Sheriff. He stands by the door for a moment looking around the bus station. He sees Mrs. Watts lying on the bench asleep. He goes over to her and looks down. He stands for a moment watching her sleep. He looks over at the ticket window and sees the Man is asleep. The Sheriff goes over to the Ticket Man. He shakes him.)

SHERIFF: Come on, Roy, wake up.

TICKET MAN: Yeah? *(He opens his eyes. He sees the Sheriff. He comes out to the Sheriff.)* Oh, hello, Sheriff.

SHERIFF: How long has that old woman been here?

TICKET MAN: About four hours.

SHERIFF: Did she get off the bus from Houston?

TICKET MAN: Yessir. I know her name. It's Watts. She left her purse on the bus and I had to call up to Don Tarle about it.

SHERIFF: Have you got her purse?

TICKET MAN: Yes. It just came.

SHERIFF: She's the one, all right. I've had a call from the Houston Police to hold her until her son can come for her.

TICKET MAN: She said she used to live in Bountiful.

SHERIFF: Yeah. I believe I remember some Wattses a long time ago over that way. I think that old ramshackly house about to fall into the Brazos River belonged to them.

TICKET MAN: That right? They must have been before my time. She asked me about a lot of people I never heard of. She claimed she was going to visit Miss Callie Davis. I told her she was dead. What do the police want her for?

SHERIFF: Police don't. It's her son. He wants to take her back home. Claims she's not responsible. Did she act crazy to you?

TICKET MAN: Not that I noticed. Is she crazy?

SHERIFF: They say so. Harmless, but hipped on running away from Houston to get back here. *(He starts over to her to wake her up. He stands looking at her for a moment. He comes back to the Ticket Man.)* Poor old thing. She's sleeping so sound. I don't have the heart to wake her up. I'll tell you what, I'll go down and call Houston…tell them she's here. Her son is coming in his car. He should be here around seven-thirty. I'll be back in ten minutes. If she gives you any trouble just call me. Keep your eye on her.

TICKET MAN: All right.

(The Sheriff goes out and the Ticket Man follows him. Comes back in carrying a crate. He bumps it accidentally against the door. This wakes Mrs. Watts up. She opens her eyes. She looks around trying to remember where she is. Then she sees the Ticket Man.)

MRS. WATTS: Good morning.

TICKET MAN: Good morning.

MRS. WATTS: Could you tell me the time?

TICKET MAN: It's around four-thirty.

MRS. WATTS: Thank you. Did my purse arrive?

TICKET MAN: Yes, Ma'm. *(He reaches under the ticket window to a ledge and gets the purse for her. He hands the purse to her.)*

MRS. WATTS: Thank you so much. I wonder if you could cash a check for me?

TICKET MAN: I'm sorry. I can't.

MRS. WATTS: It's a government check and I have identification.

TICKET MAN: I'm sorry. I can't.

MRS. WATTS: Do you know where I could get a check cashed?

TICKET MAN: Why?

(She starts to gather up her coat and suitcase.)

MRS. WATTS: I need money to get me started in Bountiful. I want to hire someone to drive me out there and look at my house and get a few groceries. Try to find a cot to sleep on. *(She has the coat and suitcase.)*

TICKET MAN: I'm sorry, lady. You're not going to Bountiful.

MRS. WATTS: Oh, yes, I am. You see…

TICKET MAN: I'm sorry, lady. You're not going any place right now. I have to hold you here for the Sheriff.

MRS. WATTS: The Sheriff?

TICKET MAN: Yes, Ma'm. *(A pause.)*

MRS. WATTS: You're joking with me!? Don't joke with me. I've come too far.

TICKET MAN: I'm sorry. That's how it is.

MRS. WATTS: What has the Sheriff got to do with me?

TICKET MAN: He came a few minutes ago while you were asleep and said I was to keep you here until your son arrived in his car this morning.

MRS. WATTS: My son hasn't got a car, so I don't believe you. I don't believe you.

TICKET MAN: It's the truth. He'll be here in a little while, and you can ask him yourself. *(A pause.)*

MRS. WATTS: Then you're not joking?

TICKET MAN: No.

(She takes her coat and suitcase and runs for the entrance. He senses what she is going to do and gets there first—blocking her way.)

MRS. WATTS: All right. But I'm going, do you understand? You'll see. This is a free country. And I'll tell him that. No Sheriff or king or president will keep me from going back to Bountiful.

TICKET MAN: All right. You tell him that.

(She comes back into the room. She is desperate.)

MRS. WATTS: What time is my son expected?

TICKET MAN: Sheriff says around seven-thirty.

MRS. WATTS: What time is it now?

TICKET MAN: I told you around four-thirty.

MRS. WATTS: Where can I get me a driver?

TICKET MAN: Ma'm?

MRS. WATTS: If you can get me a driver, I can make it to Bountiful and back way before seven-thirty....

TICKET MAN: Look, lady...

MRS. WATTS: That's all I want. That's all I ask. Just to see it. To stand on the porch of my own house, once more. Walk under the trees. I swear, I would come back then meek as a lamb. . . .

TICKET MAN: Lady...

MRS. WATTS: Last night, I thought I had to stay. I thought I'd die if I couldn't stay. But I'll settle for less now. Much, much less. An hour. A half hour. Fifteen minutes.

TICKET MAN: Lady, it ain't up to me. I told you the Sheriff...

MRS. WATTS: *(Screaming.)* Then get me the Sheriff.

TICKET MAN: Look, lady...

MRS. WATTS: Get me the Sheriff. The time is going. They'll have me locked in those two rooms again soon. The time is going...the time is...

(The Sheriff comes in. The Sheriff goes over to Mrs. Watts.)

SHERIFF: Mrs. Watts?

MRS. WATTS: Yessir. *(She looks up at him. She puts the coat and suitcase down.)* Are you the Sheriff?

SHERIFF: Yes, Ma'm.

MRS. WATTS: I understand my son will be here at seven-thirty to take me back to Houston.

SHERIFF: Yes, Ma'm.

MRS. WATTS: Then listen to me, sir. I've waited a long time. Just to get to Bountiful. Twenty years I've been walkin' the streets of the city, lost and grieving. And as I've grown older and my time approaches, I've made one promise to myself, to see my home again…before I die…

SHERIFF: Lady…I…

MRS. WATTS: I'm not asking that I not go back. I'm willing to go back. Only let me travel these twelve miles first. I have money. I can pay…

SHERIFF: I think that's between you and your son.

MRS. WATTS: Ludie? Why, he's got to do whatever Jessie Mae tells him to. I know why she wants me back. It's for my government check.

SHERIFF: I don't know anything about that. That's between you and your son.

MRS. WATTS: Won't you let me go?

SHERIFF: No. Not unless your son takes you.

MRS. WATTS: All right. Then I've lost. I've come all this way only to lose. *(A pause. She stands behind the bench supporting herself. She seems very tired and defeated. She speaks very quietly and almost to herself.)* I've kept thinking back there day and night in those two rooms, I kept thinkin'…and it may mean nothin' at all to you, but I kept thinkin'…that if I could just set foot there for a minute…even…a second…I might get some understanding of why…Why my life has grown so empty and meaningless. Why I've turned into a hateful, quarrelsome, old woman. And before I leave this earth, I'd like to recover some of the dignity…the peace I used to know. For I'm going to die…and Jessie Mae knows that…and she's willful and it's her will I die in those two rooms. Well, she won't have her way. It's my will to die in Bountiful.

(She sobs and starts to run out of the bus station. The Sheriff stops her. She suddenly seems very weak, and is about to fall. He has her arm, supporting her.)

SHERIFF: Mrs. Watts.

MRS. WATTS: Let me go those twelve miles…before it's too late. *(A pause. For a moment her strength seems to come back.)* Understand me. Suffering I don't mind. Suffering I understand. I never protested once. Though my heart was broken when those babies died. I could stand seeing the man I love walk through life with another woman. But this fifteen years of bickering.

Endless, petty bickering.…It's made me like Jessie Mae sees me. It's ugly. I won't be that way. *(An anguished cry.)* I want to go home. I want to go home. I want to go…

(She is unable to speak any more. She is on the verge of collapse. The Sheriff helps her over to the bench and settles her there. The Sheriff calls to the Ticket Man.)

SHERIFF: Roy, hurry. Call a doctor. *(She summons up her last bit of strength to get free.)*

MRS. WATTS: No. No doctor. Bountiful.…Bountiful.…. Bountiful.

(The Sheriff holds her. There is a very fast curtain.)

END OF ACT TWO

ACT III

SCENE: It is early morning. The lights are slowly brought up and we can see the house and the yard of Mrs. Watts's old house in Bountiful. The house, with a sagging porch before it, is R. The entrance to the yard is U. C.

The house is an old ramshackle, two-story country place that hasn't been painted for years. Vines are growing wild over it, coral vine and Virginia Creeper and fig vine. The roof of the front porch is sagging and one of the supporting posts is completely gone. The floor boards of the front porch are rotting away and the steps leading to the flowers are everywhere: Buttercups, dandelions and wild iris. In the early morning light there is a peace and tranquillity and a wild kind of beauty about the place that is moving and heartwarming and in its own way lovely. The Sheriff and Mrs. Watts come in U. C. walking very slowly. They stop every few minutes while she looks at the house and the yard. Mrs. Watts is carrying her purse.

MRS. WATTS: I'm home. I'm home. Thank you. I thank you. I thank you. I thank you. *(They pause for a moment in the yard. Mrs. Watts is obviously still quite weak.)*

SHERIFF: You'd better sit down and rest for a while. You don't want to overdo it.

MRS. WATTS: Yessir. *(She sits on a tree stump in the yard.)*

SHERIFF: Feeling all right?

MRS. WATTS: Yes, I am. I feel ever so much better.

SHERIFF: You look better. I hope I've done the right thing in bringing you here. Well, I don't see what harm it can do. As long as you mind the doctor and don't get over excited.

MRS. WATTS: Yessir. *(A pause. She looks around the yard again.)*

SHERIFF: Soon as you've rested for a little I'll go on back to my car and leave you alone. You can call me if you need anything. I'll stay out here until your son arrives.

MRS. WATTS: Thank you. You've been very kind.

(A bird calls. She and the Sheriff sit listening to it. It whistles once again.)

What kind of a bird was that?

SHERIFF: Red bird.

MRS. WATTS: I thought that was a red bird, but I hadn't heard one in so long, I couldn't be sure. *(A pause.)* Do they still have scissor-tails around here?

SHERIFF: Yes, Ma'm. I still see one every once in a while when I'm driving around the country.

MRS. WATTS: I don't know of anything prettier than a scissor tail flying around in the sky. *(A pause.)* My father was a good man in many ways, a peculiar man, but a good one. One of the things he couldn't stand was to see a bird shot on his land. If men came here hunting, he'd take a gun and chase them away. I think the birds knew they couldn't be touched here. Our land was always a home to them. Ducks and geese and finches and blue jays. Blue birds and red birds. Wild canaries and black birds and mockers and doves and rice birds… *(During the latter speech she gets up and begins to pick weeds out of the yard. At the end of the speech the Sheriff gently stops her and leads her to the porch of the house. She sits on step.)*

SHERIFF: Rice birds are gettin' thicker every year. They seem to thrive out here on the coast.

MRS. WATTS: I guess a mockin'bird is my favorite of them all.

SHERIFF: I guess it's mine, too.

MRS. WATTS: I don't know, though. I'm mighty partial to a scissor tail. I hope I get to see one soon.

SHERIFF: I hope you can.

MRS. WATTS: My father was born on this land and in this house. Did you know my father?

SHERIFF: No, Ma'm. Not that I can remember.

MRS. WATTS: I guess there are not many around here that remember my father. I do, of course, and my son. Maybe some old timers around Harrison. *(A pause.)* It's funny, ever since I've been here I've been half expectin' my father and my mother to walk out of the house and greet me and welcome me home. *(A pause.)* When you've lived longer than your house or your family, maybe you've lived too long. *(A pause.)* Or maybe it's just me.

Maybe the need to belong to a house, and a family and a town has gone from the rest of the world.

SHERIFF: How big was your farm, Mrs. Watts?

MRS. WATTS: Three hundred and seventy-five acres were left when my papa died and I sold off all but the house and the yard. *(A pause.)* You say the store burned fifteen years ago?

SHERIFF: Yes, Ma'm. What was left of it. You see with the good roads we have now in the county, the little town and their country stores are all disappearing. The farmers ride into Cotton or Harrison to trade....

MRS. WATTS: But what's happened to the farms? For the last five miles I've seen nothing but woods....

SHERIFF: I know. The land around Bountiful just played out. People like you got discouraged and moved away, sold off the land for what they could get. H. T. Mavis bought most of it up. He let it go back into timber. He keeps a few head of cattle out here. That's about all....

MRS. WATTS: Callie Davis kept her farm going.

SHERIFF: Yes. She did. She learned how to treat her land right and it began paying off for her toward the end. I've heard she was out riding her tractor the day before she died. Lonely death she had. All by herself in that big house.

MRS. WATTS: There are worse things.

(The sun is up full now. Filling the stage with light.)

SHERIFF: Looks to me like you're going to have a pretty day.

MRS. WATTS: I hope so. My daughter-in-law has never seen our place in the sunshine. I expect my son will bring her along with him. I'd hate for her to have to see it again in the rain.

(A pause. The Sheriff looks at her.)

SHERIFF: Feeling more rested now?

MRS. WATTS: Oh, yes, I am.

SHERIFF: Good. Then I'll be getting on back to my car. You just call me if you need anything.

MRS. WATTS: Thank you.

(He gets up and walks to the corner of the yard. Just before he goes out he turns and waves. Mrs. Watts waves back to him. She sits on the steps for a moment watching him go out U. C. When he is out of sight, she rises slowly from the steps and goes along the porch. When she comes to the front door she stops and stands for a moment. She slowly opens the door and goes inside the house as the lights fade. The lights are slowly brought up. The Sheriff comes into the yard. He goes up to the steps of the porch.)

SHERIFF: *(Calling.)* Mrs. Watts. Mrs. Watts. Mrs. Watts.

> *(He runs up on the porch as he calls her. Mrs. Watts comes out of the house. She has left her purse inside the house.)*

MRS. WATTS: Yessir.

SHERIFF: It's seven-thirty. Your son and his wife are here.

MRS. WATTS: Yessir.

SHERIFF: They're out on the road in their car. They said they had to hurry on back. I told them I'd come get you.

MRS. WATTS: Yessir. Won't you ask them to please come in for a minute?

SHERIFF: Well, all right. I'll have to be gettin' on back to town now myself, Mrs. Watts. *(He holds his hand out. She takes it.)* Good-bye, and good luck to you.

MRS. WATTS: Thank you. You'll never know what this has meant to me.

SHERIFF: Glad I could oblige.

> *(He starts away as Ludie comes into the yard U. C.)*

Oh, Mr. Watts. I was just coming to tell you your mother wanted you to come in for a few minutes.

LUDIE: Thank you.

> *(The Sheriff goes up to him.)*

SHERIFF: I've got to be getting back on into town.

LUDIE: All right, Sheriff. Thank you for everything you've done.

SHERIFF: Don't mention it. I was glad I could oblige. You folks have a nice trip home.

LUDIE: Thank you.

SHERIFF: Good-bye, Mrs. Watts.

MRS. WATTS: Good-bye, Sheriff.

SHERIFF: So long, Mr. Watts.

LUDIE: Good-bye, Sheriff.

> *(He goes out U. C. Mrs. Watts and Ludie watch him go. Ludie walks up on the porch to his mother. They both seem embarrassed and ill at ease.)*

Hello, Mama.

MRS. WATTS: Hello, son.

LUDIE: How do you feel?

MRS. WATTS: I'm feelin' better, Ludie.

LUDIE: That's good. They told me at the bus station you had another attack.

MRS. WATTS: Yes, I did. All the excitement, I guess. But I feel fine now.

LUDIE: Yes'm.

MRS. WATTS: I got my wish.

LUDIE: Yes'm. (*Ludie walks away from the porch down to the corner of the yard. Mrs. Watts follows him.*)

MRS. WATTS: I hope I didn't worry you too much, Ludie. But I just felt I had to...

LUDIE: I know, Mama.

MRS. WATTS: You see, son, I know it's hard for you to understand and Jessie Mae...understand—But...

LUDIE: Yes, Ma'm. I understand, Mama. It's done now. So let's forget about it.

MRS. WATTS: All right, sonny. (*A pause.*) You did bring Jessie Mae, didn't you?

LUDIE: Yes, Ma'm.

MRS. WATTS: Well, now she's here isn't she going to get out of the car and look around a little?

LUDIE: She didn't seem to want to, Mama.

MRS. WATTS: You asked her?

LUDIE: Yes, Ma'm. (*A pause.*)

MRS. WATTS: Did you ask about your raise, son?

LUDIE: Yes, Ma'm, and Mr. Douglas told me he liked my work and he'd be glad to recommend a raise for me.

MRS. WATTS: Oh.(*A pause.*) The sky's so blue, Ludie. Did you ever see the sky so blue?

LUDIE: No, Ma'm. (*A pause.*)

MRS. WATTS: Callie Davis died.

LUDIE: Is that so? When did that happen?

MRS. WATTS: They don't rightly know. They found her dead. She'd been ridin' a tractor the day before they found her. Buried her yesterday. (*A pause.*)

LUDIE: Mama, I should have made myself bring you here before. I'm sorry but I thought it would be easier for both of us not to see the house again.

MRS. WATTS: I know, Ludie. (*A pause.*) Now you're here, wouldn't you like to come inside, son, and look around?

LUDIE: I don't think I'd better, Mama. I don't see any use in it. It would just make me feel bad. I'd rather remember it like it was.

(*A pause. Mrs. Watts looks at the house. She smiles.*)

MRS. WATTS: The old house has gotten kind of run-down, hasn't it?

LUDIE: Yes, it has.

(*She starts back toward the house slowly.*)

MRS. WATTS: I don't think it'll out last the next Gulf storm.

LUDIE: It doesn't look like it would.

(*She turns and looks at him standing in the yard.*)

MRS. WATTS: You know who you look like standing there, Ludie?

LUDIE: Who?

MRS. WATTS: My Papa.

LUDIE: Do I?

MRS. WATTS: Just like him. Of course, I've been noticing as you grow older you look more and more like him. My Papa was a good-looking man.

LUDIE: Was he?

MRS. WATTS: You've seen his pictures. Didn't you think so?

LUDIE: I don't remember. It's been so long since I looked at his picture.

MRS. WATTS: Well, he was always considered a very nice looking man *(A pause.)* Do you remember my Papa at all, son? *(Mrs. Watts sits on the steps of the porch.)*

LUDIE: No, Ma'm. Not too well. I was only ten when he died, Mama. I remember the day he died. I heard about it as I was coming home from school. Lee Weems told me. I thought he was joking and I called him a liar. I remember you takin' me into the front room there the day of the funeral to say good-bye to him. I remember the coffin and the people sitting in the room. Old man Joe Weems took me up on his knee and told me that Grandpapa was his best friend and that his life was a real example for me to follow. I remember Grandmama sitting by the coffin crying and she made me promise that when I had a son of my own I'd name it after Grandpapa. I would have, too. I've never forgotten that promise. *(A pause.)* Well, I didn't have a son. Or a daughter. *(A pause.)* Billy Davidson told me his wife is expecting her fourth child. They have two girls and a boy, now. Billy Davidson doesn't make much more than I do and they certainly seem to get along. Own their own home and have a car. It does your heart good to hear them tell about how they all get along. Everybody has their job, even the youngest child. She's only three. She puts the napkins around the table at mealtimes. That's her job. Billy said to me, Ludie, I don't know how I'd keep going without my kids. He said I don't understand what keeps you going, Ludie. What you work for. I said, Well, Billy... Oh, Mama, I haven't made any kind of life for you, either one of you and I try so hard. I try so hard. *(He crosses to her.)* Oh, Mama. I lied to you. I do remember. I remember so much. This house. The life here. The night you woke me up and dressed me and took me for a walk when there was a full moon and I cried because I was afraid and you comforted me. *(He turns abruptly away from his mother and walks to the downstage corner of the porch.)* Mama, I want to stop remembering... It doesn't do any good to remember.

(A car horn is heard in the distance. Loud and impatient. He looks in the direction of the horn.)

That's Jessie Mae.

MRS. WATTS: Whose car did you come in?

(He crosses to her.)

LUDIE: I borrowed Billy Davidson's car. He didn't want me to have it at first. You know people are funny about lending their car, but then I explained what happened and he was nice about it.

(The car horn is heard again.)

We have to start back now, Mama. Jessie Mae is nervous that I might lose my job.

MRS. WATTS: *(Frantically trying to find an excuse not to leave.)* Didn't you ask for the day off?

LUDIE: No, Ma'm. I only asked for the morning off.

MRS. WATTS: What time is it now?

LUDIE: Must be after eight. We were a little late getting here.

MRS. WATTS: We can drive it in three hours, can't we, Ludie?

LUDIE: Yes, Ma'm, but we might have a flat or run into traffic or something. Besides, I promised Billy I'd get his car back to him by twelve.

MRS. WATTS: Son, why am I going back at all? Why can't I stay?

LUDIE: Mama, you can't stay. You know that. Now come on. *(He takes her by the arm. She starts to get up from the steps. When she is about half way up she collapses crying. She cries passionately, openly, bitterly.)*

MRS. WATTS: Ludie. Ludie. What's happened to us? Why have we come to this?

LUDIE: I don't know, Mama.

MRS. WATTS: To have stayed and fought the land would have been better than this.

LUDIE: Yes'm

(She gets up.)

MRS. WATTS: Pretty soon it'll all be gone. Ten years...twenty...this house... me...you...

LUDIE: I know, Mama.

(A pause. She looks in his suffering face. She looks around. She speaks with great tenderness.)

MRS. WATTS: But the river will be here. The fields. The woods. The smell of the Gulf. That's what I always took my strength from, Ludie. Not from houses, not from people. *(A pause.)* It's so quiet. It's so eternally quiet. I had forgotten the peace. The quiet. And it's given me strength once more, Ludie. To go on and do what I have to do. I've found my dignity and my strength.

LUDIE: I'm glad, Mama.

MRS. WATTS: And I'll never fight with Jessie Mae again or complain. *(She points out into the distance.)* Do you remember how my Papa always had that field over there planted in cotton?

LUDIE: Yes, Ma'm.

MRS. WATTS: See, it's all woods now. But I expect some day people will come again and cut down the trees and plant the cotton and maybe even wear out the land again and then their children will sell it and go to the cities and then the trees will come up again.

LUDIE: I expect so, Mama.

MRS. WATTS: We're part of all this. We left it, but we can never lose what it has given us.

LUDIE: I expect so, Mama. *(He takes her by the arm and they start walking out. Jessie Mae comes into the yard U. C.)*

JESSIE MAE: Ludie. Are you coming or not?

LUDIE: We were just startin', Jessie Mae.

MRS. WATTS: Hello, Jessie Mae.

JESSIE MAE: I'm not speakin' to you. I guess you're proud of the time you gave us. Dragging us all the way out here this time of the mornin'. If Ludie loses his job over this, I hope you're satisfied.

LUDIE: I'm not goin' to lose my job, Jessie Mae.

JESSIE MAE: Well, you could.

LUDIE: All right, Jessie Mae.

JESSIE MAE: And she should realize that. She's selfish. That's her trouble. Always has been. Just purdee selfish. Did you tell your Mama what we were discussing in the car?

LUDIE: No. We can talk it all over driving back to Houston.

JESSIE MAE: I think we should have it all out right here. I'd like everything understood right now. *(Jessie Mae opens her purse and takes out a piece of paper.)* I've gotten everything written down. Do you want to read it or do you want me to read it to you, Mother Watts?

MRS. WATTS: What is it, Jessie Mae?

JESSIE MAE: It's a few rules and regulations that are necessary to my peace of mind. And I think to Ludie's. Ludie says you may have a few of your own to add and that may be and I'm perfectly willin' to listen if you do....First of all, I'd like to ask you a question.

MRS. WATTS: Yes, Ma'm. *(Mrs. Watts sits on the steps.)*

JESSIE MAE: Just what possessed you to run away? Didn't you know you'd be caught and have to come back?

MRS. WATTS: I had to come, Jessie Mae. Twenty years is a long time.

JESSIE MAE: But what if you had died from the excitement! Didn't you know you could have died?

MRS. WATTS: I knew.

JESSIE MAE: And you didn't care?

MRS. WATTS: *(With great dignity.)* I had to come, Jessie Mae.

JESSIE MAE: Well, I hope it's out of your system now.

MRS. WATTS: It is. I've had my trip. That's more than enough to keep me happy the rest of my life.

JESSIE MAE: Well, I'm glad to hear it. That's the first thing on my list. *(She reads from list.)* Number one. There'll be no more running away.

MRS. WATTS: There'll be no more running away.

JESSIE MAE: Good. *(She takes the list up again.)* Number two. No more hymn singing, when I'm in the apartment. When I'm gone you can sing your lungs out. Agreed?

MRS. WATTS: Agreed.

JESSIE MAE: Number three.

LUDIE: *(Interrupting.)* Jessie Mae, can't this wait till we get home?

JESSIE MAE: Now, honey, we agreed that I'm going to handle this! *(She goes back to list.)* No more pouting. When I ask a question, I'd like an answer. Otherwise I'll consider it's pouting.

MRS. WATTS: All right.

JESSIE MAE: Fourth. With the condition that your heart is in I feel you should not run around the apartment when you can walk.

MRS. WATTS: All right, Jessie Mae.

JESSIE MAE: That's all. Is there anything you want to say to me?

MRS. WATTS: No, Jessie Mae.

JESSIE MAE: I might as well tell you now I'm not staying in the house and watching over you any more. I am joinin' a bridge club and going to town at least twice a week. If you go now, it'll just be your funeral. You understand.

MRS. WATTS: I understand.

JESSIE MAE: All right. *(She puts the list away.)*

LUDIE: And, Mama, we also agreed that we're all gonna try our best to get along together. Jessie Mae also realizes that she gets upset sometimes when she shouldn't. Don't you, Jessie Mae?

JESSIE MAE: Uh huh.

LUDIE: So let's start by trying to have a pleasant ride home.

JESSIE MAE: Allrightie. *(She takes a cigarette and the lighter from her purse. The lighter works and she lights her cigarette. She crosses down to the far edge of the house.)* Is there any water around here? I'm thirsty.

LUDIE: I don't think so, Jessie Mae. Mama, is there any water around here?

MRS. WATTS: No. The cistern is gone.

(Jessie Mae notices a scratch on her shoes. She is furious.)

JESSIE MAE: Look at my shoes! I've got scratches on them. They're my good pair. I ought to have my head examined for wearing my only good pair of shoes out here in this old swamp.

LUDIE: *(Looking out in the distance.)* When I was a boy I used to drink in the creek over there, Jessie Mae. We had a cistern, but I always preferred to drink out of the creek. It seemed to me the water always tasted so much better.

(Jessie Mae crosses over to the far end of the stage looking out at the creek in the distance.)

JESSIE MAE: Well, you wouldn't catch me drinking out of any creek. I knew a man once that went on a huntin' trip and drank out of a creek and caught something and died.

MRS. WATTS: There's nothin' like cistern water for washin' your hair with. It is the softest water in the world.

(A bird calls in the distance.)

That's a red bird.

JESSIE MAE: A what?

MRS. WATTS: A red bird.

JESSIE MAE: Oh. I thought you said that. They all sound alike to me. Well, come on. Let's get going. Do we go back by the way of Harrison?

LUDIE: Yes.

JESSIE MAE: Good. Then we can stop at the drugstore. I'm so thirsty I could drink ten Coca-colas. Are you all ready?

MRS. WATTS: Yes'm.

(They start out. Jessie Mae looks at her.)

JESSIE MAE: Where's your purse?

MRS. WATTS: Are you talkin' to me, Jessie Mae?

JESSIE MAE: Who else would I be talkin' to? Since when did Ludie start walkin' around with a pocketbook under his arm?

(Mrs. Watts looks around.)

MRS. WATTS: Oh, I guess I left it inside.

JESSIE MAE: Where? *(She starts toward the door of the house.)*

MRS. WATTS: I'll get it. *(She turns to go into the house.)*

JESSIE MAE: No. I want to go. You'll take all day. Where did you leave it?

MRS. WATTS: In the parlour. Right off the front hall.

JESSIE MAE: All right. I'll get it. You wait here. *(She starts in the house. She turns and sees them walking off U. C.)* I said wait here now. I don't want to be left alone in this ramshackly old house. No telling what's running around in there.

MRS. WATTS: There's nothing in there.

JESSIE MAE: There might be rats or snakes or something.

LUDIE: I'll go.

JESSIE MAE: No. I'll go. Just stay here so if I holler you can come. *(She goes inside the house. Ludie turns to his mother.)*

LUDIE: Mama.

MRS. WATTS: It's all right, Ludie, son.

(Jessie Mae comes back out with the purse.)

JESSIE MAE: Here's your purse. Now where's the money for that Government check?

MRS. WATTS: I haven't cashed it.

JESSIE MAE: Where is it?

MRS. WATTS: It's right inside the purse.

(Jessie Mae opens the purse and begins to search again.)

JESSIE MAE: No. It isn't.

MRS. WATTS: Here. Let me look.

(Jessie Mae hands her the purse and Mrs. Watts, too, begins to rummage around. All of a sudden she bursts out laughing.)

JESSIE MAE: What's the matter with you?

MRS. WATTS: That's a good joke on me.

JESSIE MAE: Well, what's so funny?

MRS. WATTS: I just remembered. I left this purse on the bus last night and caused a man a lot of trouble because I thought the check was in there. *(She is overcome by laughter again.)* And do you know that check wasn't in that purse all that time?

JESSIE MAE: Where was it?

MRS. WATTS: Right here. *(She reaches inside her dress and takes it out.)* Been here since yesterday afternoon.

(Jessie Mae reaches for the check.)

JESSIE MAE: Give it to me before you go and lose it again.

MRS. WATTS: I won't lose it.

JESSIE MAE: Now don't start that business again. Just give it to me.

LUDIE: *(Interrupting angrily.)* Jessie Mae.

JESSIE MAE: Well, I'm not going to—

LUDIE: *(With great positiveness.)* We're going to stop this wrangling once and for all. You've given me your word and I expect you to keep your word. We have to live together and we're going to live together in peace.

MRS. WATTS: It's all right, Ludie. *(She gives the check to Jessie Mae.)* Let Jessie Mae take care of the check.

(Jessie Mae accepts the check. She looks at it for a moment and then grabs Mrs. Watts's purse. She opens it and puts the check inside.)

JESSIE MAE: Oh, here. You keep the check. But don't go and lose it before you get home. *(She puts the purse back in Mrs. Watts's hand. She starts off stage U. C.)* Well, come on. Let's go.

(She leaves. Ludie goes to his mother.)

LUDIE: Mama, if I get the raise you won't—

MRS. WATTS: It's all right, Ludie. I've had my trip. You go ahead. I'll be right there.

(Ludie starts out U. C. Mrs. Watts points up in the sky.)

Look, isn't that a scissor tail?

LUDIE: I don't know. I didn't get to see it if it was. They fly so fast. *(Ludie takes one last look at the house.)* The house used to look so big.

(He goes out. Mrs. Watts stands for a moment looking into the sky. Then she drops gently on her knees, puts her hands in the dirt. She kneels for a moment holding the dirt, then slowly lets it drift through her fingers back to the ground. She begins to walk slowly out U. C. until she gets to the corner of the yard. She pauses for a moment, taking one last look at the house, speaks quietly.)

MRS. WATTS: Good-bye, Bountiful, good-bye. *(Then she turns and walks off the stage U. C. Curtain.)*

END OF PLAY

The Chase

PRODUCTION

The Chase was first produced by Jose Ferrer at The Playhouse Theatre in New York City on April 15, 1952. Milton Baron was associate producer, and settings and lighting were by Albert Johnson. The cast was as follows:

Sheriff Hawes..John Hodiak
Rip ....Richard Poston
Tarl...Lin McCarthy
Ruby Hawes..Kim Hunter
Edwin Stewart ....Sam Byrd
Mr. Douglas...G. Albert Smith
Anna Reeves...Kim Stanley
Mrs. Reeves ....Nan McFarland
Knub McDermont ....Lonny Chapman
Bubber Reeves..Murray Hamilton
Hawks Damon..Ted Yaryan

SETTING

ACT I
> Scene 1: The office of the jail, twilight.
> Scene 2: Knub's cabin. Later the same night.
> Scene 3: The jail. Later the same night.

ACT II
> Scene 1. The jail, the next evening.
> Scene 2. Knub's cabin. Later the same night.
> Scene 3. The jail. Later the same night.

ACT III
> Scene 1. The jail. Later the same night.
> Scene 2. Knub's cabin. Later the same night.
> Scene 3. The jail. Later the same evening.

The action of the play takes place in Richmond, Texas, in the present day.

PRODUCTION NOTE

The sketch and floor plan printed in the acting edition is a readaptation of the original Broadway set. It has been specifically designed to make the transition between the jail set to the cabin set as quickly and easily as possible. There are two physical changes necessary in going from jail to cabin. The desk in the sheriff's office will have to be pulled into the center of the jail set and the right wall of the cabin set, which is hinged to the center wall of the cabin set, swung down into position. To go from cabin to jail the wall of the cabin will have to swing upstage and the sheriff's desk put back in its original position. In staging the exterior parts of the cabin scenes it is suggested that the director use the whole downstage area of the stage including that space immediately in front of the jail.

—H. F.

THE CHASE

ACT I
Scene 1

It is early evening. The lights are brought up on the office of Sheriff Hawes in the back of the county jail. The room contains a desk piled high with official papers and letters, two or three old-fashioned chairs, a hat rack and a water-cooler. A small radio is on desk. There is an entrance up C. that leads to the jail and to Sheriff Hawes's living quarters. This is only entrance in the scene. On the walls are an enormous map of Texas, a stalk of cotton, a bulletin board and a few old-fashioned pictures. There is a tall window in L. wall, with a blind.

Seated at desk is Sheriff Hawes. He is thin and wiry, with a strong, kind face. He is writing. Rip, a deputy, is seated in a chair C. He is a hard-looking man of twenty-nine. He is whittling and putting shavings in wastebasket, which is just below watercooler. Phone on desk rings.

HAWES: *(Picks it up.)* Sheriff Hawes speaking. Thank you. Thank you very much. Yes'm. I'll attend to it. Yes'm. I'll see that it's attended to right away. *(Puts phone down, picks it up again.)* Red. Hawes. Call up the Magnolia Fillin' Station right away an' tell them in the name of God to turn their radio down. Miss Lydie Jackson just called an' says it's startin' her migraine again. *(Rip crosses to desk with wastebasket.)* All right. Oh, and Red, I'm expectin' Mr. Douglas to drop by in a few minutes. Send him right in when he comes. Thanks. *(Puts phone down. Goes back to his figuring. Phone rings again.)* Damn!

RIP: Go on with your work, Sheriff, I'll get it. *(Picks up phone.)* Yeah. Nope. Sheriff Hawes is busy. This is Rip. Yes, ma'am. Rip Murphy. Oh, all right. I'll see that it's attended to right away. Yes, ma'am. *(Puts phone down. Crosses to cooler R.)* That was Old Lady McAfee. She says will you please see what you can do about findin' her a cook. She wants a nigra. Mescans make her nervous.

HAWES: Isn't that a pistol? Mescans make her nervous. Like we have nothing to do except to find cooks for Mrs. McAfee.

(Tarl, a deputy, enters. He is a young man with a gentle, easy manner.)

TARL: Sheriff. *(Hangs up hat.)*

HAWES: Hello, Tarl. Did you get that trouble settled out at Booger Pete's?

TARL: Yes, sir, had to send a woman to the hospital. She was all cut up.

HAWES: Bad?

TARL: *(Takes off his holster, crosses R.)* Not too bad. She was hollerin' an' she was bleedin', but she weren't cut too bad. Hey, Rip.

RIP: Hey, Tarl.

HAWES: Tarl, did you ever see the old Weems place out at the end of the county?

TARL: I must have. I don't remember.

HAWES: I drove out there today to look at it. It's for sale. I swear, I never saw a prettier piece of land.

TARL: What they want for it?

HAWES: Hundred dollars an acre. An' that's the bottom price.

TARL: Whew! Take a rich man to buy that.

HAWES: Take a rich man to buy anything in this county nowadays. Every man ought to be entitled to his own farm.

TARL: *(Crosses to C. chair, sits.)* What's new, Rip?

RIP: Did you hear about Bubber Reeves?

TARL: No, what?

RIP: Mr. Hawes heard today they're moving him to the State Pen in Floriville.

TARL: Way out in West Texas?

RIP: Yep. I bet it can't be too far away to suit Mr. Hawes.

HAWES: Well, he's given me his share of trouble. I would like a nickel for every time I had to chase that devil—first for small things, then big things. Well, they all make their mistake when they start killin'. The minute I'd heard Bubber started killin' I said to myself there's no turnin' back for him now.

RIP: I'd rather be dead than have a life term.

TARL: So would I.

RIP: State ought to have killed him and gotten it over with.

HAWES: I don't know. It's hard to say about things like that.

(Phone rings.)

RIP: Want me to get it?

HAWES: No, I'll get it. *(Answers phone.)* Yes'm. Yes'm. Miss Lydie. I just had Red phone out there. It didn't? Yes. Yes'm. Right away. *(Puts phone down.)* Rip—

RIP: Oh, oh!

HAWES: Go over to the Magnolia Fillin' Station on the highway an' tell them to turn that damn radio down or you're gonna have to yank it out. Tell them

Miss Lydie Jackson suffers from migraine attacks an' that radio is aggravatin' her condition.

RIP: *(Crosses U. C., gets holster.)* You're too easy an' polite to people, Mr. Hawes.

HAWES: That so?

RIP: Yep. If I ever get to be sheriff, they're not gonna be callin' me up day an' night for anything that crosses their minds.

HAWES: Then you wouldn't last as sheriff very long, son. A sheriff is a public servant. The public elects him, they pay his salary, an' they have a right to call on him for anything they want, day or night. Least, that's how I feel about it. And while you're out that way, check on Miss Lydie's cow-lot an' see if she's cut down that ragweed like I asked her to. If she expects people to turn down radios on account of her migraine, she's gonna have to keep the ragweed cut for the hay fever sufferers.

RIP: Yes, sir.

(Ruby Hawes, Hawes's wife, enters. She is seven years younger than her husband. She is pretty, with a warm, open nature.)

Hello, Miss Ruby.

RUBY: Hey, Rip.

(Rip goes out.)

Hello, honey.

HAWES: Hello, Ruby.

(She goes over, kisses him very genteelly.)

RUBY: *(Crosses to chair, D. R., leaves handbag.)* Honey, Edwin Stewart's outside and he—

HAWES: Just a minute. I want to talk to you. Tarl, would you mind goin' out in the outer office with Red?

TARL: No, sir.

(He goes out. Hawes motions Ruby to come to him. She crosses to him.)

HAWES: What's the big idea?

RUBY: What?

HAWES: Don't I get a kiss?

RUBY: I kissed you. Honey, Edwin Stewart— *(Crosses to chair D. R. for handbag.)*

HAWES: Did you call that a kiss? I been sittin' here all afternoon waitin' for you to come an' kiss me an' you give me a li'l ol' peck like that.

RUBY: *(Crosses to Hawes.)* Oh, Hawes, you're a mess. *(She kisses him.)* Is that better?

HAWES: Yes, ma'am. How were the fairgrounds?

RUBY: Fine. It was hot.

HAWES: I bet. Now you're not goin' to wear yourself out runnin' around in this heat.

RUBY: No, but I have to get this fair business done. I'm your wife and certain things are expected of me.

HAWES: Promise me you'll be careful.

RUBY: I'm careful. I've waited too long for this baby. Honey, Edwin Stewart's waitin'.

HAWES: What does he want?

RUBY: He wants to talk to you.

HAWES: Oh? What about?

RUBY: Now, I want you to promise me you'll do it.

HAWES: Well, what is it?

RUBY: Now, it's a perfectly simple thing.

HAWES: Well, why don't you tell me what it is?

RUBY: All right. He's chairman of the Parade Committee and this year they want you to lead the parade.

HAWES: Want me to lead it?

RUBY: Yes, sir. They want to dress you up in a cowboy suit and put a ten-gallon hat on your head and have you ride a horse.

HAWES: Well, I'm not goin' to do it!

RUBY: Shhh, now, honey, Edwin might hear you—he's sensitive.

HAWES: I don't care if he does hear me.

RUBY: Hawes, now just calm yourself.

HAWES: I'm not goin' to make a fool of myself. This is one thing I'm gonna draw the line at. I'm not gonna be stuck up on no hoss with no cowboy suit on to lead no parade.

RUBY: Now, Hawes, you listen to me.

HAWES: I never could stand hosses an' hosses know it. Hosses know when people don't like them. No, thank you. Wouldn't I look sweet in a cowboy suit? Why, they would laugh me out of this town.

RUBY: Now, Hawes. It's part of your job as sheriff. You owe it to the public.

HAWES: All right. All right. But don't let him keep me here all afternoon talking. I've got to see Mr. Douglas on business in a few minutes.

RUBY: All right. *(Calling off.)* Edwin—Edwin—

EDWIN: *(Off.)* Yes, ma'am?

RUBY: Come on in.

EDWIN: Yes, ma'am. Thank you, ma'am. *(Edwin Stewart enters—in his early thirties, nervous and ill at ease.)* Hello, Hawes.

HAWES: Hello, Edwin. How's your papa? *(Ruby crosses to chair D. R., sits.)*

EDWIN: *(Sits C. chair.)* Fine, thank you. He works too hard, but you can't do anything about that. Everybody at the bank tries to get him to let up, but he won't. Papa's got nerves of steel. Nothin' gets him upset. I've often told Papa I envy him that quality. Why, do you know I have never known Papa to stop long enough to go out for a cup of coffee? He says that's how he got where he is. I appreciate his point of view, but like I tell him, I have to stop for coffee twice a day, because I'm more the nervous type. Did you ask him, Ruby?

RUBY: Yes, I did.

EDWIN: Well, what do you say, Hawes? Are you gonna do it?

HAWES: Well, I haven't ridden a hoss in so long—

EDWIN: Don't worry about that. We'll get a real gentle hoss. *(Crosses to Hawes.)* S. L. Barsoty said he had an old paint that a child of two would be safe ridin'.

HAWES: I appreciate that—

EDWIN: And, another thing. I thought everybody should dress up in costumes of some kind. Did Ruby tell you I wanted to dress you up like a cowboy? You know, the way you see them in the picture show. We'll get you chaps an' boots' spurs, a ten-gallon hat an'—

HAWES: Look, you're goin' to have a hard enough time gettin' me on a hoss without riggin' me up like a Christmas tree.

EDWIN: Everybody's goin' to be dressed up like somethin', Hawes. *(Crosses to Ruby.)* Pioneers, settlers, Indians, American Revolution—

HAWES: What are you goin' to be dressed up as?

EDWIN: Nothin'. I'm the chairman. What do you say, Hawes?

HAWES: Well, I guess it won't kill me—

EDWIN: Fine, fine. Thank you so much. I suggested you to the Committee to lead the parade because I think you're our most important public servant. I said to them, gentlemen, I nominate the man that has risked his life many a time so we can sleep in peace, the man who caught that crazy killer, Bubber Reeves. *(Leaves hat on chair, crosses to cooler.)*

HAWES: By the way, Ruby, this will make you happy. I got word this mornin' they're moving Bubber to a Pen out in West Texas.

RUBY: Thank goodness.

EDWIN: Well, I'm glad to hear it. I never could understand why he was sent to a Pen so close to his home town.

RUBY: They can't move him too far away to suit me.

HAWES: Ruby's always been afraid that Bubber would get out some day and come back to kill me.

RUBY: Of course I am. He swore the last time you arrested him he would kill you. The Pen he's in now is awful easy to escape from.

EDWIN: Elizabeth's scared of him, too. You all know Bubber has a grudge against me.

RUBY: No, I didn't know that, Edwin.

EDWIN: Oh, yes. Since we were kids.

HAWES: Did he ever try to bother you?

EDWIN: No, and he better not. I'm not afraid of Bubber Reeves. I'd just like him to try anything with me. But Elizabeth worries—

(Phone rings.)

HAWES: *(Picks up phone.)* Yes—all right, send him in. *(Puts phone down.)* That was Mr. Douglas.

EDWIN: Well, I declare. Is he coming in?

HAWES: Yes, he is. I've got some business to talk over with him.

EDWIN: Then I'll stay and say hello to him, if I may.

HAWES: Come on in, Mr. Douglas. *(Douglas enters. He is gray-haired and distinguished looking.)* I sure do appreciate your stoppin' by the jail. Hope it hasn't put you out any? I got stuck here an' couldn't get over to your house.

DOUGLAS: *(At C. door.)* No, it was no bother at all. How are you, Ruby, Edwin?

EDWIN: Fine, fine. Little hot.

DOUGLAS: It is hot, isn't it?

EDWIN: It certainly is.

DOUGLAS: Been keepin' you busy down at the bank?

EDWIN: Oh, yes, sir. An' I'm chairman of the Parade Committee for the Fair this year, you know.

(Phone rings.)

HAWES: *(Crosses to desk, picks up phone.)* Yes. Oh, yes. All right. Thank you.

RUBY: *(Crosses to door.)* Will you all excuse me? I've got to see about supper. Good night, Edwin. I'll come back an' say hello to you, Mr. Douglas, before you go.

DOUGLAS: All right, Ruby.

(Ruby goes out.)

HAWES: *(Hangs up phone.)* Well—

EDWIN: I've got to be goin' on myself.

HAWES: I'll be seein' you down at the bank one of these days, Edwin.

EDWIN: Fine. I'm certainly lookin' forward to it. Good night, Mr. Douglas.

DOUGLAS: Good night, Edwin.

EDWIN: Certainly glad to have seen you. *(Edwin exits.)*

HAWES: Sit down, Mr. Douglas. I asked you to stop by because I wanted to talk something over with you.

DOUGLAS: All right, Hawes. *(Sits C. chair. Hawes sits on desk, picks up phone.)*

HAWES: Red, hold the calls—thanks. *(Puts phone down.)* Mr. Douglas, I don't think I'm gonna run for re-election.

DOUGLAS: You're not?

HAWES: No, sir.

DOUGLAS: But you've done such a good job as sheriff, son. Why on earth do you want to quit?

HAWES: I don't see any future in it for me. I would like to make the change. I'm tired of politics. *(Crosses R.)* I hate havin' to do whatever people ask me. Now you take tonight. Edwin Stewart was in here wantin' me to lead a parade to open the county fair. I don't want to be in that parade. But I'm gonna have to, because I'm in politics and I can't afford to offend people. I don't have any time for Ruby—I haven't had a vacation since I've been in office. My phone rings at two in the mornin', or three, or four. It's gettin' on my nerves. And now we're havin' the baby I—well, I just can't *(Crosses L.)* see raisin' a kid around a place like this. Drunks and whores and dopeheads and thieves and murderers. It's no life to put a child into. I just can't see it. I don't want my kid livin' with the fear of Bubber killin' me, like Ruby does.

DOUGLAS: What do you plan to do?

HAWES: Well, I was goin' to see what I could do about gettin' hold of a cotton farm.

DOUGLAS: Would you spend your whole time farmin'?

HAWES: Yes, sir, I hope to.

DOUGLAS: I see. Have you thought this through, Hawes?

HAWES: Yes, sir, I've tried to.

DOUGLAS: What happens if you don't make a success of farmin'?

HAWES: I'll have to make a success of it. I think I could.

DOUGLAS: How? You've never farmed, have you?

HAWES: No, but I've lived with cotton farmers all my born days and Ruby was raised on a farm. She knows a lot about it.

DOUGLAS: And what about Ruby? She's gonna have a baby to take care of pretty soon. She'd have to work so hard on a farm.

HAWES: Naturally, I'd discuss it with her before I come to a decision.

DOUGLAS: How are you gonna manage?

HAWES: Ruby an' I are pretty well out of debt now, for the first time in eight years. I get three hundred dollars a month, an' keep. I figured if we're careful we might save a thousand dollars in the next seven months.

DOUGLAS: You can't get very far on a thousand dollars.

HAWES: I appreciate that. Do you think I would stand any kind of a chance gettin' a loan at the bank?

DOUGLAS: How much?

HAWES: *(Looks over papers.)* I figure I'll need four or five thousand.

DOUGLAS: That's a lot of money.

HAWES: I'm aware of that, Mr. Douglas. What do you think?

DOUGLAS: Hawes, you know I'm fond of you. I was your Daddy's best friend and he was mine. I watched you grow up. I've always felt like you were my own son—But I don't know, Hawes. I just don't know what to say.

HAWES: Look, Mr. Douglas. This isn't just somethin' I've thought up today. I've been tryin' to figure out a way to do this for three years. I don't like to bother people with my feelings. I realize nobody begged me to take this job. But I know it's time for me to get out. You know how I was as a kid, *(Crosses R.)* wild and cussed, fightin'—gamblin'—then I met Ruby an' married an' I settled down an' I had a change of heart an' I became a peace officer. But the fightin' for me has never stopped. It became a part of my job. I want to live in peace now with my wife and baby an' let other people live in peace.

DOUGLAS: I tell you what. You let me speak to Mr. Stewart before you go in the bank. I've done business with him for a long time and I think I can count on his friendship, if anybody can.

HAWES: Would you do that?

DOUGLAS: Certainly. I'll go over tomorrow or the next day and I'll call you as soon as I talk to him.

HAWES: I would appreciate that, sir.

DOUGLAS: *(Rises.)* No trouble at all. I'll be getting on—

HAWES: *(Calls.)* Ruby?

RUBY: *(Off R.)* Yes, honey?

HAWES: Mr. Douglas is leavin'.

RUBY: Oh. *(Enters.)*

HAWES: You sure have been a good friend to us, Mr. Douglas.

RUBY: Can you stay and have supper with us, Mr. Douglas?

DOUGLAS: No, ma'am. Thank you very much. I've had my supper.

RUBY: How is Mrs. Douglas?

DOUGLAS: She's fine. She's home now with her hat on waitin' for me to come and take her to the picture show.

RUBY: What's playin' tonight?

DOUGLAS: I swear I don't know. I never know one from the other. I only go to please my wife. I'll get back to you, Hawes.

HAWES: . Thank you, sir.

DOUGLAS: Good night, Ruby.

RUBY: Good night. *(Douglas goes out.)*

HAWES: Well, did you get the fair business all attended to?

RUBY: Yes, I did. Everybody is so tickled about us havin' the baby. They said they never saw a prouder lookin' mother, and I reckon that's right. I was thinkin' about my Mama today and how proud she would have been knowin' I was goin' to have a baby. Papa, too, though he wouldn't have let on. *(She gets up, crosses R., pulls down window shade.)* I wish you would remember to keep the shades down. If anybody wanted to shoot at you they could, as easy as anything.

HAWES: I forget.

RUBY: What were you and Mr. Douglas talkin' about?

HAWES: *(Crosses L. C.)* That's a secret.

RUBY: What were you talkin' about?

HAWES: I'll tell you later.

RUBY: *(Crosses to Hawes.)* Oh, Hawes—

HAWES: Ruby—

RUBY: Stop teasin'. Tell me now.

HAWES: Ruby, I heard about a farm that was up for sale away at the other end of the county. I took a ride up there to look it over. You'll just go crazy about it.

RUBY: Will I?

HAWES: Yes'm. It's a regular showplace. I betcha a man could get a bale and a half of cotton to the acre with no trouble at all. It's the richest lookin' land I think I ever saw. Good black dirt. Lots of pecan trees. The prettiest half-moon of a lake covered with water irises runnin' right through it. We could build a barbecue place down by the lake and ask people out to supper.

RUBY: Have a pretty house on it?

HAWES: Yes, ma'am—it's old, but it's pretty. One of those houses built way high up off the ground. Half brick and half lumber.

RUBY: Now don't go and get all excited, Hawes. We'll get a place in time. We're gonna have everything we want, in time.

HAWES: I would be so proud to have a place to call our own. No more phones ringin' at night. No more calls to hunt drunks. Ruby— *(Phone rings. Hawes picks it up.)* Red, I asked you not to call me. What? When did you hear? All right. *(Puts phone down.)*

RUBY: What is it, Hawes?

HAWES: Red just got word over the teletype that Bubber Reeves has escaped from the penitentiary.

RUBY: *(Goes to him.)* Oh, my God!

HAWES: Now, honey, take it easy.

RUBY: How can I take it easy? This is the first place he'll head for.

HAWES: I'm sure he's headin' for Houston right this minute. He's not crazy enough to come back here.

RUBY: I thought when you got him convicted the last time, it would be the end.

HAWES: I don't look for any trouble. I swear I don't—he wouldn't dare try to come back here.

RUBY: Hawes—I—I—

HAWES: Now, I just don't want you gettin' excited. There's not a thing to be excited about. You go in an' start supper. I'll be in in a little while—

RUBY: Hawes—I swanee—I—there's always trouble when that devil gets out—

HAWES: Now, will you go an' have your supper an' not worry?

RUBY: All right, all right.

(Starts out. They cross to door.)

RUBY: Come as soon as you can.

HAWES: Yes'm. *(Stands for a moment, obviously concerned. Goes to phone.)* Red? Rip back? Well, ask them both to come in.

(Crosses R., puts phone down. Rip and Tarl enter C.)

You heard the news?

RIP: Yes, sir, the sonovabitch!

HAWES: Tarl, I want you to go over and get Bubber Reeves's mother and bring her to the jail right away.

TARL: *(R. C. Puts on holster.)* Yes, sir. I sure hate to do it. She's gonna cuss me, I know, and I hate to have a woman cuss me.

RIP: Let me go—I'll just cuss her back.

HAWES: No—I want Tarl to do it—an' don't tell her anything, Tarl, except I want to see her right away.

TARL: Yes, sir. What about his wife—?

RIP: She's livin' with Knub McDermont out in the bottom. Do you want me to get her?

HAWES: No, you stay in the office with Red. Don't leave for anything without checkin' with me first.

TARL: Sheriff, do you expect Bubber to try and get back here?

HAWES: Yes, yes, I do. Don't tell anybody I said I expected Bubber back here. Not even Ruby.

RIP: Yes, sir. *(Rip and Tarl exit. Hawes straps his holster around his waist. Goes out to his supper U. C. as lights fade.)*

ACT I
Scene 2

Knub McDermont's cabin. Later the same night. The cabin is a flimsy structure made out of tin and boards. A screen door R. leads to outdoors, and U. C. is a curtain over—presumably—a door leading to kitchen. There is a window, with a shade, in L. wall. Table, chairs, etc., as in diagram. A phonograph is on table. The immediate ground in front of the cabin has been cleared or worn away by walking. Old tin cans and beer bottles are scattered in the yard.

At rise, Anna Reeves, a thin, wistful girl in her early twenties, is seated at table in cabin. A winding phonograph on the table is grinding out a honky-tonky song. She is listening to it. Over far R. on the steps leading to door in the shadows and barely visible, sits Mrs. Reeves, Bubber's mother. She has a drawn, anxious face and is neatly, but cheaply dressed. There is a window L.

ANNA: They haven't come yet, Mrs. Reeves?

MRS. REEVES: Turn that victrola off.

ANNA: Yes, ma'am.

(Anna quickly turns it off. Knub McDermont enters D.L.—i.e., not cabin, but the overall stage. He is tall and muscular with a dark, surly face. Knub goes around cabin to outside of door. Mrs. Reeves sees him, goes running to him, out of cabin.)

MRS. REEVES: Where's my son, Knub? Where's my son? Where's my son?

KNUB: Take it easy. Are you all alone?

MRS. REEVES: Yes.

KNUB: Anybody been out here?

MRS. REEVES: I haven't seen anybody.

KNUB: *(Goes into cabin.)* You seen anybody, Anna? *(Looks out window.)*

ANNA: Not since around half-past one. There was a little nigra boy around here huntin' with a BB gun. I chased him away.

(Knub goes out of cabin. He looks around, then gives a long, low whistle. Pause. Whistles again. Pause. Bubber Reeves slowly walks on from D. L. He is a small man, thin and drawn, with an intense, fanatical look. Mrs. Reeves runs to him.)

MRS. REEVES: Hello, Bubber.

(He looks at her.)

BUBBER: Hello, Mama.

KNUB: God damn it, let's get this over with. I want to get him out of here. Come on, let's go in the house. We can talk in there.

(Bubber goes into the cabin, followed by Mrs. Reeves and Knub, who stands by door. Anna is cowering back against wall as they come in.)

ANNA: *(Up L. C.)* Hello, Bubber.

MRS. REEVES: *(R. of table.)* Does she have to stay in here?

BUBBER: *(C. of table.)* What are you doin' out here, Anna?

ANNA: Knub, didn't you tell him? You swore to me you'd tell him first thing.

KNUB: *(Upstage of door.)* Shut up, I forgot. *(Turns to Bubber.)* Anna's livin' here with me now, Bubber. *(Tense silence. No one says anything. They watch Bubber anxiously. Bubber looks Anna up and down, then goes to table.)*

BUBBER: *(Sits C. of table.)* I'm hungry. Give me somethin' to eat.

MRS. REEVES: Bubber, honey, you're not gonna have time to eat. News has gotten back here about your escapin'. I hate to hurry you, boy, but the news is already in town.

KNUB: *(R. by door.)* Jesus, come on, Bubber, I'd better get you out of here.

MRS. REEVES: They announced it over the radio about half-past seven. I reckon Knub should've taken you straight on to Louisiana, but I may never see you again and I had to see you once more before I die.

BUBBER: Get me some food. I'm hungry.

MRS. REEVES: *(Sits R. end of table.)* Bubber, in the name of God.

KNUB: All right, all right, don't waste time arguin'.

(Mrs. Reeves rises, faces upstage.)

Get him somethin' to eat, Anna. Hurry, so I can get him out of here.

ANNA: Knub, we haven't got a thing to eat. I couldn't carry groceries all the way from town. All I got left is some coffee.

BUBBER: Give me some coffee. *(Anna goes to get it from up R.)*

MRS. REEVES: *(Sits R. end of table.)* Bubber, don't take time for coffee. I'll go out of my mind with you sittin' there drinkin' coffee.

BUBBER: Then go home.

MRS. REEVES: I'm not goin' home, Bubber, until Knub has you away from here.

BUBBER: Then shut up and let me drink my coffee in peace.

(Anna puts coffee on table. He drinks.)

MRS. REEVES: What are you tryin' to do to me? Kill me? Is that what you're tryin' to do?

BUBBER: Give me the money, Mama.

MRS. REEVES: It's not as much as I'd like it to be, but that H. T. Mavis wouldn't give me what I wanted for my house. The bank wouldn't even talk to me, so I had to take Mavis's offer, and then I had to pay the guard and Knub for helpin' you to escape. But it's enough to last you until you can get to Mississippi and find some kind of work. *(She has opened her purse and got money out. She gives it to him.)* I have to keep a little somethin' for myself, Bubber, until I could figure out what I was gonna do. This is all there is now, so hold on to it.

BUBBER: Give me the keys to your car, Knub.

MRS. REEVES: What do you want them for? Knub's gonna drive you.

BUBBER: I've got a few calls to make before we leave.

KNUB: *(A step L.)* Jesus Christ! I can't do it, Bubber. That wasn't part of our bargain. I can't let you take my car an' go drivin' over town. I'm in trouble now with Hawes for sellin' whiskey after hours. I've done all I can for you, Bubber.

BUBBER: Are you gonna give me the keys, or am I gonna have to take 'em?

MRS. REEVES: *(Rises, grabs Knub's arm.)* Don't give 'em to him, Knub. You're gonna get in that car with Knub an' you let him put you on the bus at Baton Rouge like you promised me. This county's gonna be wild in another hour.

BUBBER: Keep out of this, Mama. Give me the keys. *(Bubber takes revolver out of his back pocket. Points it at Knub.)*

KNUB: All right. *(Hands him the keys.)*

BUBBER: I'm not leaving town until I kill Hawes.

MRS. REEVES: Stop talkin' like that. Hawes will kill you. He'll kill you.

(Bubber rises, goes outside cabin. Mrs. Reeves follows.)

All right. Go. I hope he catches you. I'd rather see you hangin' in the courthouse square dead, than goin' on like this. So help me. *(R. C. She runs after him.)* I didn't mean that, son! Forgive me for sayin' that. Honey, listen to your old mother. Give me the gun. Promise me you'll get out of here. Promise me—promise me—

(She has grabbed his arm. He jerks away, walks off. She calls after him.)

Bubber—Bubber—Bubber—Bubber—

KNUB: *(Runs out door to Mrs. Reeves, puts hand over mouth.)* Shut up. Do you want someone to hear you?

(Anna stands up L. by window. Knub crosses L.)

MRS. REEVES: *(C.)* What am I gonna do, Knub? What am I gonna do? Go after him. Get the gun. Beg him not to do this thing. Beg him to leave. *(Knub crosses C.)*

KNUB: I've done all I can. Now go on home.

MRS. REEVES: He won't leave, Knub. He won't leave. Do you hear me, Knub?

He won't leave. I wish I'd never helped him to get out of the penitentiary. I've brought him back here for Hawes to kill.

KNUB: *(Looks out window.)* Jesus! Jesus! How did that news get back here so fast?

MRS. REEVES: He won't leave, Knub. They're gonna kill him.

KNUB: You better go on home. Somebody might have seen you comin' out here and tip Hawes off. I don't want Hawes out here.

(Mrs. Reeves crosses R. into cabin to table—starts out again, but Knub blocks her way.)

MRS. REEVES: I'm gonna get to Hawes. He's not gonna kill him.

KNUB: What are you goin' to Hawes for? *(Grabs her.)*

MRS. REEVES: Let me go.

KNUB: What are you goin' to Hawes for?

MRS. REEVES: Let me go.

KNUB: I'm not lettin' you go until you tell me what are you goin' to Hawes for?

MRS. REEVES: I'm gonna try an' buy him off.

KNUB: Are you gonna tell Hawes about me helpin' Bubber get away?

MRS. REEVES: I said, let me go.

KNUB: You heard what I asked you. Are you gonna tell Hawes about me helpin' Bubber?

MRS. REEVES: No.

KNUB: Swear to me.

MRS. REEVES: I swear.

KNUB: What are you gonna tell him?

MRS. REEVES: I'm not gonna tell him anything. Do you think I'm a fool? I'm gonna try to make him promise me that if he catches Bubber he won't kill him.

KNUB: I think I better keep you here.

MRS. REEVES: Just try it.

KNUB: I'm not sure I can trust you.

ANNA: Let her go, Knub. What do you want to keep her here for? If Hawes came aroun', there would sure enough be trouble. Let her go.

KNUB: I ought to make you get on your knees to me and beg.

MRS. REEVES: I'm gonna tell Bubber how you talk, an' then you'll be sorry.

KNUB: Tell him. Tell him. You think he'll care? He wouldn't care if you died tomorrow.

(She slaps him across the face.)

You do that again and I'll break your head open.

ANNA: Let her go, Knub.

(Knub throws open screen door. Mrs. Reeves runs off R.)

KNUB: Jesus! Jesus!

ANNA: *(Crosses to door.)* Do you think she'll tell Hawes on you?

KNUB: I don't know what the crazy fool will do. The sonovabitch takin' my car. *(Crosses C. front of cabin.)*

ANNA: How're we gonna get groceries out here if we don't have your car?

KNUB: How the hell do I know? You can walk into town and get them if you have to.

ANNA: I can't lug groceries all that way, Knub.

KNUB: Get into the house. *(Looks at her. Anna turns and goes into cabin. She winds the victrola. Knub stands smoking as lights fade.)*

ACT I
Scene 3

Later, same night. Hawes's office.

Hawes and Ruby are onstage. Ruby seated chair C., crocheting. Hawes seated at desk chair.

RUBY: I wonder how it feels to hide like that? Knowin' every county for miles around is waitin' for you to show yourself, to catch you, to kill you. *(Phone rings.)*

HAWES: *(Takes phone.)* Yep. Speakin'. No word yet. Yes'm. I'll attend to it. *(Puts phone down. Crosses to cooler.)* Somebody else imaginin' they've seen Bubber Reeves. They've seen him every place by now. Goin' toward the bank, the two gins, the graveyard, the school house, the pumpin' plant, the river, Caney, Peach Creek, Hungerford. And not one of them is a tip worth walkin' across the street for. I wish I could yank the damned phone off the hook.

RUBY: *(Seated chair C.)* Sometimes I think waitin' like this is the hardest part of all.

HAWES: *(Crosses to desk.)* It sure is. It makes me feel so helpless. You know Bubber's out there somewhere and all you can do is sit by the phone and wait for him to show himself. *(Goes and looks at map.)* Where the hell can he be hidin'? Freed Man's Town—Blossom Prairie—Egypt—Spanish Camp—in the bottom? Where in the hell can he be hidin'? *(Pause.)* I've got to get hold of Mrs. Reeves. I know she knows where he is. That's the only way I'm goin' to find Bubber. *(Takes phone.)* Red. Has Tarl come back yet? OK Send him in the minute he comes. *(Puts phone down.)* This is the fourth trip Tarl's made over to her house. God knows where she is. Well, all I can do is sit here by the phone and wait until I get hold of her. *(Phone rings. He grabs it.)* Yes. Oh. OK Send them in. *(Puts phone down.)*

Edwin and Damon are out there. Doggone it! I don't feel like foolin' with them tonight.

RUBY: I'm goin' into the house.

HAWES: All right. If they don't leave in a little, find some excuse to get me away from them.

RUBY: All right. *(She goes out. Hawes looks through papers at his desk. A knock at door.)*

HAWES: Come in.

(Edwin and Damon enter. Damon is in his late forties. He is arrogant and blustering.)

Hello, gentlemen.

DAMON: Hello, boy.

EDWIN: Hello, Hawes.

DAMON: *(Slaps Hawes on back.)* Well, how's the Lone Ranger? Called out the bloodhounds yet?

HAWES: Not yet.

DAMON: Everything under control?

HAWES: Yep.

DAMON: Good. Edwin said he had something to talk to you about, so I thought I'd tag along and watch the excitement.

HAWES: What is it, Edwin?

EDWIN: Well—

DAMON: Edwin here is a little nervous about Bubber Reeves comin' back. Well, how do you like the nerve of that sonovabitch! What's wrong with the penitentiary in this state that they can't keep Reeves inside? I was tellin' a group of my good friends just a few minutes ago at the drugstore. I said, "Gentlemen, we don't have the right men representin' us up at Austin. If we did, this walkin' out of penitentiaries would be stopped." Didn't I just finish sayin' that, Edwin?

EDWIN: Yes, you did, Damon.

DAMON: Well, I'm havin' my fun out of it. Never saw anything yet I couldn't have my fun out of. I knew Edwin was nervous so I snuck over to his place just after dark an' I crept up to the window where he was readin' his paper and gave two or three sharp raps on the screen. *(Starts to laugh.)* I declare, Edwin jumped out of his chair like he was shot.

EDWIN: Well, of course I did.

DAMON: *(Sits on chair D. R.)* Elizabeth and I laughed until I thought we'd die.

EDWIN: You and Elizabeth make me tired. *(Crosses R.)* How would you like to be readin' your paper an' have somebody knock at your window all of a sudden? I've got a right to be worried about Bubber Reeves comin' back. I've got every right in the world.

DAMON: Edwin thinks Bubber's got it in for him.

EDWIN: I know he has.

DAMON: I've been tellin' him over an' over this is the last place Bubber will come.

EDWIN: *(R. C.)* How do you know so much? I'm really worried, Hawes. Hawes, do you think perhaps I could have a man to guard my house? I'm afraid Bubber's comin' back here to get me.

HAWES: Why, Edwin?

EDWIN: I got into some trouble once an' Bubber got the blame for it.

HAWES: When did all this happen, Edwin? *(Puts coat on chair U. R.)*

EDWIN: Well, we were both workin' at Old Man Davis's grocery store. Papa wanted me to have a little business experience. I was just goin' to high school. I got all carried away one time like boys will, and I stole ten dollars from the cash register. Old Man Davis found out it was gone. He blamed it on Bubber. He called in the sheriff—you remember. Old Sunshine was in office then—and Old Sunshine called Mrs. Reeves down in front of all of us. He told Mrs. Reeves to whip Bubber. He said to whip him, or he'd send Bubber back to reform school. He made her whip him right there. Bubber was hollerin' the whole time he didn't do it. Old Sunshine made her whip him until the stick fell out of Mrs. Reeves's hand. Old Sunshine was a mean old bastard.

DAMON: Yeah—but he made us a good sheriff.

EDWIN: 'Course I felt bad about it. You know how kids are.

HAWES: *(Rises, sits on desk.)* Yeah. Did you ever tell Old Sunshine?

EDWIN: Yes, I did.

HAWES: What did the old devil say?

EDWIN: He laughed until I thought he would die. He said, well, Bubber probably needed that lickin' for somethin'. *(Puts hat on chair U. R.)*

HAWES: Did Bubber ever find out?

EDWIN: *(Sits C.)* Yep. I finally told him. I got drunk one night an' I decided to tell him about it. I looked all over town until I found him. He was over at a Mescan joint. I went in an' told him. He didn't say nothin'. He just looked at me an' walked out.

HAWES: Is that all? Well, Edwin, I wouldn't worry about it.

EDWIN: He told Knub McDermont later he was goin' to get me for it, and of course when my wife heard he was out of the Pen—she—

HAWES: Just a minute, Edwin, did he ever try to bother you?

EDWIN: No—but—

HAWES: *(Rises.)* I swear I wouldn't worry about it. First of all, I don't look for him back here. And second, Knub McDermont's a troublemaker. You can't trust anything he says. He's livin' with Bubber's wife. I'd forget about the whole thing.

EDWIN: You really don't expect him back here?

DAMON: Of course he doesn't expect him back here. Use your head, man. I've got the whole thing figured out, Hawes. They ought to have the Mescan border covered. That's where Bubber Reeves is headin' as sure as I'm sittin' here. If you should need help any time, you know you can count on me.

EDWIN: I hope he goes to Mexico and stays in Mexico.

DAMON: He will. You can put your money on that. There's some fools bettin' he'll come back an' you'll have to kill him, Hawes. I'm takin' all the bets I can on that one because I know he isn't comin' back. You ought to make yourself a little money.

HAWES: You all sure must have a lot to do.

DAMON: Well, you know how people are.

HAWES: This isn't a football game, you know, Damon. You're bettin' on a man's life.

DAMON: *(Laughs.)* Well, I guess you've got somethin' there, sheriff. This isn't a football game. *(Laughs again.)* That's pretty good, isn't it, Edwin? I hadn't quite thought about it that way.

HAWES: *(Rises.)* Well, boys, you're goin' to have to excuse me. I'm just loaded down tonight.

DAMON: *(Rises, crosses C.)* All right, Hawes! And I'd take it easy if I was you. I've spent about an hour thoroughly studyin' the situation an' it's my opinion this is the last place in the world he'll head for. The way I look at it—*(Rip comes in.)*

HAWES: You want to see me, Rip?

RIP: Yes, sir.

HAWES: All right, gentlemen. Will you excuse me?

DAMON: All right, Hawes. Don't forget, you can call me any time, day or night. Come on, Edwin.

EDWIN: Look, Hawes. *(Pause.)* You really don't think Bubber's comin' back? You just weren't tellin' me that to make me feel good?

HAWES: *(Crosses R., gives Edwin little push to door.)* No, Edwin, don't worry about it.

EDWIN: *(Steps L.)* Well, I just wanted to get your opinion. Good night. Thank you so much, Hawes.

DAMON: *(Reappearing in door.)* Come on, Edwin. I'll guard you if he comes back. I won't let Bubber Reeves get at you.

EDWIN: Shut up, Damon. Good night, Rip. *(Edwin and Damon exit. Hawes raises window shade.)*

RIP: I checked out at the pumpin' plant. There was an old bum drunk out in a rice ditch there, but that was all. I moved him on his way There wasn't any sign of Bubber. *(Phone rings. Rip answers.)* Yeah. No. Rip. Thank you very much. I'll tell him. Nope. Okay.

(Tarl enters.)

TARL: *(R. C.)* Sheriff, Mrs. Reeves still hasn't come home.

HAWES: Did you check on the picture show?

TARL: Yes, sir. Both of them.

HAWES: Did you ask uptown?

TARL: Yes, sir. Nobody had seen her.

HAWES: Did you check the bus station?

TARL: Yes, sir. I even checked the depot.

HAWES: All right. All right. We're goin' to have to keep on lookin' till we find her. It won't be easy. She always dodges us until Bubber's caught and back in the Pen.

TARL: Town's all stirred up.

RIP: It sure is.

TARL: It's all people are talkin' about. Bubber Reeves. Bubber Reeves.

RIP: God damn, I wish we could get us a good tip. I'm gettin' jumpy waitin' around. I want to get started.

TARL: Rip thinks we'll have to kill him this time if he comes here.

RIP: Think, hell, I know we're goin' to have to kill him. I know if I catch the murderin' bastard *I'm* gonna kill him.

TARL: Sheriff, do you think we'll have to kill him?

RIP: I bet we do. I'll bet a week's pay we'll have to shoot the sonovabitch.

HAWES: Rip, I don't like you talkin' that way.

RIP: And they're bettin' all over town we have to kill him.

HAWES: As long as I'm sheriff and you're workin' for me I don't want to hear talk like that. We've caught tougher men than Bubber without killin' them. We've caught Bubber before without killin' him. And that's what we're gonna do this time. That's what we're always gonna do as long as I'm sheriff.

RIP: Yes, sir. *(Phone rings.)*

HAWES: *(Takes it.)* Yep. All right. Send her in. *(Puts phone down.)* Mrs. Reeves is here. It's the first time she's ever come over here of her own accord. She must want somethin' from me. You boys go out and wait in the office.

(They go out. A knock on door.)

Come in.

(Mrs. Reeves enters.)

Mrs. Reeves, where have you been? Tarl has been over to your house four or five times.

MRS. REEVES: *(C., facing Hawes.)* I've been walkin'.

HAWES: Have you heard about Bubber?

MRS. REEVES: Yes, sir.

HAWES: Have you heard from him?

MRS. REEVES: *(Goes toward Hawes.)* Mr. Hawes—

HAWES: Now, look. We better get somethin' straight right now, lady. I'm not gonna stand for any foolishness. If you care anything about Bubber, you'll help me get him back in the Pen. I've taken all I'm gonna take from both of you.

MRS. REEVES: Mr. Hawes, listen to me.

HAWES: I'm gonna do the talkin' this time—I want you to answer my questions.

MRS. REEVES: I want you to hear what I have to say first.

HAWES: I don't want to hear it.

MRS. REEVES: Mr. Hawes…

HAWES: *(Crosses L.)* I've got no time to argue with you tonight. I'm gonna catch Bubber an' you an no one else—

MRS. REEVES: If you catch him, don't kill him. Don't kill him. That's all I ask you. Give him one more chance. Don't kill him. I'll pay you anything you want only don't kill him.

(Hawes crosses Mrs. Reeves to L.)

Don't kill him. Don't kill him.

HAWES: Mrs. Reeves, I don't want to kill your boy—*(Turns L. to her.)*

MRS. REEVES: If you want to, you can get him back to the Pen without killin' him. I'll be willin' to pay you for your trouble, just so you won't kill him. Will you please take the money?

HAWES: Hush up talkin' like that.

MRS. REEVES: Please, Mr. Hawes—take this money. I beg you to take this money!

HAWES: No, ma'am. I don't want it. All I want is to find your boy. Do you understand that? All I want is to find your boy.

MRS. REEVES: *(L. C.)* All right. I knew you'd turn it down. You've never given him a chance, you never will. None of you have. None of you ever have. *(Crosses R. C.)* That's why I hate this room. I've had to beg for him here so many times. To Old Sunshine and Carter, I begged them to help me to stop him, an' all they could say was send him to reform school, and I did—an' then they'd say whip him some more, an' I listened an' I did, an'

I wish my hands would rot off for it. I wish my hands would rot off for every beatin' I give him.

HAWES: It don't matter now, Mrs. Reeves—

MRS. REEVES: I can't sleep for thinkin' about what went wrong. I can't sleep for tryin' to see him how he was when he was little, wonderin' why he never come to me to cry. I don't sleep for wonderin' what he learned those nights when he slipped out to roam the town, for wonderin' who taught him all this. If I knew who taught him I'd kill them. I'd kill them, an' then you could hang me—

HAWES: I don't think anybody taught him.

MRS. REEVES: Then how did he learn all he's learned? From the night? From the swamps? From the prairies? Where'd he learn?

HAWES: It doesn't matter now, Mrs. Reeves—

MRS. REEVES: To me it matters. To me it certainly matters.

HAWES: Mrs. Reeves, I can't waste time like this.

MRS. REEVES: *(Crosses to Hawes.)* I did the best I could. I tried whippin' him. I tried to shame him. I kept him home. I dressed him like a girl to keep him home. I never gave him money unless he worked for it. I prayed like the preachers told me. I did whatever people said would help. I ask you to think back—what didn't I do? What else could I have done? Tell me.

HAWES: *(Rises.)* Mrs. Reeves, this won't do any good. Only one thing will do any good. If you know where he is, get him to surrender.

MRS. REEVES: I can't.

HAWES: Mrs. Reeves—

MRS. REEVES: I can't.

HAWES: Now, you can if you want to—

MRS. REEVES: *(L.C.)* I can't do anything with him. Nothing. You've all turned him into a mad dog. You and Old Sunshine an' the other sheriffs. You've turned my boy into a mad dog an' now there's no savin' him. I'll never forgive any of you for that. Never to my dyin' day.

HAWES: *(L.)* I've only done my duty, Mrs. Reeves—

MRS. REEVES: Your duty? Why is it always *my* boy you're so hard on? Why didn't you see Sam Mavis was sent to jail when he stabbed that Bohemian man at a dance?

HAWES: *(Crosses R.)* Oh, for God's sake—

MRS. REEVES: Why didn't you arrest Marcus Strachen for stealin' from the Buildin' an' Loan Funds, instead of lookin' the other way while his family put the money back? I know why, they're Weemses an' Mavises an' Strachens. They own the town an' they own you. You were paid—

HAWES: *(Turns L.)* You're a liar—

MRS. REEVES: *(C.)* You were paid an' paid plenty not to.

HAWES: You don't know what you're sayin', lady.

MRS. REEVES: I do know what I'm sayin'. Do you think some people can murder an' get off scot free an' others can get hung because they've got nobody behind them an' I'm not gonna know you an' the judges an' everybody else don't have a reason for makin' a difference? If you're not bein' paid to do it, what is the reason? Tell me any of these low-down people are better than my boy an' I'll kill you for sayin' it.

HAWES: *(Crosses in to Mrs. Reeves.)* God damn it! I've been very patient with you. Everybody knows how you and your no-good son have tried my patience.

MRS. REEVES: Don't you speak of him that way.

HAWES: I'll speak of him any way I want, lady.

MRS. REEVES: I'm not afraid of you or your pistols or your deputies or any of the people you toady to, so they'll keep you in office. I want you to understand that, Sheriff Hawes. I'm not afraid of you, so watch your step. I know you. I've been onto you for a long time. You won't rest until you find an excuse to kill my boy. Will you? Will you? *(Pause.)*

HAWES: Look, Mrs. Reeves—

MRS. REEVES: I hate you! I hate you!

HAWES: I know that. I know that—

MRS. REEVES: I hate you! I hate you! I hope they have to chase the child your wife is carryin'. I hope they have to chase him like a mad dog. I hope he's shot an' killed in some ditch—if you kill Bubber, I'm gonna kill you. I'm gonna kill you, so help me, God. If you kill him—

HAWES: *(Crosses to C. door.)* Get out of here.

MRS. REEVES: I hope he's shot and killed in some ditch.

HAWES: If you don't get out of here, I'm gonna lock you up. I've stood enough. *(Starts toward her.)*

MRS. REEVES: Don't you come near me.

HAWES: *(Turns upstage slightly.)* I mean it, now. Get out of here.

MRS. REEVES: *(Crosses U. L. of Hawes.)* All right. Drive me out of here. You can't stop the truth. I'll stand outside the jail and yell to the whole world what you are. Murderer. I hope your child is hunted and killed some day. I hope it is. I hope it is.

(She goes out. A pause. Hawes is very disturbed. He calls off.)

HAWES: Ruby! Ruby! *(Turns downstage. Ruby comes running in.)*

RUBY: *(R. of Hawes.)* What is it, Hawes?

HAWES: *(Crosses D.L.)* She's crazy. Mrs. Reeves is crazy.

RUBY: What did she say to you?

HAWES: She's got it fixed in her mind I want to kill Bubber. I thought I'd take my fist an' hit her when she said that. That's all I've heard today. Killin'! Killin'! *(Crosses R. of Ruby.)* Ruby, I just can't stand it here any more. You know that farm I saw this afternoon?

RUBY: Yes.

HAWES: *(Crosses D. R. C.)* I want it. I want to buy it.

RUBY: Buy it? What with, Hawes?

HAWES: Ruby, if we're careful and save our money the next seven months and can get some help from the bank—

RUBY: You mean—borrow?

HAWES: Yes. Mr. Douglas says he'll speak to old man Stewart and he said he knew the bank would want to cooperate.

RUBY: But, honey, we're just out of debt.

HAWES: I know, Ruby, but it's the only way we can leave here in seven months, and Ruby, I have to leave. Believe me—

RUBY: Well, all right.

HAWES: Oh, you'll love this farm. I swear to you. You've always said you wanted to go back to a farm some day.

RUBY: I know. I know. Certainly, if that's what will make you happy, Hawes— *(Suddenly from outside the jail a revolver is fired. It crashes window pane of office. Ruby falls on floor. Hawes falls down beside her. Gets up and pulls down shade.)*

HAWES: Are you all right, honey?

RUBY: Yes.

HAWES: Are you sure?

RUBY: Yes, I'm just scared.

TARL: *(Yelling from outside.)* Anybody hurt in there?

HAWES: Nope.

    (Helps Ruby up. Tarl comes in.)

    Are you feelin' all right, Ruby?

RUBY: Yes.

HAWES: Now, you're sure?

RUBY: Yes, I'm sure.

TARL: Shot was fired from a car.

HAWES: What kind of a car?

TARL: Didn't have a chance to see. Rip is out chasin' it.

HAWES: The crazy fool! The crazy bastard! Why does he always have to come back?

RUBY: Bubber?

HAWES: Yep.

> *(Ruby runs to Hawes. He takes her in his arms.)*

Take it easy, honey—

RUBY: I'm sorry. I'm sorry. It scared me so. My heart is just poundin'. Oh, Hawes, I'll be glad to leave here. I'll be glad to get to a farm.

> *(Rip comes in.)*

RIP: Everybody OK?

TARL: Yes.

RIP: That car was goin' pretty fast. Way out of sight by the time I got started.

HAWES: We've got to get busy. *(Goes to phone, picks it up.)* Alert the sheriffs in Matagorda, Luling, Eagle Lake, Victoria, Bay City, Angleton—

CURTAIN

ACT II
Scene 1

> *Next day, after twilight. Hawes's office. Ruby is seated at Hawes's desk L. Damon is seated chair C. Takes out his watch, looks at it.*

DAMON: How much longer am I goin' to have to wait?

RUBY: I know he'll be here soon, Damon.

DAMON: I've been tryin' to find him all afternoon. What the hell's goin' on?

> *(Rises, crosses R.)*

RUBY: Well, he has so much to do now, Damon. He hasn't had a moment's rest since he got the news about Bubber. He's seen to everything himself.

> *(Damon crosses L. to chair.)*

He didn't get in until just before daybreak and I made him lie down on the cot to take a nap. I don't think he rested, though. He was tossing and talking all the time. He had only been asleep a couple of hours and then he had to go to Ganado, El Campo, Blessing, and Freed Man's Town. He was terribly upset when he heard about your store.

> *(Damon turns to cooler, draws drink, throws hat on chair R.)*

He went over lookin' for you earlier this morning, but you weren't there.

DAMON: I just went out for a cup of coffee. If he had bothered to come up to the drugstore he could have found me. *(Drinks.)*

RUBY: I know. I feel terrible about his missing you, and I know he does, too.

> *(Damon sits on chair D. R.)*

Can I get you somethin' to read?

DAMON: No.

RUBY: Would you like a coke?

DAMON: No. God knows how much damage has been done.

RUBY: I know. Tarl told me.

DAMON: *(Rises, crosses up C.)* I can't sit still for thinkin' about my store.
   (Hawes and Rip enter.)

RUBY: Oh, Hawes—

HAWES: Hello, Ruby.

RUBY: Damon's here to see you.

HAWES: Hello, Damon.

DAMON: Hello.

HAWES: I'm sorry to be so late gettin' back.

DAMON: I've been tryin' to get through to you all day.

HAWES: *(Removes his holster.)* I know. Boy. I wouldn't want to live over this day
   again for a million dollars. Movin' around in this heat—I bet I traveled
   two hundred miles today if I've gone a step. The heat on the prairies was
   enough to kill a man. *(Hands holster to Rip.)* I sure was sorry to hear about
   your store.

DAMON: Yeah.

HAWES: I went over lookin' for you, but I guess I just missed you.

DAMON: Yeah, I know.

HAWES: Rip, wait in the office.
   (Rip exits. Hawes turns to Ruby.)
   How do you feel tonight, Ruby?

RUBY: Fine.

HAWES: Are you sure?

RUBY: Yes...Before I forget it, honey, Edwin has been callin' an' callin'. He says
   he has to see you.

HAWES: All right. Would you go ask Red to call him and tell him I'll be here
   for an hour? *(Crosses to desk.)*

RUBY: All right. I got a whole list of people that want you to call them.

HAWES: OK

RUBY: The phone's been ringin' every five minutes.

HAWES: *(Sits on desk.)* I don't want to talk to anybody for a while. Will you tell
   Red to hold the calls?

RUBY: Yes, I will. *(She goes out.)*

DAMON: Did you see my store?

HAWES: Yep. I took a look at it this mornin'.

DAMON: God knows how much damage has been done. Everything inside ripped with a knife—four dozen workshirts, fifteen bolts of cotton goods…

HAWES: I know. I know.

DAMON: Smashed a whole hat case to bits. Glass all over the goddamned place.

HAWES: I saw it all, Damon.

DAMON: *(Pause.)* Was it Bubber?

HAWES: *(Pause.)* Yes, sir.

DAMON: *(Crosses R.)* The low-down devil. There's at least four thousand dollars in damages been done. Where were you when my store was bein' robbed?

HAWES: You know where I was. I was out huntin' Bubber Reeves.

DAMON: *(Crosses C.)* I'm a citizen and a taxpayer. Why wasn't my store protected?

HAWES: Look, Damon, the night watchman was at the other end of town. Bubber knew his habits of makin' the rounds, and slipped in your store while the watchman was punchin' the clocks over across the tracks. The trouble with a crazy fool like Bubber is you just can't predict what he's goin' to do next. We had no idea he would do a senseless thing like goin' into your store and tearin' it up.

DAMON: Is that goin' to get me back my hat case and merchandise?

HAWES: No, I didn't say it would. I was only tryin' to explain—

DAMON: You're gonna have lots to explain when the good people of this town hear about this. Men came to my store all day and—

HAWES: Look, Damon—

DAMON: My friends, my good friends, came to me. They said, Damon, we want you to know that we think it's a shame. A cryin' shame. Where was Hawes when this happened?

HAWES: Good God, man! Don't they know how big this county is? *(Crosses C. past Damon.)* Don't they know how many calls I've had to see to—?

DAMON: An' they said this is the same question they'll be askin' at election time. Where was Hawes when this happened?

HAWES: I wish they'd ask me that. *(Crosses to window.)*

DAMON: I'm askin' you.

HAWES: And I've told you where I was. Out chasin' Bubber Reeves—

DAMON: And why isn't he caught?

HAWES: *(Turns to Damon.)* What do you mean by a question like that?

DAMON: I mean exactly what I say. Why is that killer loose after twenty-four hours?

HAWES: Look, he's not caught because it hasn't been humanly possible to catch him. *(Crosses R. to cooler.)* And if you or any other men in this town think you can do any better, you're welcome to the job.

DAMON: The good people in this town want him killed.

HAWES: I'm gonna catch him. *(Drinks.)*

DAMON: We want him killed. We want him killed. Is that clear? I've been with the good people of this town all day and we want him killed. Not caught. Killed!

HAWES: *(Crosses C.)* Damon. Damon. What in the name of God are you gettin' so excited about?

DAMON: Excited. Of course I'm excited. Wouldn't you be excited if your store had been broken into, mutilated—

HAWES: *(Crosses L.)* I appreciate that— *(Sits in chair at desk.)*

DAMON: *(Crosses R.)* Wouldn't you be excited if a killer was runnin' loose for twenty-four hours—

HAWES: All right, Damon. All right.

DAMON: *(Crosses R. C.)* Excited? By God, you're right I'm excited. I'm excited enough to get a gun and go out and hunt that crazy killer myself so that the good people of this town can sleep at night—

HAWES: All right, Damon. Calm down. Calm down.

DAMON: Don't ask me to calm down. I won't calm down until he's dead—

HAWES: *(Sharply.)* Will you let me talk, for Chris' sakes? *(Rises.)*

DAMON: All right, talk. *(Pause.)*

HAWES: Have I ever failed to catch Bubber Reeves before?

DAMON: No.

HAWES: Have I ever in any way let the people of this town down before?

DAMON: No.

HAWES: And I won't this time. I'll catch Bubber. I'll catch him and get him back to the Pen.

DAMON: The good people of this town want him killed.

HAWES: *(Crosses to Damon C.)* No, they don't. They think they do right now because they're excited, but they don't. Now, look. I know people. Remember when that Houston nigra come here an' cut up a white man. I had to hold 'em off with a pistol to keep them from lynchin' him. In their excitement they thought they wanted him killed, but they didn't. And after it was over and I got him away without their killin' him, everybody in town wrote me or called me sayin' how glad they was I kept that nigra from them. An' after I've gotten Bubber back to the Pen alive, I know you an' everybody else is gonna be glad. An' I'm confident you'll be the first to tell me so. *(Pause.)* Damon, I've always played fair an' square with you. I like you. I'm your friend. I've always considered you mine. Please, please, don't give me any trouble here tonight. Will you give me your word on that?

DAMON: Well—I—

HAWES: Look, Damon. You and I both know how the people here listen to you. Now if you want to help me smooth things down, you can. That's all I'm askin' you to do. Just help me smooth things down until I can have a fair chance to catch Bubber.

DAMON: How am I gonna do that?

HAWES: By goin' home an' mindin' your own business. If people ask you about your store, tell them you don't know who robbed it—

DAMON: Why can't I tell them who robbed it?

HAWES: Because they'll be lots easier to handle if they find it out after Bubber's caught.

DAMON: Look, Hawes—

HAWES: I'm beggin' you, Damon. *(Pause.)* Help me keep sanity an' order here tonight.

DAMON: Well—I—

HAWES: I appeal to you. As a leader, I appeal to you. I'm beggin' you, Damon. I'm beggin' you as a friend—as a friend—

DAMON: Well, all right. Since you put it that way, all right.

HAWES: Thank you, Damon. And I swear to you you'll never regret it.

DAMON: But you're gonna keep right after him until you catch him?

HAWES: Oh, yes, and I'll catch him, Damon. I swear to you, I will.

DAMON: All right, Hawes. *(Crosses Hawes to door.)*

HAWES: And thank you, Damon. *(Damon stops near door. Hawes offers his hand.)*

DAMON: Well—

HAWES: Thank you again.

DAMON: All right.

> *(He goes out. Hawes stands a moment, thinking. Goes to the chair D. R. and sits. Ruby enters.)*

HAWES: There isn't a man in this town can't talk the best line of sheriff you ever heard.

RUBY: I'd like for them to try it. I'd just like for any of them to try it. No more word about Bubber?

HAWES: No, ma'am. Well, I guess nobody begged me to take this job. Where are the names of the people that called, Ruby?

RUBY: Here. *(Hands him list.)*

HAWES: Lord, there's not one of them isn't gonna tell me something I don't already know. Well, I'd better get it done. It'll make them feel better.

RUBY: Honey, relax a little first. You've been drivin' and drivin' yourself today. Let me get you some music on the radio. *(Starts to turn radio on.)*

HAWES: No, Ruby, I don't want music—just stay here close to me.

RUBY: All right.

(She gently strokes Hawes's shoulder. He leans his head against her.)

It's been hot today, hasn't it?

HAWES: It was so hot I almost died. I don't think I ever felt the heat quite like this. What did you do all day, honey?

RUBY: Oh, I just fooled around the apartment until late afternoon. And I wanted to go for a walk but I didn't want to go to town because I knew everybody would be askin' a lot of questions about the shootin' here last night, so you know where I went?

HAWES: Down the railroad tracks?

RUBY: No, over by the river. I walked down the riverbank as far as I could. It was so quiet down there. The willows an' the oaks an' the pecans seemed so cool and friendly, I forgot all about what a hot day it had been. I took off my shoes an' waded a little in the water. Wrote my name an' your name in the sandbar. Oh, I had a ball down there by myself.

HAWES: When I was a kid there used to be alligators in the river.

RUBY: I know. I was thinkin' about that today. I wonder where they all went to?

HAWES: Killed 'em all off, I guess.

RUBY: You know what I knew about myself today, Hawes?

HAWES: What, honey?

RUBY: I'm restless.

HAWES: Are you?

RUBY: Uh-huh. Because I'm waitin'. Sometimes I can hate waitin'. I hate waitin' here for you to go out on night calls when there's any kind of danger like last night. But this kind of waitin' I don't mind. Knowin' the baby's inside me, growin' an' growin'. My heart was so hungry for a baby, Hawes.

HAWES: And so was mine.

RUBY: I never gave up hope, Hawes.

HAWES: I know you didn't.

RUBY: *(Crosses to Hawes.)* I never gave up hope that we were gonna have our own family to love an' take care of. *(Puts arms around him.)* Oh, honey, I love you so. And it hurts me to see you lookin' so tired. I think it's the best thing in the world we're leavin' here in seven months.

HAWES: You mean that, honey?

RUBY: I swear I do.

HAWES: Oh, Ruby, I want to get that farm so—that's all that's kept me goin' this whole blessed day. The thought of you and the baby on our place. *(Phone rings.)*

RUBY: Let me get it. *(She answers it upstage.)* Yes? Oh, Hawes, Edwin Stewart is out there.

HAWES: All right. Ask him to come in.

RUBY: Couldn't you see him some other time, Hawes? You should rest now if you can. You may have to be up most of the night again.

HAWES: Better not put him off.

RUBY: All right. Tell him to come in, Red.

(Puts phone down. Edwin enters. He is very nervous. Ruby sits on stool below desk.)

EDWIN: Hello, Ruby, Hawes.

HAWES: Edwin.

EDWIN: I've been tryin' to see you all day—

HAWES: I know, and I wanted to get by the bank, but I had my hands full today.

EDWIN: *(Crosses R.)* I thought you said Bubber wasn't comin' back.

HAWES: I reckon I was mistaken.

EDWIN: *(Crosses C.)* I'll say you were—I just saw Damon down the street. He said you all had found out it was Bubber who broke into his store.

HAWES: *(Jumping up from his chair.)* Jesus!

EDWIN: What's the matter?

HAWES: He just got through swearin' to me he wouldn't say a word about it.

EDWIN: Why not?

HAWES: Because I didn't want him to. *(Goes to phone.)*

EDWIN: Hawes—

HAWES: Red, send Tarl or Rip out to find Damon. Tell them to bring him back here as fast as they can. And, Red—

EDWIN: I'd appreciate your puttin' the phone down and talkin' to me.

HAWES: *(Into phone.)* Never mind. *(Hangs up, sits.)* What is it?

EDWIN: Remember what I was tellin' you last night about Bubber Reeves and me?

HAWES: Yes. And I told you I wouldn't worry too much about it.

EDWIN: Well, I *am* worried and I'm gonna stay worried until he's caught. I want you to send one of your men over to guard my house.

HAWES: I can't do that, Edwin. I haven't a man to spare.

EDWIN: *(Crosses to Hawes.)* You mean you won't do it.

HAWES: Don't put it that way, Edwin—I would if I could.

EDWIN: I don't see any other way to put it. Look, Hawes, I wouldn't ask you if I could help it.

HAWES: *(Rises, crosses R.)* I appreciate that, Edwin, but we've had our hands full since Bubber got out. We've had four cuttin' scrapes, three cases of—

EDWIN: Look, Hawes—Bubber said he was gonna kill me.

HAWES: Edwin, if I gave you a deputy, every person in Richmond that has a reason to be afraid of Bubber would be wantin' someone at his house until he's caught an' back in the Pen—

EDWIN: You don't need to talk to me like a child, Hawes.

HAWES: I don't mean to talk to you like a child—I'm just explainin'—

EDWIN: All right. Then don't act so high and mighty when I ask for a little protection.

HAWES: I wasn't actin' high and mighty.

EDWIN: Yes, you are. I tell you, I wouldn't have come to you if I didn't think it was necessary.

HAWES: Look, Edwin, I'll tell you what I can do. You and Elizabeth are welcome to come over here and stay with us.

EDWIN: Thank you very much. *(Crosses L.)* What the hell kind of a man do you take me for? I can't ask my wife to come and sit in a jail while you take your time about catchin' a man who threatened to kill me.

HAWES: I'm not takin' my time. I'm doin' everything a human bein' can do.

EDWIN: Look, I'm tired of arguin'. I'm goin' to ask you one more time.

HAWES: And I've told you all I can do.

EDWIN: All right. I'm glad to find this out. *(Crosses L. and back, picks up hat.)* Then I'll take my wife and go to Houston and put up at a hotel until this is all over—

HAWES: Now look, Edwin—

EDWIN: And don't be comin' to me or my father and askin' for any favors, because you're not gonna get them. Do you understand that?

HAWES: Edwin—Edwin—

EDWIN: You're not gonna get them. Let Mrs. Reeves loan you the money.

HAWES: All right, you can get out of here.

EDWIN: Thank you, but I want to tell you one more thing, Hawes, before I go. You're a public servant, and you better remember that. My money and my vote, and the money of my friends and the votes of my friends, put you in office and pay to keep you there—and I have a lot of friends. And my wife has a lot of friends, and every one of them is gonna hear of your treatment of us. *(He goes out.)*

HAWES: Boy, I'll be glad when the day comes when I can say what I please when I please. This business of servin' the public can be mighty hard sometimes.

(Tarl comes in.)

TARL: Mr. Hawes, old man Billy Reynolds says someone smashed up a car out near his farm as he was comin' down the road. He said he seen a man jump out as soon as it smashed and he swears it was Bubber.

HAWES: Did he get the number of the car?

TARL: Yes, sir. I checked the number against the files. It's Knub McDermont's car.

HAWES: Knub McDermont! Well, this is the first real break we've gotten. Ruby, will you watch things here for me? I've got to get out to Knub's right away.

RUBY: All right.

HAWES: Come on, Tarl.

(They exit.)

CURTAIN

ACT II
Scene 2

Later same night. Knub's cabin. Anna is looking out door. Knub is seated R. of table.

ANNA: Mama said she expected to pick up a paper in Victoria and see where Bubber's killed us both. I was thinkin' last night how I first met Bubber Reeves. It was at a Bohemian dance. He weren't no Bohemian and I wondered what he was doin' there. He weren't drinkin' at all and he asked me to dance with him. Just kind of mumbled it. I thought to myself at the time, he's got mean-lookin' eyes. *(Crosses to table, L. end.)* Do you ever get to thinkin'?

KNUB: No.

ANNA: I wish I wouldn't. I swear I wouldn't care what happens to me if I didn't think. I told Mama today she was gonna have to give me my baby back, but she says she won't until I start in livin' right, an' I said, how am I gonna start in livin' right if Knub can't marry me, and he can't marry me until I divorce Bubber, an' I can't divorce him until I get the money for the lawyer? But you can't argue with Mama. I've known that for a long time. Jesus, if I ever saw more than ten dollars at one time, I think I'd go crazy with happiness. *(Pause.)* I bet you never see your old car again.

(From L. in the distance is heard "Knub, Knub.")

What is it?

KNUB: *(Rises.)* Shhhhh.

ANNA: Oh, my Father.

(Knub looks out window. Again "Knub" is heard. Bubber enters up L., crosses R. [i.e., in yard, not cabin] to stoop.)

KNUB: It's Bubber.

ANNA: Oh, my God, you better get him away from here. *(Jumps out of her chair.)*

KNUB: Sit down and don't act crazy.

(Goes to door. Bubber calls "Knub," Knub goes out on steps.)

Get away from here, Bubber, it's too late for me to help you. Now get away from here.

BUBBER: Give me a gun.

KNUB: I'm not gonna give you nothin'. This whole county's wild. They would string me up if they knew I ever helped you.

BUBBER: I gotta have a gun.

KNUB: You got money. Buy yourself one. Fat Boy will sell you one.

BUBBER: I don't want to go to Fat Boy. I want you to give me one.

KNUB: Jesus Christ—you had a gun! What did you do with it?

BUBBER: I left it in your car.

KNUB: Where's my car?

BUBBER: I wrecked it.

KNUB: Jesus! Jesus! I'm not goin' to give you a gun, so clear out of here.

(Knub pushes Bubber downstage. Bubber goes into cabin—back of table, followed by Knub.)

Where the hell you going?

BUBBER: I'm not leavin' here until I get that gun.

KNUB: Bubber, Hawes will be high-tailin' it out here when he finds my car wrecked. Do you want him to catch you out here?

BUBBER: *(Sits C. table.)*. Give me somethin' to eat, Anna.

(Knub crosses to door.)

ANNA: Bubber, you go on. You don't want Hawes—

BUBBER: What did you say?

ANNA: Nothin'.

BUBBER: That's better. Now give me some food.

ANNA: Yes, sir. All we got left is a little leftover chili an' some greens. I was about to throw that out. I was just sayin' to myself—

BUBBER: All right. Get the food.

(Anna goes out upstage, gets food out of a pan. Knub stands in doorway, watching. She drops something.)

KNUB: *(Crosses up C.)* What the hell's the matter with you?

ANNA: I'm nervous. I told you that.

KNUB: Well, get over bein' nervous or I'll run you back to town.

(Anna re-enters with food on tray, puts it in front of Bubber. He wolfs it down.)

Where did you wreck my car, Bubber?

BUBBER: 'Bout a half mile away from here.

KNUB: *(Sits R. of table.)* Did anybody see you wreck it?

BUBBER: How the hell do I know?

KNUB: Is the car ruint?

BUBBER: I don't know. I don't know. I don't know. *(Shoves plate aside, puts his head on table.)*

KNUB: Jesus! *(Turns away from Bubber.)*

BUBBER: I'm tired. Oh, my God, I'm tired! When I was in the Pen waitin' to get out I thought I'd never get tired again until I come back here an' get this done. But I only been out a day an' I'm tired, bone tired.

(Knub crosses to door.)

I can't rest. I'm tired an' I can't rest. I couldn't rest in the Pen. They worked us like niggers, choppin' cotton an' workin' the fields an' I thought if I get out of here I can rest, but I can't rest. I lay down in the woods last night an' I kept sayin', stay quiet an' you can rest, nobody will find you. But I couldn't. I couldn't. The hoot-owls an' the possums an' the tree frogs wouldn't give me no rest. If I could just kill that devil, I could rest. If I could just kill that devil, I could rest.

(Knub goes to door, looks out.)

KNUB: God damn it, get out of here, Bubber. Hawes and Tarl are out there snoopin' around.

BUBBER: Give me a gun, Knub. Let me kill him. Let me kill him.

KNUB: Will you stop talkin' crazy and get out of here! *(Drags Bubber to window L.)*

BUBBER: Knub—

KNUB: Hurry. Get out the window.

BUBBER: All right, but I'm comin' back. You hear me? I'll be back.

(Knub shuts door, Bubber climbs out window. Knub pushes Anna into chair L. of table. Hawes and Tarl enter from down R. They stand a moment at edge of stage and look around. They go up to cabin door, and knock.)

KNUB: Go talk to him.

(Knub sits L. of table.)

ANNA: *(Calling.)* Who is it?

HAWES: Open up, Anna—it's Sheriff Hawes.

(Anna goes to door.)

ANNA: Yes, sir.

HAWES: I want to talk to Knub.

ANNA: Yes, sir.

(She opens screen door. He enters, followed by Tarl.)

HAWES: Knub—

KNUB: Sheriff—

HAWES: Did you all know Bubber was out of the Pen?

KNUB: Yep.

HAWES: Have you seen Bubber?

KNUB: Nope.

HAWES: Have you, Anna?

ANNA: No, sir.

HAWES: *(Looks into kitchen U. C.)* Are you sure about that?

ANNA: Yes, sir.

HAWES: All right. Where's you car, Knub? *(Looks out window.)*

KNUB: Sir?

HAWES: Where's your car?

KNUB: I don't know?

HAWES: You don't know?

KNUB: It was stole from me some time last night. I went out this mornin' to ride into town and it was stolen from me.

HAWES: Why didn't you come in and tell me about it?

KNUB: Well—I—

HAWES: You're lyin' to me, Knub.

KNUB: No—I'm not lyin', Mr. Hawes.

HAWES: Your car was found wrecked out by old man Billy Reynold's place.

KNUB: Yes, sir.

HAWES: Bubber Reeves was seen drivin' it.

KNUB: That so?

HAWES: You think he was the one that stole it?

(Noise outside window.)

What's that? Come on, Tarl.

(They leave cabin. Knub runs to window, looks out. Anna moves chair, straightens table, pushes barrel under it. Hawes and Tarl throw their flashlights all around. Bubber has run into the brush. Hawes and Tarl come back inside.)

All right, now, Knub, I want you to stop foolin' around. I want the truth out of you.

KNUB: I'm tellin' you the truth.

HAWES: How did Bubber get hold of your car?

KNUB: I don't know.

HAWES: *(Crosses R., turns.)* Now look, Knub, I haven't come over here to make trouble for you. I need your help. I need your help bad. This county is gettin' ugly. I been sheriff a long time an' I know when bad trouble is startin'. A lot of people here want Bubber killed. His Mama thinks I want to kill him. Believe me, I don't. I'm the sheriff and it's my duty to catch him. I ask you, I beg you. If you know where he is, tell me so I can catch him.

KNUB: I don't know nothin' about him.

HAWES: Knub.

KNUB: I told you, I don't know nothin' about him.

HAWES: *(Pause.)* You know, if this goes on much longer I'm gonna have a lynchin' mob on my hands. *(Pause.)* Is that what you want to happen to Bubber?

KNUB: I don't know.

HAWES: God damn it, Knub— *(Pause.)* All right. I guess you're not gonna help me. I guess I can't make you. If you see him, will you tell him this? Tell him that I don't want any trouble. All I want is to get him back to the Pen safe. If he's got any sense left, try to make him understand that the only chance he has is to surrender to me.

KNUB: I'm not gonna see him.

HAWES: OK *(Goes outside.)* Come on, Tarl, I swear I heard somethin' out there.

TARL: Yes, sir.

(Hawes looks around. He and Tarl start off.)

HAWES: Let's go back to the jail. What the hell. We're just chasin' shadows out here.

(They cross R., exit. A moment passes, then Knub comes out of cabin. He looks after Hawes. Anna comes out.)

ANNA: You think they've gone for good?

KNUB: I don't know.

ANNA: Bubber says he was comin' back. Do you think he'll be back?

KNUB: I don't know.

ANNA: I pray Bubber don't come back here botherin' us. I pray—I pray—I wish I hadn't seen Bubber again. It always gets me upset to see him.

(Knub goes into cabin. Anna follows, back of table.)

Knub, honey, give me a bottle of whiskey.

KNUB: *(Seated R. end of table.)* No, ma'am. I don't want you drunk.

ANNA: *(Crosses R. of Knub.)* Knub, honey, give me the whiskey. I'm nervous. I'm always nervous when Bubber's out this way. I stay nervous until he's locked up again. Give me the whiskey.

KNUB: I don't want you drunk.

ANNA: I won't get drunk, honey. I swear to you I won't get drunk. I've got to do somethin' for my nerves, that's all.

(Knub goes to U. L. behind curtain, comes out with bottle and glasses. Crosses R.)

KNUB: Here.

ANNA: Thank you.

KNUB: Now I got thirteen bottles more in there an' I want to find thirteen bottles there in the mornin'.

ANNA: Look at me. I'm tremblin'. *(Drinks.)* You better have a drink, too, honey.

KNUB: No.

ANNA: Knub, when this is all over, will you take me out on the highway some night to that new church they got out there? They tell me the preacher lets snakes crawl all over him an' bite him. People say them snakes are full of poison. Cottonmouths and water moccasins and rattlers. Do you believe that, Knub?

KNUB: I don't know.

ANNA: Will you take me some night, Knub, so I can see?

KNUB: No.

ANNA: Why won't you take me, Knub? Edna Lee pointed the preacher out in town to me the other Saturday. They say he just stands there an' lets them snakes crawl all over him. Edna Lee seen him. She said she fainted when she seen it and she had to be carried out to Randolph's car. She said she dreamed about them snakes for a whole week afterwards. Knub, won't you take me?

(Knub crosses to door. Bubber comes onstage, not yet into cabin. He crosses yard. He stands looking a moment. Goes into cabin.)

KNUB: Jesus, Bubber!

BUBBER: All right, Knub—now, give me a gun.

KNUB: I'm not gonna give you a gun—Hawes and Tarl—

BUBBER: Knub, I don't have any time to argue. Where's the gun? I'm goin' to get Hawes.

KNUB: You're not goin' to get Hawes with any gun of mine. God damn it, get out of here! I told you I helped you all I was goin' to.

BUBBER: Take your hands off me.

(Knub pulls him from behind curtain U. C. Bubber pulls free.)

I'll ask you one more time. Will you give me a gun?

KNUB: No.

(Bubber takes a piece of pipe out of his back pocket. He hits Knub with it. Anna screams.)

BUBBER: All right, Anna, tell me where the gun is, or I'll beat his brains in.

ANNA: Under the mattress.

(Bubber goes out through curtain U. C., returns with revolver, checks it. Anna runs to Knub, kneels beside him.)

Honey—honey—honey—Knub, answer me—honey, honey, are you all right?

KNUB: *(Stirs.)* Yeah.

ANNA: Oh, my God, I thought he had killed you. I can't stand any more of this. What are we gonna do, Knub, what are we gonna do?

KNUB: I don't know. I don't know.

LIGHTS FADE

ACT II
Scene 3

Hawes's office. Later same night. Ruby and Douglas are seated. Hawes enters. He is very upset.

RUBY: Hello, Hawes.

HAWES: Hello, honey. Hello, Mr. Douglas.

DOUGLAS: Hello, Hawes. I just came by to see how you all were after last night. I found Ruby alone, and I thought I'd stay a while and keep her company.

HAWES: Thank you.

DOUGLAS: How are you bearin' up, Hawes?

HAWES: *(Hangs up his holster.)* Not so good—I'm so sore right now I'd like to tear this town apart.

RUBY: What happened?

HAWES: Ruby, I couldn't get a thing out of Knub or Anna. *(Sits at desk.)* Nothin'. They just sat there and acted like they never heard of Bubber Reeves. I've had my belly full of it. People callin' every five minutes. Expectin' me to check on every kind of silly rumor. Edwin Stewart demandin' a deputy to guard his house. Damon promisin' he wouldn't spread it around town about Bubber robbin' his store and five minutes later tellin' the first person he met.

RUBY: Hawes, we'll be away from here in seven months and then we won't ever have to think about these things again. Just try and get through tonight.

HAWES: *(Rises, crosses R. to cooler.)* I know. Did you get to speak to Mr. Stewart about the farm, Mr. Douglas?

DOUGLAS: Well, yes, I did. *(Crosses up R.)*

HAWES: What did he say?

DOUGLAS: Well, he was very nice about it at first and I thought it was all arranged. But he called just before I come over and said he wouldn't do it.

RUBY: Did he give any reasons?

DOUGLAS: He said Hawes had never farmed and would probably lose the money.

HAWES: That's not the reason.

DOUGLAS: Well, I said, give him a chance. He's strong. And he said Hawes hadn't saved any money in the eight years he's been sheriff.

HAWES: And that's not the reason.

RUBY: He hasn't saved any money because he's been payin' back every penny he's ever owed. He went all over town and even looked up debts he had as far back as a kid of seventeen. Mr. Stewart knows that. I've heard him say he admires him for it.

HAWES: Edwin's sore at me. He's spiteful. He said Bubber had a grudge against him and was goin' to try to kill him. Wanted me to send a deputy over to guard his house. Christ, what difference does it make!

(Phone rings. Ruby answers.)

RUBY: Yes, oh, yes. He's here now. *(Puts phone down.)* Hawes, it's Dixie Graves. She's been callin' an' callin'. Can you talk to her?

HAWES: No, Ruby, not now.

RUBY: I wouldn't ask you, but it's about her little boy. He ran away from home again.

HAWES: *(Into phone.)* Hello, Dixie. I'm sorry. I'm short of men tonight. It will have to wait until tomorrow. I know, Dixie, and I'm sorry. All right, Dixie, and I'm sorry. All right, Dixie. I'll see what I can do. *(Puts phone down.)* He's twelve. Her boy's twelve and she says she can't control him. She talks just like Mrs. Reeves used to. Another five years, if he keeps on, we'll have to send him to reform school. Another five, hunt him like I'm huntin' Bubber tonight. And the Damons and the Edwins will be after me to kill him and the chase will be on. How does it begin? How does it start? How does it end?

RUBY: I don't know that Hawes. I don't know that.

HAWES: And that's what's drivin' me crazy. I don't know that.

(Rip enters.)

RIP: I found Damon. He was over at Edwin Stewart's.

HAWES: All right, bring him in.

RIP: There were about ten men over there with him.

HAWES: What were they doin'?

RIP: Just sittin' on the front gallery.

HAWES: Have they got guns?

RIP: They didn't say and I didn't ask them. But I know they have.

HAWES: What were they talkin' about?

RIP: Buyin' some whiskey. They wanted to know from me if the whiskey store was closed, and I said I didn't look to see.

HAWES: All right. All right. Bring Damon in.

RIP: Yes, sir.

(He goes out. Damon enters.)

DAMON: I come over here with Rip to tell you once and for all—

HAWES: What the hell do you mean by givin' me your word you wouldn't tell anybody about Bubber robbin' your store, and then walkin' out of here—?

DAMON: I changed my mind.

HAWES: Oh, you changed your mind! I wish I could lock a man up for changin' his mind. If I could I'd lock you up so fast!

DAMON: People have a right to know who robbed my store.

HAWES: All right. All right. Rip tells me you men have got guns over there at Edwin's.

DAMON: That's right. There isn't a man in this town that isn't carryin' a gun tonight or sleepin' with one under his pillow. The good people of this town are gonna get Bubber Reeves and you're not goin' to keep them away from him. Understand that. Not you or twenty sheriffs.

HAWES: *(C.)* Now, look, Damon, I'm the sheriff. I'm gonna see that Bubber's taken alive for the law to punish—

DAMON: *(Interrupts.)* The law's too good for this murderin'—

HAWES: That isn't for you to say. That's not for me to say. I don't care who he is or what he's done. I'm gonna take him alive for the law to punish him. I'm not gonna let you or any other men keep me from doin' that. I'm gonna catch him.

DAMON: All right, catch him. We'll take him away from you because this time we're gonna see he's killed.

RUBY: Damon!

HAWES: Damon, how can you talk like that? You know you don't mean that.

DAMON: I do mean it. We should have killed him before. That's the mistake we made. We waited to see what the law would do, and it did nothin'. Well, we're gonna get him tonight. We're gonna run the bottoms until we find him. And when we find him we're gonna kill him. And I hope I'm the one to pull the trigger.

HAWES: If any man in this town touches him, so help me God I'm gonna—

DAMON: You're gonna do what? *(Pause.)* You're gonna do nothin'. Because they'll tear any man to pieces if you try to get in their way. I've never seen people like this, Hawes, so I warn you to stay out of their way. They'll tear you to pieces if you try to get in their way.

(Ruby runs to Hawes.)

RUBY: Hawes! Hawes!

(She sways. He grabs her.)

HAWES: Honey. Honey. What's the matter, Ruby—what's the matter?

(She is crying.)

RUBY: I'm all right. I'm all right. Only get him out of here. Talk like that makes me sick. It makes me sick.

DAMON: How the hell do you expect me to talk? If that sonovabitch—

HAWES: *(Grabs him.)* Now, you get out of here. You get out of here as fast as you can before I—I—

DOUGLAS: *(Taking Hawes' hand away.)* Let him go, Hawes. Let him go. Now, get out of here.

DAMON: All right, I'll go—but we're goin' to get our dogs and run the bottom till we find him, and when we do we'll tear him to pieces and we'll tear you to pieces if you get in our way. *(He goes out.)*

RUBY: It makes me sick. It just makes me sick to hear men talk like that. Why, he's no better than Bubber. He's just as cruel and brutal as Bubber. I'm afraid for you. I'm afraid for my baby when I hear talk like that.

HAWES: Oh, Ruby—Ruby— *(Goes to her, takes her in his arms.)* I was so afraid somethin' had happened to you.

RUBY: Now, don't worry. I'm all right. I'm all right.

HAWES: Are you sure? Are you sure?

RUBY: Yes. Yes.

HAWES: Do you think I'd better call a doctor?

RUBY: No, no, I'll be all right. I just hope this ends tonight. Bubber isn't bein' chased out there. We are. How's it goin' to end, Hawes, how's it goin' to end?

HAWES: I don't know. I don't know.

DOUGLAS: You've got to get to Bubber before the men do, Hawes. You have to.

HAWES: And how do I do that? How do I do that? Stand outside the jail and holler his name? Take a gun and stand off the whole of Richmond until he decides to give himself up? I'll do anything to catch him. Only tell me how. My God, why is it so hard? Why is it always so hard? All I want to do is to save a man's life. Why is it so hard?

CURTAIN

ACT III
Scene 1

Hawes's office, later the same night. Ruby is lying on cot. Hawes is pacing up and down.

HAWES: Ruby, I wonder what you ever saw in me to marry me? Wild and cussed, and not worth killin'—debt-ridden—

RUBY: *(Sitting on chair D. R.)* Now, hush talkin' like that. You know what I saw in you. The fine man you are now.

HAWES: I just plain wasn't worth killin', Ruby, until I married you.

RUBY: Oh, hush up, Hawes. I don't like you to talk like that. Marryin' you was the nicest thing in the world that ever happened to me. And don't worry about us. Even if everyone here turns against us, we'll find a place that we can farm on shares. My mother and father worked a place all their lives that they didn't own. They made a living for us—a good living sometimes. We're strong. We'll work hard together and we'll make out all right. You'll see.

HAWES: What would I do without my partner?

(Knock on door. Tarl enters.)

TARL: Mrs. Reeves and Knub McDermont just come into the front office. They said they had to see Mr. Hawes.

HAWES: All right, you bring them in here.

TARL: Yes, sir.

(Hawes crosses L., sits in desk chair. Mrs. Reeves and Knub come in.)

MRS. REEVES: Hello, Mr. Hawes.

HAWES: Hello, Mrs. Reeves.

(Mrs. Reeves crosses R. C.)

KNUB: *(C.)* Hello, sheriff.

HAWES: Hello, Knub.

MRS. REEVES: Knub has somethin' to tell you about Bubber, Mr. Hawes. I just want you to know that I haven't come here to fight you, but to help in any way I can.

KNUB: I would have been here earlier but I couldn't catch a ride on the highway so I cut across some cotton fields to save time. As I was starting to cross the highway to get into town, I saw some men stopping cars about fifty feet ahead so I had to swing back and come in on the old school house road. I came out by Mrs. Reeves's house. She seen me going by and asked if she could come over here with me. Bubber Reeves has gone crazy, Mr. Hawes. He's gone ravin' crazy. He tried to kill me about an hour ago.

He took a lead pipe and hit me over my head and tried to kill me because I wouldn't give him a gun. He hit me and left me for dead and took my gun and ran off. About half an hour later I was standing outside my cabin smoking, thinking what to do, trying to get the strength to come into town, when I heard a noise. Something told me to hide in the brush until I knew what it was. I did, and Bubber come back to my house.

HAWES: Is he there now?

KNUB: Yes, sir. I stayed long enough to hear Anna beg him to leave. He said he wasn't goin' to. He said he wasn't goin' to run no more. He said he was gonna wait for you to come out there and get him.

HAWES: All right. Would both of you mind goin' into the outer office for a minute?

KNUB: *(Starts out.)* Yes, sir. I ought to warn you. He's been hurt. He tried to take a car away from a nigger and the nigger almost clawed his face off. He said he shot the nigger and was afraid someone would hear the shot so he ran for the cabin. I heard him tell Anna he had to kill the nigger.

HAWES: All right, go out in the office.

(Knub goes out. Mrs. Reeves starts out. As she gets to door she turns.)

MRS. REEVES: *(At door.)* Mr. Hawes—Mr. Hawes—they've come to my house lookin' for Bubber. They've wrecked my house lookin' for Bubber. Dan and Al Roberts and Ludie. When they couldn't find him they jumped in their cars and drove away. I know what's happening. All over town men are gettin' in their cars with their guns to hunt my boy. Don't let them get him. I beg you. Whatever we've done to you, don't let them get him. I know what he is but don't let them. Bubber's killed again. I know that. And if the law has to kill him now, I won't try to stop it. I swear to you I've learned my lesson. But don't let them get him and drag him to a swamp to hang and burn. Don't let my boy die that way. Not that. Not that.

HAWES: All right, Mrs. Reeves. You go on out with Knub.

MRS. REEVES: Yes, sir. *(She turns and goes.)*

HAWES: *(Turns to Ruby.)* I'm goin', Ruby. *(Rises, crosses C.)*

RUBY: *(Rises.)* All right, honey.

HAWES: I've got to go.

RUBY: I know that.

HAWES: Pray this is the end of it. Pray I get by the men. Pray I get to Bubber in time. Catch him. Get him out of the county alive away from the men.

RUBY: All right, honey. Take care of yourself. Promise me.

(They embrace.)

Promise me. I love you so much, Hawes. I love you so much.

HAWES: I love you, honey.

RUBY: When will you be back?

HAWES: I'm goin' to try to get him to the Jackson County jail. I guess won't be seeing you until in the morning.

(He goes out. Ruby stands for a moment. She goes to the chair, sobbing.)

CURTAIN FALLS

ACT III
Scene 2

The cabin. Later the same night.

Lights are brought up in cabin. The lamp is burning. Anna is seated at table C. Bubber is seated on floor, leaning against door.

ANNA: Bubber, Bubber—Bubber, what are you gonna do?

BUBBER: I ain't gonna run no more. I'm tired an' I'm stayin' here.

ANNA: You can't stay here in the daytime. If they know you're here they're bound to call out the bloodhounds.

BUBBER: They can burn this shack down around me and I ain't gonna leave. They can set the whole Goddamned bottom on fire and I won't leave now.

ANNA: It must be almost four in the morning. It'll be daylight before you know it. Why don't you go hide in the bottom until you get your strength back? Knub could slip food out to you until they are quieted down around here and he could get you out of the state. I could give you a blanket—

BUBBER: I told you to let me do the worrying.

(Hawes comes on stage quickly, creeping into yard R. His revolver is drawn. Pauses, crouches low, listening and looking around. He leaves Tarl R.—creeps L., signals Rip and Third Deputy who crawls on L. Hawes goes back R., joins Tarl.)

ANNA: I wish you'd let me go to the pump and get some water to wash your face. I can't stand lookin' at the blood all over you *(Pause.)* I'm hungry. I feel like I haven't eaten for a week. I'm so hungry.

BUBBER: *(Hears noise outside cabin.)* What's that?

ANNA: Probably an old dog.

(The two listen.)

BUBBER: Shhh. Turn out the light.

ANNA: Bubber, I'm scared of the dark.

BUBBER: God damn it. Do like I say. Turn out the light.

ANNA: *(She blows out lamp.)* Oh. Jesus. He won't listen to me and daylight's comin' an' they're gonna call out the dogs and catch us here. Oh, Jesus.

HAWES: *(Calling.)* Bubber.

(Bubber falls flat on floor.)

ANNA: *(Whispering.)* Oh, Jesus.

HAWES: *(Calling.)* Bubber, can you hear me? *(To Tarl.)* Get Mrs. Reeves.

ANNA: Oh Jesus! Jesus! Jesus!

BUBBER: Shhh—

ANNA: It's Hawes.

HAWES: *(R.)* Bubber. I know you're in there. I've got my men all here with me and the house is surrounded.

(Tarl creeps off R. Comes back with Mrs. Reeves.)

All right, speak to him, Mrs. Reeves.

MRS. REEVES: Bubber, son, listen to me. Mr. Hawes knows you're in there. Come on out and surrender. There are posses out lookin' for you.

(Bubber sneaks to L. of cabin, crouching against wall.)

I'm so afraid they'll lynch you if they find you. They'll hang you to a tree until you're dead. Please don't let that happen. Mr. Hawes don't want that to happen. So, now, listen to me and hurry and surrender to Mr. Hawes, so he can get you out of the county, before they get to you. Bubber, answer me. Answer your mother. Please come on out. *(She is crying.)* Bubber—Bubber—

HAWES: Rip, I want you to take Mrs. Reeves over there out of range.

(Rip takes Mrs. Reeves over L. to Third Deputy. He takes her offstage.)

I'll give you five minutes to give yourself up. Do you hear me, Bubber? Five minutes.

ANNA: *(Whispering.)* What are you gonna do, Bubber? Bubber, don't let them hurt me. Who'll take care of the kid if I get hurt?

BUBBER: Keep quiet. You won't get hurt. He's right there where I could kill him and I got no gun. I got no gun to kill him with. I'm licked, Anna. I knew it when I got here. I knew it when I killed that nigra. I knew it—I knew it—

ANNA: Then give yourself up, Bubber. Your mama will help you if you do. Go on and be good and she'll help you. I will. I swear.

BUBBER: What the hell, I'm licked. I'm tired. Let the sonovabitch kill me.

ANNA: Don't say that, Bubber. Surrender. Don't talk that way.

BUBBER: *(Screaming.)* I'm comin' out, you yellow-bellied sonovabitch. I'm comin' out so you can kill me. Hawes, I'm comin' out. I'm comin' out—

HAWES: OK Listen to me. I want you to behave yourself and surrender peacefully. If you do, there won't be any trouble, and I'll see you get back to the

Pen without gettin' hurt. Do you hear me? Bubber? I'll tell you when to start—

BUBBER: Kill me, you sonovabitch—come in an' get me.

ANNA: No, Bubber—no.

HAWES: You know we've got you surrounded, Bubber, so come on, get it over with. *(Rises.)* Now, come on out walkin' backwards with your hands up. *(Hawes has door covered with his gun. Bubber crosses L. to R. in cabin.)*

BUBBER: *(Screaming.)* Shoot me, you sonovabitch. Get it over with. Right here. Shoot me.

HAWES: Keep movin', Bubber. I don't want to shoot you. I'm takin' you back to the penitentiary alive—keep movin'. Do you hear me?

BUBBER: I'm not goin' back to the penitentiary. I'm comin' out. You can kill me here. I know you want to kill me.

(Mrs. Reeves comes running back in from L. She gets away from Third Deputy, runs past Rip. He grabs her. She gets away. Hawes turns and crosses to C.)

TARL: *(Screaming.)* Look out, Sheriff. She got loose. The old lady got loose—

MRS. REEVES: *(Screaming and running toward Hawes.)* Let me speak to him again. Don't kill him. Don't kill him—

HAWES: Watch out, Mrs. Reeves.

MRS. REEVES: *(Trying to run past Hawes.)* Don't kill him. Kill me. Don't kill him. Bubber—Bubber—

HAWES: Grab her. Grab her.

(Hawes tries to block Mrs. Reeves. Rip takes Mrs. Reeves L. as she struggles. Bubber comes out of cabin. He starts toward Hawes. Hawes doesn't see him coming.)

TARL: Look out, Sheriff. Look out. Bubber's comin' towards you. Look out. Look out.

(Hawes whirls and sees Bubber coming toward him. He goes wild. He shoots. Bubber falls. Mrs. Reeves screams. Hawes lets revolver fall from his hand. Tarl goes to Bubber.)

HAWES: Jesus! Jesus Christ! Sweet Jesus—

(Silence. Tarl is examining Bubber.)

Jesus, Jesus—Jesus—

MRS. REEVES: Bubber—Bubber—

(Tarl comes to Hawes. Rip joins them.)

TARL: You better get her away from here. You riddled him pretty bad—

MRS. REEVES: Is he dead?

HAWES: Yes, ma'am.

MRS. REEVES: He's dead. Bubber's dead. *(Pause.)* I pray he has some rest now. I pray he has some peace now. What's goin' to happen to your mother, honey? How'm I gonna find peace? How'm I gonna rest? I dug up one of your old toys, rusty and rotten, under the fig tree today. How'm I gonna rest? *(Pause.)*

HAWES: Tarl had better take you home.

(She doesn't answer. Tarl crosses from up R. to Mrs. Reeves L., takes her by arm, leads her out. She is sobbing but offers no resistance. The men silently watch her go. When she has gone, Rip turns to Hawes.)

RIP: He didn't even have a gun on him.

HAWES: He didn't have a gun?

RIP: No. I just searched him.

HAWES: Rip, you go on. Send somebody back for the body. I'll stay here until they come—

RIP: You're tired. Go on.

HAWES: No, I'll stay here.

RIP: All right.

(He goes out. Knub enters L. Crosses over R. Anna rises, comes out of cabin, looks at Hawes, then at Bubber.)

CURTAIN

ACT III
Scene 3

Later the same night. Hawes's office. Ruby is seated in a chair.

TARL: *(Tarl enters.)* I'm goin' on home, Miss Ruby. Mr. Hawes ought to be along any minute. He stayed with the body.

RUBY: I know.

TARL: I don't know if I'll be in tomorrow unless Mr. Hawes calls me. It's my day off.

RUBY: All right. Do you know if anyone got in touch with the family of the colored man that Bubber killed?

TARL: *(At cooler.)* Yes'm. Red got word to his wife, he told me.

RUBY: Did she take it awful hard?

TARL: Yes'm. From what Red said, she did.

RUBY: The poor thing.

TARL: Yes'm. I swear I can't help feelin' sorry for Mrs. Reeves. All the family she's got is some cousin livin' in Lagoon.

RUBY: Did anybody notify him?

TARL: No, ma'am. I understand she don't speak to him. Methodist preacher and his wife are over there with her.

RUBY: Have the men gone off the streets?

TARL: Yes'm. The men have put their guns away and all gone home.

RUBY: Then the town's quiet?

TARL: Yes'm. Quiet as the grave.

RUBY: Quiet until next time.

TARL: Ma'am?

RUBY: Nothin'.

TARL: We were lucky there weren't more killin's or accidents before it was all over. There were about seventy-five men roamin' around the town. I hate to think what would have happened if any of them had seen us goin' for Bubber an' tried to follow us.

RUBY: I know.

(Hawes enters.)

TARL: Sheriff—

HAWES: Tarl.

TARL: Well, I'm tired. I'll be gettin' on.

(He exits. Ruby and Hawes embrace.)

HAWES: I killed him, Ruby. I killed him.

RUBY: I know. I know.

HAWES: Mrs. Reeves broke and tried to get to him. My back was turned. Tarl yelled. I swung around and there was Bubber coming toward me.

RUBY: Hush, Hawes.

HAWES: I lost my head, Ruby. I gave in to fear and panic just like the rest of them and I killed him.

RUBY: Shhh, honey, shhh.

HAWES: I failed. I failed. *(Crosses R.)* The chase is over and I've lost.

RUBY: Hawes—

HAWES: *(Turns L.)* I did. I lost. I'm no better than the rest of them.

RUBY: Hawes, please—

HAWES: I'm no better than the rest of them. I did the very thing I tried to keep them from doing—I killed him.

RUBY: Don't talk that way, Hawes.

HAWES: Why couldn't I have saved him, Ruby? Why couldn't I have saved him?

RUBY: I don't know that, Hawes. All I know is you did your best. You tried. That's all we can ask. All right, he's dead, but you can't change that now. You've got to go on and keep goin' on, even if you fail. This chase didn't start tonight. It didn't end tonight. Don't run away, Hawes. Keep on livin'. Keep on tryin'.

(Phone rings. Hawes turns back. Ruby takes it.)

Yes, yes. I'll tell him. All right. I'll ask him. *(To Hawes.)* Hawes, it's Dixie Graves. Her little boy just come home. He won't talk about where he's been or what he's been doin'. She wants to know if she can speak to you.

HAWES: *(Pause—takes phone.)* Hello, Dixie. All right. *(Puts phone down.)* She wants to send him over in the mornin' for me to talk some sense into him and I'll try. I guess that's all a man can do is try. Just try and try and try.

CURTAIN

END OF PLAY

The Traveling Lady

For Lillian, Barbara Hallie and Brother

PRODUCTION

The Traveling Lady was presented by The Playwrights' Company at The Playhouse, New York City, on October 27, 1954. It was directed by Vincent J. Donehue and the setting was by Ben Edwards. The cast was as follows:

Mrs. Mavis	Mary Perry
Slim Murray	Jack Lord
Judge Robedaux	Calvin Thomas
Georgette Thomas	Kim Stanley
Margaret Rose	Brook Seawell
Clara Breedlove	Helen Carew
Sitter Mavis	Katherine Squire
Mrs. Tillman	Kathleen Comegys
Henry Thomas	Lonny Chapman
Sheriff	Tony Sexton

SETTING

ACT I: An early spring day. Eleven o'clock.

ACT II: Scene 1: Five hours later.

Scene 2: Two hours later.

ACT III: Two days later. Ten-thirty in the morning.

The scene is the sun parlor, side porch and yard of Clara Breedlove's house in a small Texas town.

FOREWORD

We must have all grown accustomed by now to the ways of criticism. I have met with one reviewer who professed to regard a certain play as a monument of great thought and majestic pattern, and for the same play another reviewer who said that anybody with any brains could see how bad it was. So that I should not have been too much surprised to find one critic saying that in Horton Foote's play the characters were well-drawn and natural enough as to South Texas and all that, but were of very poor interest for us at this distance; it might be all very well, but—

In a country where all men are equal, if we grant there might be such a place, all opinions are equal. We may then dismiss as mere Attic chatter Plato's remark about democracy; that "It is a charming form of government, full of variety and disorder, dispensing a kind of equality to equals and unequals alike. So that the pupil is as good as the master, and even horses and asses have a way of marching along with all the rights and dignities of freemen.

Everything is ready to burst with liberty." Our critic has, therefore, as much right to his opinion as anybody else.

Nevertheless, these Texas characters, though of so little interest to our localized critic, do speak. And one of the ironies of our playwriting is that for all its sticking to realism and the school of common life, one of its chief weaknesses is its speech, the writing itself. One of the chief merits of *The Traveling Lady* is its speech. We may ask our critic one question: If that far-off South Texas speech is so far-off in interest, what happens about plays with the North Shore or the Maine accent and dialect, or the solid old Pennsylvania Dutch, or the tangy Vermont folks, or the quaint heritage of language in some of the Irish dramatists? The answer is very likely that from long acquaintance with Broadway these forms of speech have become critically absorbent. The interest in them and our response to them is now easy, even as the ancient island of Capri, at home among us now as Capree, is everywhere responded to as the very lap of sinful luxury and song.

I had a backsliding once into six or seven years of Texas, and now I have gone twice to *The Traveling Lady* and read it twice, and I have not found a word or phrase that did not seem to me true, almost unnoticeably true even, to what I heard and saw in that far-off place. It is not always the kind of talking that many Texans I knew had, the more cultivated people as it were. Their grammar was the standard kind, though their idioms and figures of speech were not always so vivid or close to the earth. To write such speech as this we find in Horton Foote's play is anything but a small order. Simple as such a feat may seem, you will not be likely to find any too many cases of it. The people in *The Traveling Lady* do not by any means talk as the best people in the Old South talk, though, for that matter in the South itself there are numberless variations. Most Southern writers themselves have not solved the problem; the speech they may write may have a kind of surface effect of Southern but the basic elements are not there at all.

How often in Texas have I heard those idioms, localisms and voluble outbursts and that ranging vocabulary in *The Traveling Lady!* It all belonged mostly to plain people and people who lived largely in plain towns and circumstances that were all their own and that belonged to themselves and their region. Their speech tended to be alive, unselfconscious and rural. As for Horton Foote's dialogue there is everywhere present a kind of elusive and glowing accuracy. And there is never any sense of arch intention or any sign of the playwright's coquetting with quaintness.

We find the same kind of truth in the creation of the characters. The young woman with her child, trying to find her husband again, the young cotton-buyer and the sister he lives with, the judge, the cracked old woman and her old maid daughter whose life is bound up with hers and forever thwarted, the managing neighbor with her mushy mania for saving the down-and-out; the worthless, just-out-of-the-penitentiary drunken husband, they are all there for us to see; each of them is clearly separated from the rest, each one complete. It is almost as if these people, instead of being written, had merely been standing by, ready for making a play. But it must be said that, having been written, they constitute roles that are shrewdly and almost graciously actable.

In the story of the young wife whose husband has left her desolate and worse, and the young cotton-buyer whose passionate marriage has been clouded and lost with some hidden and inexplicable retreat on his wife's part, despite her love for him, we might seem to arrive simply and romantically at an ending long familiar in novels and drama. But the author knows better than that. Two people with such marks of life as these two have on them come together, when they do come together, with far more shy and tragic depths.

There is one motif in the play that might if we chose be dwelt upon at some length. This involves Henry Thomas, the husband, with his degeneracy, whiskey, and music and all the rest of it. He has been raised as a child by a Miss Kate Dawson, an old maid in the town, who in a so-called effort to "break his will" had subjected him to such beatings as brought the neighbors to protest. And now it is the day of this woman's funeral. Only a score of people, twenty-four in fact, are there. Henry has gone on a drunken spree, and has stolen his benefactress's silver and is running away with it. Meanwhile he goes to the cemetery lot of this old maid who has been his guardian, to put it mildly; he tears the flowers on the grave and scatters them in all directions.

This might pass simply as a part of the story. But taken otherwise it might be as dark and hideous as anything in Strindberg. That all depends on the dramatist, but taken either way, the motif itself is per se a knockout. Just how the dramatist, and not only in this instance, comes on such an image, such a rich motif, perhaps he himself does not know. It might remind us of what Coleridge, in one of those winged moments of his, said of science: All science, he said, begins in wonder and ends in wonder, and the interspace is filled with admiration. In drama the same is doubtless true with many a fine image, ultimate and expressive beyond the dramatist's calculation.

There is one point about this play of Horton Foote's that I have thought over a good many times, but would never settle on an answer for—yes or no. Running over in my mind various plays, not only by the masters in drama, Molière, Benavente, Ibsen and so on, but also by the sure-fire plays on a lower entirely popular plane, I have wondered if it is not true that this play of *The*

Traveling Lady might gain by more projection. More scoring, or theatre under-scoring, for some of its ideas, instances, motifs, images, whatever we may call them. As matters go at present it is possible that in places there is not any full economy for the projection, the landing, of some of the genuinely significant and the profound things that are being said.

That remains a definite question in the aesthetics of the theatre, and in fact in the aesthetics of all creative art. The final art must lie, of course, in what we may call the author's comment on what he tries to recreate into art and make us receive, the extent to which he puts meaning into the material he draws from or presents, and gives to his matter a larger humanity and dilation.

Meanwhile we shall have to let Horton Foote, with his talent and the fine fluency of his responses, work all this out to his own purposes and as the case may be.

We need not invite comparisons with immortality exactly, but we may at least be reminded of Aristotle's remark that Homer, deserving to be praised for many things, is most to be praised because he knows what part to take himself.

Stark Young
New York City
March, 1955

THE TRAVELING LADY

ACT I
Scene 1

It is eleven o'clock in the morning of an early Spring day. A beautiful day, not too hot and the sky is blue and very clear. The action of the play takes place in the sun parlor, side porch, and yard of Clara Breedlove's house. The sun parlor, from R. to R. C., is a large, pleasant room with screens all the way around the sides facing the porch and the backyard. The doors and woodwork are painted ivory. There are three white wicker chairs (one of them a rocker), a small table, low stool and a wicker settee, also white, in the room. The settee is R., the rocker just L. of it, and the other two chairs are at L. The stool is D. C. in front of the chairs. The table is behind the settee. On the table are a dust cloth and a sewing basket with socks, etc., in it. U. L. of sun parlor there is a door which leads off to the rest of the house and D. L. is a screen door that leads out to the side porch. There is a window R. of the house door, another U. R. of C., facing the porch. The side porch, or the part that is visible to us, is part of a long porch that extends along the whole side of the house from U. R. of C. to D. C. and halfway to the front of the house off U. R. Entrances are made by people coming presumably from the front of the house along the porch. Just as the yard that we see is part of a huge front and backyard. On the porch are two light chairs (rockers) that can be brought easily down the steps into the yard. There are three wide steps D. C. The side yard has two flowering bushes, a crepe myrtle and an oleander, one huge pecan tree and flower beds, along the edge of the side porch. The flowers growing in the bed are nasturtiums, hollyhocks and verbena. Upstage separating the side yard from the front is a fence and a low privet hedge. There is an entrance in and out of the side yard through a gate U. L. of C. U. L., coming out like a little square, is another tall hedge. It extends to D. L. It is part of the old cemetery that cuts into the Breedlove yard. Partly visible behind the hedge are two or three very old tombstones, the graves now flattened with the ground. There is a strip of yard running in front of the sun parlor that is used as a pathway to go across to downstage R. Entrances are also made from D. L. through the hedge. A wooden box with garden tools is D. R. of C. A small trowel and a small stick are on the ground. Below sun parlor, D. L. are two garden armchairs. They are now turned over on their sides.

AT RISE: Mrs. Mavis, an incredibly old woman, clutching a package of dates, comes darting into the side yard through the hedge upstage. She seems to be in fear of being followed. She pauses from time to time and looks around to see if anyone is coming. She runs up the steps of the porch and starts to knock at the screen door when in the distance a Woman's voice can be heard calling: "Mama. Mama. I see you in Miss Clara's yard. Now you come on home." She sits on the steps paying not the slightest attention to the voice. The Woman calls again: "Now you come on home." Slim Murray comes out of the house and onto the sun parlor. He is lean, tanned, wearing a shirt open at the collar. He has been working on an old automobile carburetor and fuel pump which is on the garden toolbox, which is D. R. of C. below the sun parlor. He sees Mrs. Mavis sitting on the steps. She has opened the package of dates. She is stuffing herself, as he goes out onto the porch and down the steps to toolbox.

SLIM: Good mornin', Mrs. Mavis.

MRS. MAVIS: 'Mornin'.

SLIM: What are you doin' out here?

MRS. MAVIS: Eatin' dates. Want one?

SLIM: No, ma'm. Thank you. It's a nice morning.

MRS. MAVIS: Yessir.

(We hear the Woman's Voice calling again: "Mama. Mama." She still pretends she doesn't hear a thing.)

SLIM: Isn't that your daughter callin' you, Mrs. Mavis?

MRS. MAVIS: I reckon so. She's always callin' somebody.

SLIM: Why don't you go on home, Mrs. Mavis, if she's callin' you? My sister isn't home. You can come back later and visit when she's here.

(Mrs. Mavis doesn't answer if she hears him. She just goes on stuffing herself with dates. The Woman calls again: "Mama.")

Mrs. Mavis, I think you ought to go on home.

(She still doesn't answer. She goes on eating dates.)

MRS. MAVIS: I remember the day this house was built. I remember your sister comin' here as a bride and bringin' you with her to raise. *(A pause. She eats another date.)* They're buryin' Miss Kate Dawson today, but they wouldn't let me go to the funeral. I miss going to funerals worse than anything in the world.

(Slim sits on the toolbox, turns away and continues to work.)

I remember Laura Ewing's funeral. You tried to jump into the grave. Took four men to hold you. *(A pause. She takes another date.)* Yep. I remember all of it. I remember everything that happened in this town. *(She takes still another date. She gets up and goes to the hedge U.L.)* You cut that hedge down I bet you could see Laura Ewing's grave from your side gallery. If you were standing up. *(A pause. She takes another date.)* She was buried in the old cemetery. Miss Kate is being buried across the street in the new part. *(A pause. Coming back and sitting down on steps again.)* We got our lots in the old cemetery. I consider that very lucky because the trees are prettier there. *(She calls in to him.)* What part of the cemetery are they buryin' you? *(She waits a moment for an answer and then calls loudly in to him.)* I said what part of the cemetery are they buryin' you, Slim?

(Slim pretends not to have heard the question. The Woman calls again: "Mama. Mama. If you don't come home this minute I'm coming after you." A man in his late sixties comes into the side yard through the gate U. L. of C. It is Judge Robedaux. He calls.)

JUDGE: Slim?

SLIM: Good mornin', Judge.

JUDGE: *(Coming down to Mrs. Mavis.)* Good mornin', Mrs. Mavis. Didn't you hear your daughter calling you, Mrs. Mavis? *(A pause.)* She said to tell you she was comin' after you if you didn't come right this minute.

(Mrs. Mavis sits for a moment thinking over that threat and then pops one last date into her mouth, gets up slowly and moves offstage D. R.)

You aren't going to the funeral, Slim?

SLIM: No, sir.

JUDGE: *(Putting a foot on steps.)* I didn't go to the Funeral Home. I thought I ought to go to the service at the cemetery. I guess I'm a little early. There's nobody there yet. *(A pause. Looking over at the graveyard.)* Well, she was a funny little woman, Miss Kate Dawson. To meet and talk to her you'd think she was the gentlest little soul alive. Never raised her voice above a whisper. *(Back to Slim.)* And I guess she was most of the time, but she used to beat that Thomas boy, used to beat him until the neighbors would complain. I once had to threaten to take Henry Thomas away from her if she didn't quit it. I went over and talked to her about it. She said she had to whip him. She said she had to whip him to break his spirit. *(He walks over to the fence gate.)* Do you think I can hear the funeral procession from back here as it comes by?

SLIM: I don't know.

(The Judge walks out through the gate. He comes back in.)

JUDGE: They haven't started from the funeral parlor yet. *(He goes to the steps and takes out his handkerchief.)* A little warm with your coat on.

SLIM: Yessir.

JUDGE: I hear they've got that cotton gin over in Stafford up for sale today.

SLIM: *(Getting up.)* Yessir. I heard.

JUDGE: We were talking the other day about what makes a good cotton buyer or farmer or gin man. It's in the blood, I say. A God-given talent. *(Going to Slim.)* Whatever it is that makes a good cotton buyer, you've got it. Now who taught you?

SLIM: *(Walking away to D. L.)* I don't know. I just picked up whatever I know working around the gins.

JUDGE: Thurman told me he offered you your old job back at his gin.

SLIM: Yes. He did.

JUDGE: *(Going to L. of C.)* Are you going to take it?

SLIM: *(Wiping the grease off his hands.)* I don't know.

JUDGE: You ought to take it. This being a deputy at the jail is nothing for you to be doing. You have a trade…

SLIM: I'm only doing it temporarily.

JUDGE: Clara go to the funeral?

SLIM: Yessir.

JUDGE: It's amazing how that cemetery has grown. They tell me all the lots in it are taken. Does Clara have a lot reserved?

SLIM: I don't know, sir.

JUDGE: *(As he sits down on the steps.)* We got one about two years ago. Had to get it in the new part. *(A pause.)* Slim. Do me a favor and walk to the front of the yard and see if you can see the cars coming.

SLIM: All right.

(He goes out behind the gate and looks off R. The Judge fans himself with his hat.)

JUDGE: Have they started yet?

SLIM: No, sir. Not yet.

(He comes back into the yard. A Woman's voice off R. is heard calling: "Mister. Mister." A Woman and a Little Girl come to the entrance of the fence from U. R.) Were you calling me?

GEORGETTE: Yessir. I was. I hope you'll excuse me. I tried to holler to you from the street but you didn't hear me. I wonder could you direct me to a Judge's house that's around here. A man told me his name and I forgot it. He rents houses I believe.

SLIM: Do you mean Judge Robedaux?

GEORGETTE: Yessir. That's the name.

SLIM: This is Judge Robedaux here.

(Judge gets up off the steps.)

JUDGE: How do you do.

GEORGETTE: How do you do.

(She and the little girl come into the yard and over to the Judge. The little girl is a towhead of six. Her name is Margaret Rose. The woman, a slim young blonde, neatly, but inexpensively dressed, is her mother, Mrs. Georgette Thomas. She is carrying a large suitcase and handbag.)

JUDGE: What can I do for you?

GEORGETTE: I was directed to you by a man I went to see about a house. A Mr. Burton, I believe.

MARGARET ROSE: *(Tugging at her mother.)* Mama…

GEORGETTE: Can my little girl sit down? We have been ridin' a bus all night an' we're dead for sleep.

JUDGE: Surely. Slim, draw up some chairs for the lady.

(Slim goes up on porch.)

GEORGETTE: Thank you. Of course, I was all excited about gettin' here, but I never could sleep on a bus, could you?

SLIM: *(Handing small rocker to Judge.)* I expect the Judge can sleep any place any time.

JUDGE: I never noticed you havin' any trouble. *(He places rocker L. of steps.)*

GEORGETTE: I said to Margaret Rose, "Look at these people sleepin' all around us." I never saw anything like it. I wish to heavens I could have slept. 'Course I haven't traveled so much, and every time the bus would stop for a rest, I'd be bound to get out and look around. "Shucks," I said to myself, "I don't know when I'm goin' to get another ride like this one, an' I might as well enjoy myself."

(Slim has given the other rocker to the Judge.)

JUDGE: Puddin', get you a seat over there. *(He places rocker R. of steps.)*

GEORGETTE: Her name's Margaret Rose. Stop hangin' onto your mother, love, an' get in the seat. You hear me, Margaret Rose? *(Margaret Rose goes and sits in L. rocker. Georgette puts suitcase down beside rocker.)*

JUDGE: *(Turning to Margaret Rose.)* How old are you, Puddin'?

GEORGETTE: Tell the nice man how old you are, Margaret Rose.

(A pause. Margaret Rose doesn't answer. She hangs her head.)

She's shy with strangers. Speak to the nice man, Sugar. *(A pause.)* What's the matter, girl, cat got your tongue? Speak nicely now.

(Margaret Rose sticks her tongue out of her mouth.)

MARGARET ROSE: Cat hasn't got my tongue.

GEORGETTE: *(Laughing.)* I declare. I've never seen Margaret Rose act so. That's 'cause she's tired from ridin' on the bus.

MARGARET ROSE: I want a piece of gum.

GEORGETTE: Sh, Sugar.

MARGARET ROSE: I want some Juicy Fruit.

GEORGETTE: Can't have none now.

MARGARET ROSE: I want a piece of Juicy Fruit. *(Margaret Rose starts to cry. Georgette searches in her purse for chewing gum.)*

GEORGETTE: Have any of you gentlemen got any chewin' gum?

(Slim and Judge look at each other.)

SLIM: No, ma'm.

JUDGE: I sure don't believe I do.

GEORGETTE: I usually keep it in my pocket. *(She sits on the suitcase.)* Be quiet, Margaret Rose, while I talk to the gentlemen, then mother will get you some chewin' gum.

(Margaret Rose continues crying.)

My heavens. I guess I better run out an' get her some. She's just cryin' from tiredness.

SLIM: *(Coming down off the porch.)* Why don't I take her out an' buy her some?

GEORGETTE: Oh, I wouldn't want to put you to any trouble. I can run out.

SLIM: I'd like to do that. How about comin' with me, young lady?

JUDGE: Run along, honey.

GEORGETTE: I'd sure be much obliged. You want to go with the man to buy some chewin' gum, Margaret Rose?

MARGARET ROSE: Ma'm?

GEORGETTE: The man is goin' to take you to buy some chewin' gum.

MARGARET ROSE: Which man?

GEORGETTE: *(Pointing to Slim.)* This one here.

SLIM: My name is Slim.

GEORGETTE: Mister Slim.

MARGARET ROSE: Has he got a little girl?

GEORGETTE: I declare, Margaret Rose. I don't know. You better ask him.

MARGARET ROSE: Have you got a little girl?

SLIM: No, ma'm.

MARGARET ROSE: Can you sing "New San 'Tonia Rose?"

SLIM: No, ma'm.

MARGARET ROSE: My daddy can. When he comes here, he's just gonna sing it, night and day.

GEORGETTE: You better go on and get your chewing gum, Margaret Rose.

MARGARET ROSE: *(Gets up.)* Yes, ma'm.

SLIM: Will you come go with me?

MARGARET ROSE: *(Going to Slim.)* Yes, ma'm.

GEORGETTE: Sir, Margaret Rose. You ma'm your Mama, but you sir Mr. Slim.

MARGARET ROSE: Yessir.

SLIM: Tell your mama we'll be right back.

MARGARET ROSE: We'll be right back.

> *(They start out. Georgette is unwinding a white handkerchief. She gets up and goes to her.)*

GEORGETTE: Take a nickel, Margaret Rose.

SLIM: The treat's on me.

GEORGETTE: Oh, no, please. I've got a nickel right handy here in my handkerchief. *(She finds the nickel. She gives it to Margaret Rose.)* Here, Margaret Rose. See you behave yourself.

MARGARET ROSE: Yes'm.

> *(Slim takes her by the hand and they go on out the gate and off U. R.)*

JUDGE: It's a nice little girl you've got.

GEORGETTE: *(Coming back.)* Thank you. She's just the sunshine of my life. I called her Margaret after my mama that's dead, and Rose because it's my favorite flower. I like verbena, too, but I didn't like the sound of Margaret Verbena.

JUDGE: What can I do for you? *(He sits in R. rocker.)*

GEORGETTE: Well...I...I...I guess I've gone an' done a plain foolish thing.

JUDGE: How's that?

GEORGETTE: *(Going to him.)* Well—you see—I was workin' in Tyler, an' I got laid off because things were slow at the drive-in. I was the last girl taken on, so it was right it was me that was the first to go. I waited there a week tryin' to find other work, an' I couldn't. So, as I was to meet my husband here in another week, I decided to come on ahead. I got off the bus this mornin' an' a man at the bus station told me to look up a Mr. Burton, that he had houses to rent cheap. So Margaret Rose and I walked out to his house about a mile from the bus station. Do you know where it is?

JUDGE: Yes, ma'm.

GEORGETTE: Well, he was real nice an' polite an' said he had a lovely house for twenty a month, but he rented it the evenin' before. He said the only thing he had was for seventy-five dollars, at present, an' that as far as he knew he didn't think I could find anything else under that....

JUDGE: Houses are awful hard to get here, ma'm. Gulf Coast is on a boom.

GEORGETTE: That's what he said. I asked him if he knew of anybody that could find me a place to stay until my husband gets here. He thought for a minute an' said you were the person for me to see. Do you know of a house?

JUDGE: Let me think for a minute. I don't offhand, Mrs. ...

GEORGETTE: Thomas

(The Judge thinks for a moment, obviously stalling. He looks at her slyly.)

JUDGE: When will your husband get here?

GEORGETTE: I don't rightly know. That is, not down to the exact minute. I look for him the early part of next week.

JUDGE: Where is your husband?

GEORGETTE: I'm not at liberty to say.

JUDGE: I see. Do you have a family back in Tyler?

GEORGETTE: No, sir. Lovelady. I was born in Lovelady. My daddy is still there, the last I heard. My mama's dead. She died when I was a little girl of ten. My daddy is a cotton farmer. He's got a farm about five miles out from Lovelady. I left Lovelady before Margaret Rose was born. Margaret Rose has never seen Lovelady.

JUDGE: I see. Did you and your husband rent a house back in Tyler?

GEORGETTE: No, sir. I lived with him in Lovelady. We only had six months together...

JUDGE: And you haven't seen him in all this time?

GEORGETTE: No, sir.

JUDGE: I see. Where's he been, in the Army?

(Georgette looks uncomfortable.)

I said, has he been in the Army?

GEORGETTE: Yessir. I heard you...Don't keep askin' me where he's been, Mr. Judge. I can't tell you that, but I know he's comin' here to meet me. ...

JUDGE: I see.

(A pause. He thinks a moment. He looks at her. She is very uncomfortable.)

Mrs. Thomas, I'm sorry, but if you want me to help you, you're goin' to have to answer my questions. I can't rent to people I don't know anything about. I'll keep everything in perfect confidence, but I have to know whether you're worthwhile takin' a chance on.

(A pause. She looks away.)

Do you want me to help you find a house?

GEORGETTE: Yessir.

JUDGE: Then you'll have to answer my questions.

GEORGETTE: Yessir. *(A pause.)*

JUDGE: All right. Now, where's your husband been? *(A pause.)* I'm waitin', Mrs. Thomas. *(A pause.)*

GEORGETTE: I just can't bring myself to say it. You ask me some more questions.

JUDGE: The service? Oh, I asked that. *(A pause.)* Has he been in the penitentiary?

(Georgette looks at him for a moment. She begins to cry. She covers her face with her handkerchief.)

Now, there's nothin' to be ashamed of, Mrs. Thomas. You can't help it. I guess that's where he was. Now don't be afraid of tellin' me. I won't say anything to anybody.

GEORGETTE: Yessir. *(She dries her eyes.)* That's where he's been. At Huntsville. *(She cries again.)*

JUDGE: Now, now, Mrs. Thomas. You don't have to be ashamed of it.

GEORGETTE: I know that. I know. I don't have to be. But people certainly make it hard not to be. My Lord, the first question they ask me is where is my little girl's daddy. I never was good at lyin' an' I make up an excuse that I figure will satisfy them. But the minute my back is turned, they're after Margaret Rose to find out if she'll tell them. The last lady we lived with in Tyler told her to say he was a millionaire an' away seein' Europe an' that would stop them an' she's smart an' bright an' she does, an' I try to laugh about it.

JUDGE: Why is your husband in the penitentiary?

GEORGETTE: He got to drinkin' too much an' cuttin' up about six months after we were married an' stabbed a man in Lovelady. There was a big to-do, the man almost died, an' they tried him an' sent him away. I thought it was best I leave Lovelady. My daddy never did care for my husband an' when he got sent to jail my daddy as good as asked me to leave. I hope I've done the right thing comin' here. I only decided yesterday. I wrote Henry an' told him that I was tired unto death of Tyler. An' then, too, I thought it would be better for him to start in again making his living where he was known an' loved.

JUDGE: What was his first name again?

GEORGETTE: Henry. Henry Thomas.

(The Judge looks away.)

Do you know him?

JUDGE: Yes, ma'm. He grew up here. I remember Henry. *(A pause.)* Mrs. Thomas, suppose you didn't find work right away, an' Henry wasn't able to find work?

GEORGETTE: Yessir?

JUDGE: What I'm gettin' at is this. How would you be able to keep the rent goin'?

GEORGETTE: Well…

JUDGE: Would your father be able to help you?

GEORGETTE: My daddy? Oh, I guess he could if he would, but I wouldn't ask him. I sent him a picture of Margaret Rose on her third birthday, an' he didn't even write to thank me for it.

JUDGE: I see.

GEORGETTE: Oh, it doesn't matter. He's just peculiar. My daddy has always been peculiar. I'm not sorry I left Lovelady, I can tell you that. You know how it is, Mr. Judge, when your husband gets into trouble and everybody knows you. Seems it's time, jus' naturally time to move on. Margaret Rose weren't born then, an' I cried terrible when I heard but I said shucks, I've got to pull myself together and I went off. I'm not a bit afraid of work an' a nice lady in Tyler took me in for room an' board an' spendin' money until Margaret Rose was born, then her husband turned out not to care for children, an' I had to move. So I went an' got a room with another lady, who had no husband an' I did her washin' an' ironin' at nights 'cause her back gave her trouble an' she hated stoopin'. She took care of Margaret Rose while I worked days an' early evenin's as a carhop.

JUDGE: I see. Has Henry finished servin' his sentence?

GEORGETTE: No, sir. He's gettin' pardoned. That's why I had to work so, earnin' the money to pay the lawyer for his pardon. It took me six years to get it together. He wrote such nice letters all the time he was in jail and I was makin' money for the pardon, how much he was gonna do for me an' the baby. How he appreciated my workin' so hard. I tell you, some of the letters were enough to make you cry. I just feel now in my heart everythin' is gonna be fine. Of course, I haven't heard from him in a month, but that's nothin'. Sometimes it's three months before he gets aroun' to writin'. Then I'll get six or seven letters one on top of the other.

(Margaret Rose and Slim come in through the gate from U. R.)

MARGARET ROSE: *(Holding up a package of gum.)* I got my Juicy Fruit.

GEORGETTE: Did you thank Mr.…

(Judge gets up.)

SLIM: *(D. L. of C.)* Slim.

MARGARET ROSE: *(Sitting on the steps.)* Yes'm. Three times.

JUDGE: This is Henry Thomas's wife, Slim.

SLIM: Is that so?

MARGARET ROSE: Did my daddy come?

GEORGETTE: No, honey. Now you know he won't be here until next week.

(The Judge and Slim exchange a quick look.)

SLIM: Excuse me, but he's here now.

GEORGETTE: He is? *(She looks at the Judge, then at Slim.)*

SLIM: Yes, ma'm. He's working for a lady not far from here.

(A pause, Georgette gets up.)

GEORGETTE: I declare, I don't understand that.

SLIM: I'd be glad to take you over to where he works.

GEORGETTE: Thank you, I'd sure appreciate that. I just don't understand at all his not getting in touch with us.

SLIM: Maybe he tried to and couldn't. I expect you're going to find he had a good reason.

GEORGETTE: Yessir, I expect so.

JUDGE: Won't he be at Miss Kate's funeral, Slim?

SLIM: I'm sure he was, but it's over.

JUDGE: *(Looking at his watch.)* Is that so?

SLIM: I saw the people leaving the cemetery as I was coming back with the little girl.

JUDGE: Oh. Well, I got so interested in helping the young lady here, it slipped by mind. Well, I'll go on. Good-bye, Mrs. Thomas. *(He goes to her and shakes hands.)*

GEORGETTE: Good-bye, Judge. Say good-bye to the Judge, Margaret Rose.

MARGARET ROSE: *(Getting up.)* Good-bye.

JUDGE: Good-bye, young lady. *(He goes up onto the porch to the far end.)*

MARGARET ROSE: Mama, is Daddy here?

GEORGETTE: Yes, honey. You heard what the man said.

MARGARET ROSE: Where is he?

GEORGETTE: I don't know. We're going to find him now, Sugar.

SLIM: *(Picking up her suitcase.)* Let's go out this way, Mrs. Thomas. We could cut through the back here, but I think we'd better go in my car.

GEORGETTE: Thank you. Thank you so much.

(She and Margaret Rose go out of the yard through the gate and off U. R. as Slim follows. Clara Breedlove comes in D. S. L. She is a large friendly woman in her late fifties. Wears hat and gloves, carries purse. She doesn't see them leave. As she takes her hat off and goes toward the steps, Sitter Mavis and Mrs. Mavis come in from the backyard, D. R.)

MISS CLARA: Hello, Sitter. Hello, Mrs. Mavis.

(Sitter comes over to her. She goes up the steps onto the porch and into the sun parlor. Her mother follows her and sits on the settee.)

Well, you can't tell me Harrison hasn't changed.

SITTER: It certainly has. I only counted twenty-four people at the funeral this morning. How many did you count?

MISS CLARA: Twenty-seven.

SITTER: Twenty-four or twenty-seven. Imagine that's all that cared enough about poor Miss Kate Dawson to come and tell her good-bye.

MISS CLARA: Did seein' the hearse pass upset your mother, Sitter?

(Clara puts her hat, gloves, and purse on table behind settee.)

SITTER: No, ma'am. She didn't get to see it. I made Papa play checkers with her the whole mornin' out in the backyard under the fig trees. She can't see the street from there. She didn't know a thing about it, I'm happy to say, until I came home and told her I'd been to see Miss Kate Dawson put to rest.

MRS. MAVIS: *(Sits on settee.)* That's what you think. I saw the whole thing. Your papa dozed off an' I snuck out front just as the hearse turned the corner.

(Miss Clara gets her sewing basket from table, sits in chair L. and mends socks.)

SITTER: *(Sitting in rocker L. of settee.)* Oh, Mama. I can't do a thing with her any more, Miss Clara. She runs away from home all the time. It just keeps me so upset.

MRS. MAVIS: Did you know Sitter whips me? All the neighbors have been complainin'.

SITTER: Mama. Somebody's gonna believe that talk some day. Did you see Henry Thomas at the funeral?

MISS CLARA: Yes. I noticed him come in with Mrs. Tillman. He'd changed so I hardly recognized him.

SITTER: I thought it was sweet of him to attend. Didn't you?

MISS CLARA: Well, after all, Miss Kate gave him the only home he ever had.

SITTER: He has a home at the Tillmans now. They're very thick, you know—I declare, Mrs. Tillman always picks up with the strangest people. You remember last year she had that young man that was arrested for being a draft dodger or something working in her yard?

MISS CLARA: Yes, I remember.

SITTER: They're usually drunks and she tries to reform them. Which is very commendable, I suppose, but I think she's gotten a little fanatical on the subject myself. Don't you?

MISS CLARA: Yes, I do.

SITTER: I won't say she's not a good woman, because she is, but she is a little fanatical.

MISS CLARA: I know.

(Mrs. Tillman comes in onto the porch from the front of the house U. R. She is a stern-faced humorless woman about Miss Clara's age. Wears hat and gloves,

carries a purse. She opens the screen door to sun parlor. Clara gets up and draws a small rocker for her.)

Hello, Mrs. Tillman. Come in.

MRS. TILLMAN: Thank you. It's goin' to be another beautiful day.

MISS CLARA: Yes, it is.

SITTER: I've often thought to myself if I have to die and get buried, which I know I do, I hope it's the Spring of the year. And not a rainy Spring, but a dry one like this year.

MRS. TILLMAN: I'm ready to meet my Maker at any time, I'm thankful to say. *(She sits down on rocker.)*

SITTER: Well, I certainly hope I'm ready to meet my Maker, honey, but I'd just prefer a dry Spring, that's all.

(Clara sits down in chair L. and resumes her mending. Mrs. Mavis has closed her eyes and dozed off. She is snoring slightly. Sitter shakes her.)

Mama, wake up now. You'll be roaming around half the night if you sleep the afternoon through.

(Mrs. Mavis opens her eyes.)

MRS. MAVIS: I wasn't asleep.

SITTER: You were, too. Mrs. Tillman, we were just talkin' about Henry Thomas. Miss Clara saw him at the funeral and said he'd changed so she hardly recognized him.

MRS. TILLMAN: Oh. When was the last time you saw him, Clara?

MISS CLARA: I don't know. Seven or eight years ago.

MRS. TILLMAN: Well, I'd expect him to change in that time, wouldn't you? Particularly after the life he's led. I think it's remarkable what a cheerful disposition he still has. Well, we can all see where whiskey leads. I told Mr. Tillman in 1916, when he was still drinking. I said, "You might as well take a gun an' blow your brains out as keep on in this way." Of course, he was one of those with character enough to stop. He marched in one mornin' an' said, "Mrs. Tillman, I'm quittin'." And he did. He took the whiskey bottles, threw them out in the yard, an' busted them on the fig trees. The '22 storm got the fig trees. I have always felt bad about losin' them. And he never took another drop, Praise God. He used to beg me not to march in the parades, but I said, "I will so march."

SITTER: What parades, honey?

MRS. TILLMAN: The temperance parades.

SITTER: Oh.

MRS. TILLMAN: He said, "I've given it up. Why are you marchin'?" I said, "to try an' keep it from bringin' the sadness to other homes it once brought to mine."

SITTER: I'll never forget those parades. Everybody dressed in white. I loved them. *(She sings half to herself to the tune of "Bringing in the Sheaves.")*

"Texas goin' dry.

Texas goin' dry.

Come an' take the pledge, boys,

Texas goin' dry."

MRS. TILLMAN: *(Interrupting.)* Well, the parades have stopped, but I haven't stopped. I've given my life to helpin' others overcome the habit. Miss Kate herself asked me to help Henry, you know. When Henry got out of the penitentiary, she come to Mr. Tillman and asked him to please give him any kind of honest work. Mr. Tillman sent him out to the house to see me. I put him to work hoeing the weeds in the garden. I went away that first afternoon to go to the picture show, an' I didn't lock my house. I never lock my house. but on the way downtown, somethin' inside me told me to go back an' see to the safety of my possessions. So halfway down to town, I turned around and came back. An' there he was.

SITTER: There who was, honey?

MRS. TILLMAN: Henry Thomas.

SITTER: What was he doin', honey?

MRS. TILLMAN: Stealin'!

SITTER: Stealin'!

MRS. TILLMAN: Yes, ma'm.

SITTER: Oh, my Lord. I would have fainted.

MRS. TILLMAN: He had all the silver piled up on the table tryin' to wrap it up in the *Houston Chronicle.*

SITTER: What did you do?

MRS. TILLMAN: I just marched right up to him, and said, "Henry Thomas, put every bit of that right back where you found it."

SITTER: I declare! She doesn't know the meanin' of the word fear. I'd 'a' fainted. I'd 'a' fainted dead away. Then what did you do, honey?

MRS. TILLMAN: I stood there and glared at him until he put all the silver back. He looked just like a whipped dog. When he was finished I said for him to come on with me, I was gonna take him down to the Sheriff's office. An' then he broke out cryin'…

SITTER: Well, I declare!

MRS. TILLMAN: Yes, ma'm. Broke out crying. Sobbed and sobbed. He begged me not to tell Miss Kate or the Sheriff. He said he would be sent back to the penitentiary if I did. He said he was stealin' it to get money to buy whiskey. He said he was a slave to the habit. Well, I stood there and watched him for a minute. Then I told him to have a seat, an' I got the Bible down an' I read some Psalms to clear my mind. An' then it come to me what to do. It came to me clear as day that he'd been sent to me to break of the whiskey habit, and I said I wouldn't take him to the Sheriff if he promised never to drink again.

SITTER: And did he promise?

MRS. TILLMAN: Yes'm

SITTER: Did he keep his promise?

MRS. TILLMAN: Yes, I'm happy to say.

SITTER: I hope you keep your things all locked up now.

MRS. TILLMAN: No, ma'm. And what's more I leave ten dollars out in full view of the kitchen table whenever I leave the house. Just to show him I trust him, and I'm grateful to say it's always there when I get back.

(Mrs. Mavis has fallen asleep again. Sitter shakes her.)

SITTER: Mama, wake up now.

(Mrs. Mavis opens her eyes.)

Well, Hallie Davis got her fo'th oil well.

MRS. TILLMAN: Fifth.

SITTER: Fo'th. One at Peach Creek—

MRS. TILLMAN: Fifth.

SITTER: Fo'th. If you can name five I'll eat them.

MRS. TILLMAN: Peach Creek, Blossom Prairie, Hunger Ford, Bonus—Well, I guess you're right. I guess it was four—

(Henry Thomas has come into the yard from D. L. He is in his late twenties. He still has on his suit and tie from the funeral and is more dressed up than he usually is. He is nice looking, but still a little pale from his long stay in prison. He comes to the D. L. of C. and calls.)

HENRY: Mrs. Breedlove. Is Mrs. Tillman there? *(A pause.)*

MISS CLARA: Yes, she is. *(Pause.)* Won't you come in, Henry?

(She gets up and opens the screen door.)

HENRY: Thank you, ma'm. *(He goes up into the sun parlor.)*

SITTER: Henry, do you remember me? I'm Miss Sitter Mavis.

HENRY: *(Shaking her hand.)* Yes'm. How do you do. It's been a long time since I've gotten to speak to you.

(Clara sits down again in chair L.)

SITTER: It has been a long time, truly. I've been noticing you over in the Tillmans' yard. Are you planning to be around for a while, Henry?

HENRY: Yes, ma'm. I hope so. I'm working for Mrs. Tillman, you know. I've never done yard work before, but I guess she's satisfied.

MRS. TILLMAN: Perfectly satisfied, Henry.

SITTER: We all feel so bad about Miss Kate, Henry.

HENRY: Yes, ma'm. She was the only mother I ever knew, Miss Sitter. She could be hard and she was at times, but I know now it was for my own good. I caused her many a tear and I'm sorry she had to die before I could prove to her... (*A pause. He seems too moved to go on and turns away.*) Well, all my tears are too late now, ladies.

MRS. TILLMAN: Don't say that, Henry. Miss Kate knew you were behavin' yourself and I'm sure she died happy in the knowledge of it.

(*He turns back.*)

She told me last Friday when I went to see her that it gave her a great deal of gratification to see you take hold this way.

HENRY: Yes, ma'm. I hope so. I think she was happy about my taking up my music again, don't you?

MRS. TILLMAN: Yes, I think so.

HENRY: She'd rather hear me sing than eat, you know, ladies. She used to rather hear me sing, I believe, than anything in this world. Miss Kate used to say, "Henry. Any man can lay bricks or sell insurance or work in a filling station. But you've got a call, Henry. Just as much as a man gets a call to preach. You've got a call to sing and that don't come to everybody."

SITTER: Are you startin' your string band again, Henry?

HENRY: Yes, ma'm. I've been practicing for about three weeks. Honey Jeffers and Delbert Price and myself. We played for a Bohemian dance the other night. 'Course we didn't charge too much because we hadn't worked ourselves up yet to where we ought to be.

MRS. MAVIS: I never heard him sing. I want him to sing me a song.

SITTER: Sh, Mama.

HENRY: We're playin' for a dance over in Cotton this Saturday and next Thursday beyond Glen Flora...

SITTER: You don't say.

HENRY: Yes'm.

SITTER: What are you calling the band, Henry?

HENRY: I can't decide, Miss Sitter. I was trying to think up a name coming out here. The South Texas Ramblers. How do you like that?

SITTER: That's a nice name. ...

HENRY: Do you like that better than the Dixie Five?

MRS. TILLMAN: I do.

SITTER: I don't know. I just naturally like anything with Dixie in it.

MRS. MAVIS: Why don't he sing us a piece instead of talking so much?

SITTER: Sh, Mama. Now I'll take you home if you get insulting——

HENRY: She's not botherin' me any, Miss Sitter. *(Sitting on arm of settee.)* What song would you like me to sing you, Mrs. Mavis?

MRS. MAVIS: I don't care, just as long as you sing.

HENRY: All right. Lessee. *(Henry stands and sings "True Love Goes On and On." Henry looks around at the ladies. They all seem fascinated. Sitter gives a sigh.)*

SITTER: That's just lovely.

MRS. MAVIS: I never heard a prettier voice in my life—and he's handsome as a picture, too.

MRS. TILLMAN: I told Mr. Tillman that's why I think he keeps so happy. He's always singing.

HENRY: Mrs. Tillman says I'm mighty lucky to get paid for what I like to do.

MRS. TILLMAN: Yes, you are.

HENRY: *(Going to her.)* Mrs. Tillman, can I have the keys to the car so I can back it into the yard and wash it? I would have waited until you come home, but I have to get it done right now because we're having a little band practice this afternoon.

MRS. TILLMAN: *(Reaches into her purse searching for her keys and finds them. She is about to give them to Henry when she suddenly puts them back in her purse.)* I tell you what, Henry. I think I better go back with you.

HENRY: Yes, ma'm.

(She gets up. Clara and Sitter get up.)

MRS. TILLMAN: I'll see you ladies later.

SITTER: Good-bye, Mrs. Tillman. Mama, say good-bye to Mrs. Tillman.

MRS. MAVIS: Who's that?

SITTER: Mama, you know who Mrs. Tillman is. She's standing right there in front of you. You've known her all her life.

MRS. MAVIS: I've never set eyes on her before.

SITTER: Oh, Mama. She's just bein' naughty. Don't pay any attention to her, Mrs. Tillman.

MRS. TILLMAN: I don't. Come on, Henry.

HENRY: *(Holding screen door open.)* Yes, ma'm. Good-bye, ladies.

SITTER: Good-bye, Henry.

MISS CLARA: Good-bye, Henry.

(Henry and Mrs. Tillman go out the screen door, down the steps and out through the yard and off D. L.)

SITTER: Well, he certainly has her eating out of his hand. But, Mama, I don't want you ever to repeat to Mrs. Tillman that I said that. Mama has a bad habit of repeating things I say.

MRS. MAVIS: You shouldn't say things you don't want repeated.

SITTER: But isn't he polite?

MISS CLARA: He seems to be.

SITTER: I hadn't remembered he had such nice manners. And he's very grieved and I think that's commendable.

MRS. MAVIS: Sitter, I want to go for a walk.

MISS CLARA: Now, Mrs. Mavis, you just got here.

MRS. MAVIS: I can't help it. I want to go.

SITTER: Now, Mama.

MRS. MAVIS: I want to go for a walk. I'll fall out on this floor if you won't take me.

SITTER: *(Going to her.)* All right. I might as well. She'll give me no rest until I do. Come on, Mama.

(Mrs. Mavis gets up and goes out onto porch.)

MISS CLARA: *(Getting dust cloth from table.)* You all come back later on.

SITTER: *(Going out on porch.)* All right. I don't know where on earth we're going to walk to.

MRS. MAVIS: *(Going down the steps toward hedge L.)* Let's go to the graveyard. I want to see Kate Dawson's grave.

SITTER: Oh, Lord, Mama. We're certainly not goin' to any graveyard. Mama has graveyards on the brain.

(She goes down the steps to her mother. Miss Clara follows behind them and goes out onto porch.)

Now, you start on toward the house, Mama. I'll be right along.

(Mrs. Mavis goes off D. R. Clara comes down the steps.)

Miss Clara, I was surprised not to see Slim at Miss Kate's funeral.

MISS CLARA: I know. *(She goes and picks up R. garden chair and wipes it off.)*

SITTER: I suppose they still upset him. I can hardly realize Laura's been dead over a year. *(A pause. Going and picking up L. chair.)* Oh, well. I never see a boy and girl walking by that I don't think of Slim and Laura Ewing. I can see them now at sixteen or seventeen walking in front of the house at night or riding around town in that old secondhand car Slim bought working at the gin. And when Slim came home from the Army that time and she told him she didn't want to marry him, I just couldn't believe it when I heard it. Everybody in town was so upset. And when she changed her mind and they finally married everybody in town was so glad. Did you ever see a sweeter looking young girl than Laura Ewing?

MISS CLARA: No. I don't believe so. *(She wipes L. garden chair.)*

SITTER: I wish they'd gotten married here. I'm sorry it wasn't my privilege to see her as a bride. I know she was pretty as a picture.

(A pause. Clara goes to toolbox, puts in cloth and takes out cutting shears. Sitter follows.)

I was so worried about Slim right after she died. Many a night I'd be out looking for Mama and I'd come through your backyard and see him just walking back and forth. I don't think Slim'll ever love anybody else.

MRS. MAVIS: *(Off R., calls.)* Sitter! You come on now!

MISS CLARA: *(Starting R. with Sitter.)* I'll walk to the edge of the yard with you.

SITTER: Your yard always looks so pretty, Miss Clara.

MISS CLARA: Thank you.

(Miss Clara and Sitter go off D. R. Slim and Georgette come into the sun parlor from U. R. door to house and go out on the porch.)

SLIM: My sister must be out in the yard.

GEORGETTE: Yessir. I sure hope we're not putting you out any.

SLIM: No, ma'm....I wish you'd try and get some rest.

GEORGETTE: I couldn't sleep. I'd be worrying the whole time that I'd miss Henry some way.

SLIM: Now, please don't worry—we'll find him—I'll check over at the Tillman's every few minutes. ...

(Miss Clara comes back into the yard from D. R. and comes to the steps.)

Clara, this is Mrs. Thomas. This is my sister, Mrs. Breedlove.

MISS CLARA: How do you do, Mrs. Thomas.

GEORGETTE: How do you do.

SLIM: Mrs. Thomas is married to Henry Thomas.

MISS CLARA: Oh, is that so?

SLIM: Their little girl is taking a nap in the front bedroom. They were riding a bus all night. We weren't able to locate Henry, so I insisted she...

MISS CLARA: Did you look over at Mrs. Tillman's?

SLIM: Yes, we tried there twice. There was nobody home.

MISS CLARA: They were both here just a few minutes ago. The said they were going right home.

(Henry comes in through the hedge D. L. He sees Miss Clara and no one else.)

HENRY: Miss Clara, did Mrs. Tillman leave her glasses over here? She...

GEORGETTE: *(Coming down the steps.)* Hello, Henry.

(He looks up and sees her.)

HENRY: Why, Georgette. How did you get here?

GEORGETTE: I just came in on the bus. We've been looking all over town for you. We just heard you were here.

(*They go to meet each other. They do not kiss, but shake hands. They seem very shy and self-conscious with each other.*)

HENRY: I just can't get over it. This sure is a surprise. You're looking good, Georgette.

(*Clara goes up into sun parlor and off into house. Slim follows.*)

GEORGETTE: Thank you. You're looking good, too, Henry.

HENRY: I bet you were surprised when you heard I was here.

GEORGETTE: Yes, I was.

HENRY: I wrote you a letter yesterday. Did you get it?

GEORGETTE: No.

HENRY: I guess it didn't get there until today. I told you all about my getting out earlier in that letter. I've been out for a month.

GEORGETTE: That's what Mr. Slim told me.

HENRY: I got out for good behavior. I was determined to have a little something ahead before I wrote to you, so I came back here and got me a job and was savin' my money. I just couldn't see comin' to you all broke.

GEORGETTE: That was thoughtful of you, Henry.

(*Georgette and Henry still seem a little embarrassed with each other.*)

HENRY: How are things back in Tyler?

GEORGETTE: Pretty good.

HENRY: I believe you said you came in on the bus?

GEORGETTE: Yes, I did.

HENRY: You're looking good, Georgette.

GEORGETTE: Thank you. You look good, too, Henry.

HENRY: Do you think you would have recognized me?

GEORGETTE: Oh, sure. Right away.

HENRY: Where's our little girl?

GEORGETTE: She's in there asleep. Want me to go and wake her so she can say hello to you?

HENRY: No. No. Let her get her sleep out. I can see her later. She must be tired.

GEORGETTE: She is. Neither of us could sleep on that old bus.

HENRY: Well, I have to find us a place to stay tonight. I'd better get a move on.

GEORGETTE: Maybe I better wake up Margaret Rose so we can go with you. ...

HENRY: No. No. Don't do that. Let her get her sleep out. I'll go ahead and make arrangements about a house and then I'll come back and get you.

GEORGETTE: Do you think it'll be all right with them?

HENRY: I'm sure it will. Want me to ask them?

GEORGETTE: If you don't mind.

HENRY: All right. *(He goes up to the screen door and knocks.)* Miss Clara——

MISS CLARA: *(Coming out from house into sun parlor.)* Yes, Henry?

HENRY: I was wondering if it was all right with you if my wife waited here while my little girl got her nap out. You see, I want to go and see about a house and the little girl was awful tired…

MISS CLARA: It's perfectly all right with me, Henry.

HENRY: Thank you, ma'm.

> *(He comes back to Georgette. Clara goes back into house.)*
>
> It's OK I better get started. I was gonna wash a car for the lady I work for and I had my string band practice for this afternoon, but I'll postpone all that. Did you know I was starting a string band, Georgette?

GEORGETTE: No.

HENRY: Yep. Played our first dance last week. I wrote you all about it in the letter.

GEORGETTE: That's nice. *(A pause.)*

HENRY: Well, I'll go on.

> *(He starts out D. L., stops, comes back and kisses her.)*
>
> I should be back no later than an hour. And you'll wait here for me?

GEORGETTE: I sure will.

> *(He goes out D. L. Miss Clara comes out of the house and goes on the porch.)*

MISS CLARA: Well, do you feel better?

GEORGETTE: I sure do. I'm so relieved to see Henry. *(Going above yard chairs.)* He doesn't look a bit different than he did when I first met him.

> *(Slim comes out from house into sun parlor and stands in the doorway to porch.)*

MISS CLARA: *(Going down the steps to R. chair.)* Where did you meet Henry, Mrs. Thomas?

GEORGETTE: *(Turns to her.)* Ma'm?

MISS CLARA: I said, where did you meet Henry?

GEORGETTE: Oh, excuse me. My mind was a thousand miles away. I met him back in my home town of Lovelady. It was on a Saturday and he was riding through town with a bunch of boys. One of the boys knew the girl I was with, and they stopped their car and we were introduced. They asked me to go for a ride but I couldn't as I had to meet my papa to go see the picture show. And then the next night I went to a dance and there he was singing with a string band and he asked me to dance and I said I would, and he'd sing a while and then we'd dance a while and he'd sing a while and we'd dance a while….It was love at first sight, I guess. Everybody that knew Henry back in Lovelady was just crazy about him. He had Sis Roberts just wild about him, and they tell me her papa offered to set him up in a grocery store just to get him to marry her. They say she took to her bed and cried for a week when she heard how I got him. *(She holds her hand up.)* Here's the ring Henry gave me. Of course, for a long time I thought it was a genuine diamond. Then some mean old devil in Tyler proved to me it wasn't. But I don't care. I like it just the same. It usually looks prettier, but it kind of turns green when my hands perspire, and ever since I got on that bus my hands have just been wringing perspiration.

(Margaret Rose comes out into sun parlor from the house past Slim and goes out onto the porch.)

SLIM: *(Following.)* Look who's here.

(Georgette goes to the steps and picks Margaret Rose up in her arms.)

GEORGETTE: Why, honey, I thought you were asleep.

MARGARET ROSE: I was, but I woke up.

(Clara sits in R. yard chair.)

GEORGETTE: Guess who was just here?

MARGARET ROSE: I don't know.

GEORGETTE: Your daddy.

MARGARET ROSE: No, he wasn't. You're just teasing me.

GEORGETTE: Honey, why would I want to do a thing like that? Of course, he was.

MARGARET ROSE: Did he sing "New San 'Tonia Rose"?

GEORGETTE: No, not yet.

MARGARET ROSE: I bet he's going to sing "New San 'Tonia Rose"—first thing he sees me. …

GEORGETTE: Of course he will. Oh, excuse me, Margaret Rose. You haven't met Mrs. Breedlove. Mrs. Breedlove, this is my little girl, Margaret Rose. I was so excited over the news about Henry I forgot my manners.

MISS CLARA: How do you do, young lady.

MARGARET ROSE: Hello. You sing it, Mama.

GEORGETTE: Sing what, Sugar?

MARGARET ROSE: "New San 'Tonia Rose."

GEORGETTE: No, honey.

MARGARET ROSE: Please.

GEORGETTE: Now, Daddy will be back in a little while and then he'll sing it.

MARGARET ROSE: Sing just a part of it, please.

GEORGETTE: Well, all right. *(She turns to Miss Clara.)* Do you mind if I sing, Mrs. Breedlove?

MISS CLARA: No, go right ahead.

(Georgette sits in rocker L. of steps, puts Margaret Rose in her lap.)

GEORGETTE: I don't sing worth listening to, but Margaret Rose likes it. It comforts her.

(She hugs her. Slim goes down and sits on toolbox.)

I just can't get over how it's all worked out. Can you, Margaret Rose?

MARGARET ROSE: No, ma'm. Sing it, Mama.

GEORGETTE: All right, honey. *(She starts to sing part of "New San Antonio Rose."*
She stops and covers her face with her hands.)

MARGARET ROSE: Mama's crying.

GEORGETTE: Sh, Margaret Rose. Mama's happy. I'm crying because I'm happy.

MARGARET ROSE: Why are you happy?

GEORGETTE: Because people here have been nice to us, and because Daddy's
home.

(Margaret Rose snuggles up to her mother. Georgette begins to sing again. She
is singing as the...)

CURTAIN FALLS

ACT II
Scene 1

The sun parlor five hours later. Miss Clara is seated in the rocker alone,
mending a shirt. Mrs. Mavis comes scurrying into the yard through the gate
and up the steps. She pauses, looks around, and then comes inside and into
parlor.

MRS. MAVIS: Lock the door. Lock the door!

MISS CLARA: Mrs. Mavis, what has gotten into you?

MRS. MAVIS: That devil is after me.

MISS CLARA: What devil?

MRS. MAVIS: Sitter.

(Sitter comes into the yard through the gate calling: "Mama. Mama." Mrs.
Mavis screaming.)

Lock the door. Lock the door.

MISS CLARA: *(Getting up.)* I'll do no such thing. Now keep quiet. There's a
woman and a little girl asleep in there.

(Mrs. Mavis runs into the house and closes the door. Miss Clara goes out on
the porch.)

Sh, Sitter. Sh....Your mother's in here.

SITTER: I'm sorry. Is someone asleep?

MISS CLARA: Yes. Henry Thomas's wife and little girl.

SITTER: *(Going up to the porch.)* Hasn't he come back for them yet?

MISS CLARA: *(Going back into sun parlor.)* No. And I'd like to know where he is.

SITTER: *(Following.)* Mama was telling me they were over here.

MISS CLARA: He said he'd be gone an hour. He's been gone nearer three. Slim went off to see if he could find what's happened to him. *(Sitting down on rocker and resuming her mending.)* I tried to keep up a conversation with them but they were so tired they began to yawn in my face.

SITTER: *(Opening door to house and looking around the room.)* Mama. Mama. I vow she's run off again. *(Closing door and coming down and looking around the yard.)* I swear I don't know what I'm going to do. I feel like bustin' out cryin' sometimes. She just does it to devil me.

(Margaret Rose comes sleepily into the sun parlor from the house, with a small rag doll.)

MARGARET ROSE: Has my daddy come?

MISS CLARA: No, honey. Not yet.

SITTER: Is that Henry's little girl?

MISS CLARA: Yes.

SITTER: She doesn't look a thing like Henry. Does she?

MISS CLARA: No. She favors her Mama.

SITTER: *(Sitting on stool.)* Hello, there, little lady.

MISS CLARA: Margaret Rose, this is Miss Sitter Mavis.

SITTER: Are you going to live here with your daddy?

MARGARET ROSE: Yes, ma'm.

MISS CLARA: Is your mother still sleeping?

MARGARET ROSE: Yes, ma'm.

SITTER: Couldn't you go back to sleep?

MARGARET ROSE: No, ma'm.

SITTER: Are you excited about seeing your daddy?

MARGARET ROSE: Yes, ma'm. I've never seen my daddy.

SITTER: You haven't?

MARGARET ROSE: No, ma'm. He's been away seeing Europe. He's a millionaire.

SITTER: Well, I declare.

MARGARET ROSE: Can you sing "New San 'Tonia Rose"?

SITTER: No, honey. I don't sing.

MARGARET ROSE: My daddy can. *(To Clara.)* Have you all got a chinaberry tree?

MISS CLARA: Uh huh.

MARGARET ROSE: Where is it?

MISS CLARA: There are two of them out in the backyard.

MARGARET ROSE: Can I go climb them?

MISS CLARA: Does your mother allow you to climb trees?

MARGARET ROSE: Yes, ma'm.

MISS CLARA: Well, go ahead then.

MARGARET ROSE: Yes, ma'm. *(Margaret Rose goes down the steps of the yard, in front of sun parlor and off D. R.)*

SITTER: She's a sweet looking little thing. Now wouldn't you know it would be just like Slim to turn up with Henry's wife and little girl? If there's anything stray, Slim will be bound to find it.

MISS CLARA: That's the truth.

SITTER: I bet you hope they don't stay as long as that Mexican family he brought home to live in your backyard. Did you ever hear from that Mexican family?

MISS CLARA: I haven't. I don't know whether Slim has or not.

(Mrs. Mavis comes scurrying into the yard from U. R.)

SITTER: Here comes Mama.

(Sitter jumps up and goes out on the porch. Mrs. Mavis goes running out of the yard, past the sun parlor and off D. R. Sitter runs down after her.)

Mama. You come here.

(Miss Clara goes out on the porch.)

MISS CLARA: Don't chase her, Sitter.

(Sitter stops D. R.)

That's all she wants you to do. If you didn't run after her I bet she'd come on home with no trouble at all.

(Slim comes into the yard through the gate.)

SLIM: Where's Mrs. Thomas?

MISS CLARA: She's in there asleep. Didn't you find Henry?

SLIM: I couldn't find a trace of him. I went all over town.

SITTER: Did you ask Mrs. Tillman if she knew where he was?

SLIM: Yes, I went by there first thing. She said she'd loaned him her car for the emergency. I checked at her house just before coming here. The car wasn't there so I figured he wasn't. *(He goes and sits in L. yard chair.)*

SITTER: I'm going to go see if she's heard anything from him. I bet she's in a state.

(She goes out through the hedge, D. L. Mrs. Mavis has sneaked into the house through the door in front of the house. She comes out of the house through door into the sun parlor and on to the porch.)

MRS. MAVIS: Where's Sitter off to?

MISS CLARA: She went over to ask Mrs. Tillman a question. You wait here. She'll be right back.

MRS. MAVIS: I don't care if she comes right back or not. I don't care if she ever comes back.

MISS CLARA: *(Going down the steps to Slim.)* Mrs. Mavis, you ought to be ashamed of yourself as good as Sitter is to you.

MRS. MAVIS: You tend to your business and I'll tend to mine. *(She goes down the steps and off D. R.)*

MISS CLARA: You know, she's just plain mean, Slim. I feel so sorry sometimes for Sitter. *(A pause. She sits down in R. chair and continues to mend the shirt.)* What do you think happened to Henry?

SLIM: I can't figure it. He's probably having trouble finding a house. *(He looks off R.)* Is that the little Thomas girl up in the chinaberry tree?

MISS CLARA: Yes. She told me her mama lets her climb them.

SLIM: She's a nice little girl.

MISS CLARA: Yes, she is.

SLIM: Did you give them anything to eat?

MISS CLARA: Yes, I gave the little girl a sandwich and a glass of milk. Mrs. Thomas said she was too excited to eat.

SLIM: How was the funeral?

MISS CLARA: Very sweet. Pitiful crowd though.

SLIM: Clara, I got an offer to work for a gin down in the valley. *(He gets up and walks over to the porch railing.)*

MISS CLARA: A better job than the one Thurman offered you here?

SLIM: About the same. *(A pause. He picks up a small trowel from ground.)* I think I'm going to take it.

MISS CLARA: But if it's no better than the job here…

SLIM: I want to take this one. I want to be on the move again. I… *(He doesn't finish what he was going to say. He walks to the toolbox, puts trowel in and picks up a small stick from ground.)*

MRS. MAVIS: *(Inside house—starts to sing.)*

> I like coffee,
> I like tea,
> I like the boys
> And the boys like me.

MISS CLARA: *(Calling in.)* Mrs. Mavis, if you're gonna make noise I'll have to ask you to leave. There's a woman trying to get a nap in my front bedroom.

MRS. MAVIS: *(Offstage on her way out R.)*

> I like coffee,
> I like tea,
> I like the boys
> And the boys like me.

MISS CLARA: Mrs. Mavis, did you hear what I said?

(*Mrs. Mavis goes out of house—offstage.*)

Slim, what makes you so restless and want to wander like this? You didn't used to be this way. Why, I remember as a boy and a young man I could hardly drive you out of this yard. And when you came home from the Army you said you never wanted to leave again, then a month later you walk in an announce you're leaving your job and going off. You wander around four or five years, come home, stay a year and now you tell me you're restless again. What is it? What's the matter? If you know, I wish you'd tell me.

(*He doesn't answer.*)

Slim, I'm your sister. I raised you. You're all I have. I don't mean to be prying, but I don't like to see you this way. You should get married again and have a home and children. Laura's been dead for over a year. You can't go through life grieving for a dead girl.

(*A pause. He sits in* L. *chair next to his sister. It is obviously difficult for him to talk.*)

SLIM: I've never talked about this before, Clara, and I don't want to talk about it again. Six months after we were married Laura left me.

MISS CLARA: She left you? Why did she leave you, Slim?

SLIM: (*Looks away.*) I don't know. I've never known. She said she didn't know. She just said that she guessed she wasn't ready for marriage. I asked her if she wanted a divorce and she said no, that she just wanted to go off by herself for a while. When I came home from work next day, there was a note saying she had gone to Dallas. Three months later I heard from a friend that she was living in Fort Worth. She never called or wrote after she left or would come to the phone when I called her or answer any of the letters I wrote. Even when she was so sick and I heard about it finally from her mama and I came back here to be near her and I'd go to the house everyday and her mama would go into her room everyday and say, "Slim's here. He wants to see you. Don't you want to see him?" (*He looks at Clara.*) Her mama said she wouldn't even answer, just shake her head no. And those nights you and everybody else thought I was sitting at her bedside and waiting, I wasn't. (*He looks away.*) I was sitting outside the door to her bedroom. (*A pause.*) And then the night just before she died she asked to see me and I went into her room and she asked me to forgive her and I said there was nothing to forgive her for and she said yes there was and then she took my hand and held it for a minute and then she said she was tired, and would I stay while she slept, and I said I would.... (*A pause. He rises and walks about the yard, then comes back and sits.*) I've done a lot of thinking, Clara, since her death. I used to come out here and sit by myself and think of Laura as she was when I first met her, her sweetness, my love for her and her love for me and wondering what went wrong and if I had failed her and how I failed her. Then it came to me the other night that I couldn't even answer, now, those questions. That right or wrong I did the best I could and that if I had it to do all over again, I wouldn't know what else to do, but what I did. *(Getting up walking to C.)* And that I can't spend the rest of my life sitting in this backyard and worrying over the past. *(Sitter comes running in from D. L.)*

SITTER: *(Going above chair to Clara.)* He's drunk. He's drunk. He's over at Mrs. Tillman's drunk as a hoot-owl.

MISS CLARA: Who is?

SITTER: Henry Thomas. And you should see Mrs. Tillman. Just as calm. I took one look at him and almost fainted, but not her.

(Mrs. Tillman comes in from D. L.)

MRS. TILLMAN: *(Going to Clara.)* Now, I ask you both not to worry about a thing. I'll have him sober in no time.

SITTER: She just said don't be nervous, Sitter.

MRS. TILLMAN: I've got him in the kitchen pouring coffee down him. I want to get right back to him and keep up the treatment but I just wanted you to know I have everything under control.

SITTER: I'm terrified of drunk men.

(Clara and Slim shush her. Slim moves up to L. of porch and looks toward the house door.)

…but there she was, just as calm, busy making him coffee. *(Going above to R. of Clara.)*

She thinks the shock made him do it, don't you, Mrs. Tillman?

MISS CLARA: Shock? What shock?

MRS. TILLMAN: What shock? Miss Kate Dawson's funeral and seeing his wife and little girl all the same day. That's what shock.

MISS CLARA: Shock, my grandmother. Personally, I wouldn't trust him as far as I could throw him.

MRS. TILLMAN: Clara, he's had a shock!

MISS CLARA: I had a talk with Mrs. Thomas, Slim, right after you left…

(Slim comes D. C.)

and I think she's a very nice lady. And I don't know how you feel, but if it was up to me, I'd tell her exactly how Mr. Henry is behavin'.

MRS. TILLMAN: *(Going to Slim.)* Oh, I wouldn't do that.

MISS CLARA: And why wouldn't you?

MRS. TILLMAN: *(To Clara.)* Because he's had a shock. *(To Slim.)* I'll get him sober and then he'll be sorry and she won't ever have to know. And I'm sure Sitter agrees with me, don't you, Sitter?

SITTER: *(Going to Mrs. Tillman.)* Yes, I think I do. Why, you've never seen anything like it. She's just pouring black coffee down that boy...

SLIM: That's all well and good, Mrs. Tillman, but what am I supposed to tell Mrs. Thomas when she wakes up and wants to know what has kept him all this time?

MRS. TILLMAN: Tell her...tell her he's been detained. Why hurt the poor thing unnecessarily when it all may work out just fine?

MISS CLARA: Well, I want to go on record as saying I don't agree... *(Georgette, off in the house, calls: "Margaret Rose.")*

SLIM: Sh...sh...

MRS. TILLMAN: *(Whispering.)* I'm running now. I don't dare leave him alone any longer. I beg you to listen to my counsel. I've had vast experience in matters of this kind.

(She goes out the hedge D. L. Georgette, in the house, calls again, "Margaret Rose.")

SLIM: *(Moving U. L. of steps. Calling into the house.)* We're out here, Mrs. Thomas.

(Georgette comes out of the house and onto the porch.)

GEORGETTE: Did my little girl come out this way?

MISS CLARA: *(Rises and takes a step toward Georgette.)* Yes, she asked permission to climb my chinaberry tree. I said it was all right. I hope you don't mind.

GEORGETTE: No. My goodness, I must have just slept and slept. Has Henry come back?

SLIM: No, ma'am. Not yet.

(He turns away and sees Miss Clara looking at him.)

GEORGETTE: Oh, I thought sure he'd be here by now.

SITTER: *(Tugging at Miss Clara's sleeve.)* Miss Clara, I haven't met the lady.

MISS CLARA: Oh, excuse me, Sitter. Mrs. Thomas, this is my neighbor, Miss Sitter Mavis.

SITTER: How do you do.

GEORGETTE: How do you do.

(Outside twilight is beginning. In the distance, far away, can be heard a Mexican dance band playing a waltz. Margaret Rose comes in from the backyard D. R.)

MARGARET ROSE: Mama.

GEORGETTE: *(Going down the step to R. of C.)* Hello, honey. Been climbing the chinaberry tree?

MARGARET ROSE: *(Coming to her.)* Yes, ma'm. Has my daddy come yet?

GEORGETTE: No, honey, not yet.

MARGARET ROSE: When's he coming?

GEORGETTE: He'll be along in a little while.

MARGARET ROSE: Are we gonna eat supper with him?

GEORGETTE: I expect so. Are you getting anxious to see your daddy?

MARGARET ROSE: Yes, ma'm. Are you?

GEORGETTE: I sure am, honey.

SITTER: It'll be dark before long. I better start looking for Mama again. She's always harder to find once it's night. Nice to have met you, Mrs. Thomas.

GEORGETTE: Thank you. Nice to have met you.

SITTER: Good-bye, you all.

MISS CLARA: Good-bye, Sitter.

SLIM: Good-bye, Miss Sitter.

(Sitter goes out the gate and off U. R.)

MISS CLARA: *(Going up onto porch.)* I'm going to have to see about supper. You all excuse me. *(Turns to Slim.)* Slim, remember what I told you I would do. I don't care what Sitter says, or Mrs. Tillman says.

SLIM: All right, Clara.

(She goes off into the house. Slim is about to tell Georgette.)

MARGARET ROSE: *(Sitting on the steps.)* I wish I had my cry-baby doll.

(Slim stops and moves away to yard chair.)

GEORGETTE: I wish you did, too, honey. We'll buy you another one tomorrow or the next day. We left her cry-baby doll sitting in the Houston bus station. We didn't discover it until we were on our way here.

(Georgette, Margaret Rose, and Slim listen to the dance music a moment.)

Where is that music coming from?

SLIM: The Mexican dance hall. They have them every Thursday night.

GEORGETTE: It sounds pretty. I haven't been to a dance in so long I bet I've forgotten how. My daddy didn't approve of dancing, but I used to go anyhow. Do you like to dance?

SLIM: I used to.

GEORGETTE: Don't you go anymore either?

SLIM: No, ma'm. I haven't gone to a dance in about two years.

GEORGETTE: Why did you stop going?

SLIM: My wife died—and I—

GEORGETTE: Oh. *(A pause. The music has stopped. Margaret Rose gets up.)*

MARGARET ROSE: I want to go back and climb the chinaberry tree.

GEORGETTE: All right. I'll come and get you when it's dark.

MARGARET ROSE: Yes, ma'm.

>*(She goes off D. R. Georgette follows to D. R. A pause. ...)*

GEORGETTE: She'd spend her life up in one of those old trees if she could. I hope we can get a house with one, for her sake. *(Coming back to C.)* I always wanted a tree in our yard when I was a little girl. I used to beg Papa to plant one, but he couldn't listen. He'd had cotton growing up to the front door if he'd had his way.

SLIM: *(Going to her.)* Miss Georgette...

GEORGETTE: Yessir?

SLIM: It was...uh...too bad for you have to wait for Henry this way.

GEORGETTE: Yes, it is. But I guess he's having trouble finding a house. Where's Henry living now, Mr. Slim?

SLIM: *(Moving away to D. L. of C.)* He has a room in the lady's backyard he works for.

GEORGETTE: I wonder if it's big enough for me and Margaret Rose if he can't get a house right off.

SLIM: Yes, ma'm. I think so. For a while anyway. *(A pause. He goes to her again.)* Miss Georgette...

GEORGETTE: Yessir.

SLIM: Uh...Do you feel more rested now?

GEORGETTE: Yes. I do. I had the funniest dream while I was asleep. I dreamt I was on the bus, and Papa was driving that bus, and every time we'd pass Harrison I'd holler for him to let me off, but he wouldn't listen to me. *(A pause. The Mexican band starts another tune.)* I wonder what time it is now?

SLIM: Around seven. *(He turns away.)*

GEORGETTE: I hope Henry get's here by supper. It would be nice having supper together. Margaret Rose would enjoy having supper with her daddy. *(A pause. She moves R. of C. and looks off R., then turns to him.)* Sometimes back in Tyler I thought the six years would never go by. Well, they have. Now we're here waiting for him to come and get us. *(A pause.)* I hate to keep getting in the way of you all. *(Going to him.)* Maybe the baby and I should go over to his room and wait for him.

SLIM: You're not in anybody's way.

GEORGETTE: You're sure I'm not keeping you from doing anything?

SLIM: No, ma'm. I haven't a thing to do.

GEORGETTE: Did you lose your job, too?

SLIM: No, ma'm. It's my day off. *(Moving away to the yard chairs.)* I'm quitting my job tomorrow, though—I'm leaving town tomorrow or the next day.

GEORGETTE: Do you have another job?

SLIM: Yes. If I want to take it. If I don't I'm just gonna travel around for a while until I find something I do like.

GEORGETTE: Do you like to travel?

SLIM: *(Coming over to L. of steps.)* Pretty well.

GEORGETTE: *(Sitting on the steps.)* I do. My idea of heaven would be to travel. Have you traveled much?

SLIM: Quite a lot.

GEORGETTE: Where to?

SLIM: *(Sitting beside her.)* Around Texas mostly.

GEORGETTE: Have you been all over Texas?

SLIM: No, ma'm. Just the Eastern part and the Northern part. I've been to Louisiana. *(Pause. The music has stopped. It is very still now.)*

GEORGETTE: The stars are coming out. Where's the moon?

SLIM: I reckon the moon will be late tonight.

GEORGETTE: I guess it will. *(Pause.)* I don't know how I can ever thank you for all your kindness.

SLIM: *(Looks away.)* I haven't done anything.

GEORGETTE: Oh, yes, you have. *(A pause. She touches his arm.)* Mr. Slim, you know I don't know your last name.

SLIM: Murray. My first name is Tom. But everybody's always called me Slim. Ever since I was a kid. I used to be real skinny. It used to worry my sister to death because I was so skinny. *(Pause. Looks at her.)* My sister has taken to you, Miss Georgette.

GEORGETTE: She has?

SLIM: Yes'm. And she doesn't take to everybody.

(A pause. They both seem embarrassed. A train whistle is heard in the distance.)

GEORGETTE: Do you ever worry?

SLIM: Sometimes.

GEORGETTE: Worry is my middle name.

SLIM: What do you worry about?

GEORGETTE: Lots of things. Mostly I used to worry about Margaret Rose and her daddy. Wondering what was going to happen to us all. I knew so little about Henry, and I was so young when we got married. Sometimes I'd worry that he wouldn't be good to the baby.

(Slim looks away. The Mexican band begins a waltz.)

Lady back in Tyler said I was a fool to worry about it. That I'd find out soon enough if he was gonna be good to her. Then I got a letter after that from Henry telling me all he was gonna do for Margaret Rose when he was free.

(He looks at her.)

It was a beautiful letter. I never worried any more about how he'd treat her after that. Then I started to worry about how he'd find a job. You know some men have trouble once they've been in the Pen. But now he has one, so that was all foolishness, too, wasn't it.?

(The music fades out. The train whistle is heard again.)

SLIM: Yes, it was.

GEORGETTE: I'm trying to break myself of the habit of worrying. I knew a girl in the restaurant that had turned her hair white at twenty-five from worrying. Of course, she had a lot to worry her, her husband had deserted her. Left her with four small children. I don't see how a man could desert his little children. Do you?

(Slim seems embarrassed and uncomfortable. In the distance the train whistle can be heard again.)

What train is that?

SLIM: *(Getting up.)* The Texas and New Orleans.

GEORGETTE: Is New Orleans far from here?

SLIM: Pretty far.

GEORGETTE: *(Looking toward backyard D. R.)* Is it? I don't know my geography too well.

SLIM: Miss Georgette…

GEORGETTE: *(Turns to him.)* Yessir.

SLIM: Miss Georgette. Suppose things hadn't worked out like they have and Henry had turned out different?

GEORGETTE: How do you mean?

SLIM: I mean, if he hadn't gotten a job and he was drinking and gambling again. What would you do?

GEORGETTE: I don't know. I used to ask myself that. Sometimes I think I'd just want to throw myself in the river.

SLIM: *(Getting up again.)* Oh, I wouldn't do that.

GEORGETTE: Don't worry, I wouldn't. I meant I'd just feel like it. I'd feel so discouraged. I don't really know what I'd do. Why do you ask me that?

SLIM: *(Walking away to D. L.)* Nothing. I just wondered. *(Pause.)*

GEORGETTE: I smell Cape Jessamines. Are they in your yard?

SLIM: *(Coming back to L. of C.)* No, ma'm. That's from the graveyard.

(Miss Clara comes on from the house. She comes out to the porch.)

MISS CLARA: Supper is about ready. Will you eat with us, Mrs. Thomas?

GEORGETTE: *(Gets up.)* No, ma'm. I think I'll wait for Henry, thank you. It's getting kind of dark for Margaret Rose to be climbing trees. I think I'd better get her down. *(She goes out through the yard and off D. R.)*

MISS CLARA: You didn't tell her, did you?

SLIM: *(Going across to D. R.)* I couldn't, Clara. I tried, but I just couldn't bring myself to it. *(A pause. He looks off R. then goes back to L. of steps.)* I wonder what will become of them?

MISS CLARA: *(As she fastens vine growing along porch post.)* What always becomes of women like that? I've seen her kind so many times in town on Saturdays coming in to buy what they can with what they have left over from their husband's drinking. Old before their time; stooped and bent from overwork. Wasting their youth. Sitting around… *(Going down steps to toolbox for a ball of cord.)* waiting for some old man to change, that probably couldn't change if he wanted to, until they have a house full of kids, and at forty look like old women.

SLIM: Yes'm.

MISS CLARA: And then one morning they wake up and find they're deserted.

(Sitter comes into the yard through the gate.)

SITTER: *(Coming D. L. of C.)* Has Mama been back this way?

MISS CLARA: No, ma'm.

SITTER: She hasn't been seen anywhere in the neighborhood.

SLIM: *(To Clara.)* I'm going to tell her. I swear, this time I'm going to tell her…
(He goes out D. R.)

SITTER: I hope he doesn't tell her in front of the little girl.

MISS CLARA: *(Going up onto porch.)* I'm sure he won't. *(She begins to tie the cord to vine and fasten it to post.)*

SITTER: It would be cruel to tell her in front of the little girl.
(In the distance, Slim can be heard calling: "Mrs. Thomas…Mrs. Thomas…" The music from the Mexican dance can be heard again.)
The Mexicans are going to have another dance. It's been a long time since I've watched them dance. They're pretty waltzers.
(A pause. In the distance Slim is heard calling: "Mrs. Thomas. Mrs. Thomas…!" As Sitter sits on arm of R. yard chair.)
If I had my life to live over again I'd learn to dance.
(She starts up, as if to stand on her feet, but for a second only, she sits back down as she goes on with the speech.)
I swear my whole life would have been different if I'd just learned to dance.
(Pause. Slim comes back in from D. R.)

SLIM: I can't find them.

MISS CLARA: What do you mean?

SLIM: They're not out back. I looked up and down the side street. *(He goes out the gate toward the front yard and looks off U. R.)* They couldn't have been gone long. I was talking to them not more than five minutes ago.

SITTER: *(Looking off L.)* And I don't see them out there. Isn't that strange?

SLIM: *(Coming back in to Clara.)* I'm going to walk down the street a ways and see if I can't find them.

(He goes out the gate and off U. R. calling: "Mrs. Thomas. Mrs. Thomas…" as the…)

LIGHTS FADE

FAST CURTAIN

ACT II

Scene 2

Clara Breedlove's. Two hours later. It has now gotten quite dark outside. The yard chairs have been turned on their sides. The porch light is on.

Miss Clara is seated on the steps of the porch. After a moment, Slim comes into the yard through the gate.

SLIM: *(Coming down to the steps.)* Have they come back?

MISS CLARA: *(Getting up.)* No. I don't understand it.…

SLIM: I'm worried sick about them.

MISS CLARA: I don't blame you. Do you realize it's been two hours since they left?

SLIM: Yes, I know it. I don't know where else I can look. I've checked the depot and the bus station. I think I'd better go call the Sheriff.

(As he goes up the steps Mrs. Tillman comes in through the hedge D. L. She is very upset.)

MRS. TILLMAN: *(Coming to L. of C.)* Miss Clara. Miss Clara…

(Slim stops.)

MISS CLARA: *(Going to her.)* What in the world is the matter, Mrs. Tillman?

MRS. TILLMAN: Oh, he's disappointed me. He's just broken my heart. Henry's gone. He's run off.

SLIM: *(Coming back down.)* He's run off?

MRS. TILLMAN: Taken everything in sight. Where's his wife?

MISS CLARA: She's gone too. We don't know where.

MRS. TILLMAN: *(She is crying now.)* Oh, the treachery of it! I did everything for him that I could think of. I poured black coffee down him. Sent him out to his room for a nap. Gave him every encouragement in the world. Then

I made Mr. Tillman take me out to supper because I was too nervous from all the excitement to cook and when we got back Henry was gone and he'd taken everything in sight with him. *(As she sits on back of R. yard chair.)* Fifty dollars out of my wardrobe, the ten dollars off the kitchen table, all my sterling silver and a black traveling bag.

MISS CLARA: *(Going to her.)* Did you call the Sheriff?

MRS. TILLMAN: Mr. Tillman did. He's on his way here now. I just had to talk to somebody. Oh, I feel so betrayed.

SLIM: I'm going on over to Mrs. Tillman's, Clara. I want to talk to the Sheriff. *(He goes out D. L.)*

MRS. TILLMAN: Mr. Tillman says it serves me right. Oh, I feel so betrayed. *(Standing up.)* Mr. Tillman is not speaking to me.

MISS CLARA: Well, I'm awfully sorry, but you'd just better try to quiet yourself. You won't do yourself any good being in a state like this. …

MRS. TILLMAN: Would you come back with me? Stay with me, while the Sheriff is there?

MISS CLARA: Why, certainly. *(She goes up into sun parlor, reaches inside the door and turns off the porch light.)*

MRS. TILLMAN: Thank you. You're a good, kind, dear friend….You warned me. You certainly warned me. But I was so sure I could trust…

MISS CLARA: *(Coming back down to her.)* Now, Mrs. Tillman. Just try and forget it. It's done.

MRS. TILLMAN: Mr. Tillman is fit to be tied.

MISS CLARA: *(Going toward L.)* I know, but we better go back to your house.

MRS. TILLMAN: *(Backing away.)* Oh, I can't face the Sheriff.

MISS CLARA: Now, yes, you can. Come on.

MRS. TILLMAN: I can't. I can't.

MISS CLARA: You're going to have to, Mrs. Tillman, sooner or later.

MRS. TILLMAN: I guess you're right.

MISS CLARA: Now, let's go.

MRS. TILLMAN: All right, dear. Thank you for your kindness.

(She goes out D. L. Miss Clara follows her. Mrs. Mavis has been hiding around the corner of the house U. R. She sneaks over to the graveyard, peers through the shadows. She carries a small black traveling bag. She comes quietly back to the steps again, looks once more to be sure she's not being seen, then opens the bag and quietly takes out some silverware. She hears a noise, puts the silverware back in the suitcase, shuts the top and shoves it under the steps. She hides again around the corner of the house, D. R. Georgette and Margaret

Rose come in from the front of the house U. R. Georgette is leading Margaret Rose by the hand. They both look exhausted.)

GEORGETTE: *(Coming down to the screen door.)* They must be in the back, honey....I'm just as lost as I can be. Well, it won't hurt to ask. *(She knocks at the screen door.)* Mr. Slim! *(Pause. She knocks again.)* Mrs. Breedlove! *(Pause.)* Everything's dark. Nobody's home.

MARGARET ROSE: I'm hungry.

GEORGETTE: I bet you are, honey. We'll get you something to eat in a little.

MARGARET ROSE: I'm so tired, Mama.

GEORGETTE: *(As they sit down on the steps.)* All right, honey. Let's sit down on these steps and rest a minute. Put your head in my lap. You'll rest better that way. I know we'll find Daddy before long if we're just patient. Somebody's bound to come soon.

(Margaret Rose puts her head in her mother's lap. Georgette hums and sings to her and strokes her head. Margaret Rose soon falls asleep. Georgette's voice trails away. The Mexican band can be heard again. She gently shifts Margaret Rose onto the edge of the porch. Mrs. Mavis comes scurrying in from D. R.)

MRS. MAVIS: Howdy do.

GEORGETTE: *(Getting up.)* Howdy do. Excuse me, could you tell me is this where Mr. Slim lives?

MRS. MAVIS: *(Coming to R. of C.)* Who?

GEORGETTE: Mr. Slim Murray or his sister, Mrs. Breedlove.

MRS. MAVIS: *(Moving below to L. of C.)* I don't know whose house it is. My memory ain't so good any more. I used to know everybody in town and all the houses, but I'm slippin'.

GEORGETTE: Well, I declare.

MRS. MAVIS: Yes'm. I'm slipping. *(Turning to her.)* I've run off from home so don't tell them you've seen me.

GEORGETTE: Oh, I wouldn't tell nobody. I don't know nobody to tell. But if I was you, I'd think twice before I'd go running out in the night this way.

MRS. MAVIS: I have to run off, honey. I'm running from my daughter. She won't let me have my supper.

GEORGETTE: She won't?

MRS. MAVIS: No, ma'm. She twisted my arm yesterday until it was black and blue.

GEORGETTE: I declare.

MRS. MAVIS: *(Moving L. a step.)* I'm gonna catch lightning bugs. *(Turns back.)* You want to help me catch 'em?

GEORGETTE: I don't think I better, thank you.

MRS. MAVIS: You want to go to the river swimmin'?

GEORGETTE: I don't swim, thank you.

MRS. MAVIS: What's your name, honey?

GEORGETTE: Mrs. Thomas. Mrs. Georgette Thomas.

MRS. MAVIS: What's the name of your little girl?

GEORGETTE: Margaret Rose.

MRS. MAVIS: Ain't that the name of the Queen of England?

GEORGETTE: Nope. Her sister.

MRS. MAVIS: Did you name it after her?

GEORGETTE: No, ma'm. I named her Margaret after my mama, that's dead, and Rose because it's my favorite flower.

MRS. MAVIS: *(Looking toward graveyard.)* Oh, Lord, honey. You hear that?

GEORGETTE: No, ma'm.

MRS. MAVIS: There's a dove in the yard. Hear it? Doves mean death. Go chase it away.

GEORGETTE: I don't hear any dove in the yard.

MRS. MAVIS: I do. Doves mean death. Go away, dove. I'm terrified of dyin', honey. Old as I am. I'm just terrified of dyin'. I live on this old road to the graveyard and the funerals come and go. Sitter hides me out back where I can't see 'em, but I know the sound of the hearse rumblin' by. Stay away from the graveyard. *(Moving L. a step.)* Yonder goes that dove again. Go away, dove. Scat!

(Georgette goes to her.)

There're ghosts in the graveyard. There's a headless woman that walks out there most every night. Her husband cut her head off because she was unfaithful and they say she can't rest until she finds her head again. Well, I gotta be goin'. I won't tell on you if you don't tell on me.

GEORGETTE: Tell on me for what?

MRS. MAVIS: There's a man out in the graveyard throwing the flowers on Miss Kate Dawson's grave all over creation. I crept up to that iron gate and peeked at him. I tell you it just makes your blood run cold to see it.

GEORGETTE: Oh, it's not true.

MRS. MAVIS: Yes, it is. The things I can see running around in the night like this. I caught Mrs. Ethan and Mr. Davenport in a car parked outside Mr. Davenport's house one night buck naked, doin' the act of darkness. Sitter don't like me to tell that, but I did. 'Course, they're both Yankees, so what can you expect? Sh! Look yonder… *(Going to hedge U. L.)* back in those shadows?

GEORGETTE: No. I don't see any man. I wish you'd stop talking like that. *(She goes back to Margaret Rose.)*

MRS. MAVIS: *(Coming back to her.)* I bet it is, and I know what he's looking for. That black traveling bag I have under there.

GEORGETTE: Aw, foot. You're just making the whole thing up.

MRS. MAVIS: No. I'm not. He hid a black bag outside the graveyard gate in the Buffalo grass. I grabbed it and ran off. Look and see. It's hid right under there…

SLIM: *(From off L., calls.)* Miss Georgette…

(Mrs. Mavis takes the bag and scurries off D. R. Slim comes in from D. L.)
Where in the world have you been?

GEORGETTE: *(Running to him.)* Mr. Slim. Oh, I'm so glad to see you.…

SLIM: I've looked all over town for you. I just asked the Sheriff to help start a search for you.

GEORGETTE: Oh, I'm so sorry to have worried you. But we got lost.

SLIM: You did?

GEORGETTE: Yessir. I was out in the back with Margaret Rose and I happened to look up and I saw a man walking about a half block away under the street light and I said to Margaret Rose, "That looks like your daddy to me," and I thought for a minute what to do and then I decided to take out after him to make sure. I was gonna tell you we were going but I was afraid he'd get away because by that time he was turning the corner…

SLIM: *(Interrupting.)* Well, it's all right as long as you're safe. I was so worried, Mrs. Thomas——

GEORGETTE: Have you heard anything from Henry? I'm worried to death——

SLIM: Yes'm. I just heard that Henry wasn't able to come for you tonight…

GEORGETTE: He wasn't able to come tonight?

SLIM: No, ma'm. You see…

GEORGETTE: Why, Mr. Slim?

SLIM: Well…you see…It's this way, Miss Georgette…Henry…well…he…
(Sitter comes in with her mother from D. R.)

SITTER: Slim. Mama just told me a long story about… *(She sees Georgette and starts toward her.)* My dear, I'm so sorry all this had to come to you.
(Slim tries to motion her to keep quiet.)

SLIM: Miss Sitter, please…

SITTER: What?
(She steps C., looks up and sees the expression on Slim's face. She is genuinely shocked.)
Oh. Oh, my heavens. I thought she knew. Oh, my Lord. What have I done?

GEORGETTE: What is it, Mr. Slim?

SLIM: Well, I was just about to tell you…

GEORGETTE: Has something happened to Henry?

SLIM: Yes, ma'm.

GEORGETTE: Is he hurt?

SLIM: No. It's not that…

GEORGETTE: Then what is it? Tell me, Mr. Slim. I'm going crazy if you don't tell me.

SLIM: He's in trouble.

GEORGETTE: What kind of trouble? Is it bad trouble?

SLIM: *(Looking away.)* He's run off. He got to drinking and stole some things from the lady he worked for and he's run off…

GEORGETTE: Oh.

SLIM: *(Turns to her.)* I'm sorry. I'm so sorry.

SITTER: Honey, I thought you knew. I'm so sorry.

(Georgette is crying. She turns away and hides her face behind porch post.)

MRS. MAVIS: What's she crying for?

SITTER: Come on, Mama. *(Sitter takes her mother by the hand. She leads her out D. R. A pause. The Mexican orchestra is playing another piece.)*

SLIM: *(Going up to her.)* You'll never know how bad I feel about the whole thing. I feel responsible because I told you a lie today. I didn't have the heart to tell you the truth. I don't know whether it would have made any difference if I'd told you the truth, but I'm sorry I had to lie to you. *(A pause.)*

GEORGETTE: I've been afraid. I've been so afraid all night. Something inside me kept saying, something's wrong. Something's not right.

(A pause. She is crying. Slim looks miserable.)

What am I gonna do? What in the name of God am I gonna do?

SLIM: You'll think of something. Try not to worry. Please, try not to worry.

(Again there is silence except for the music of the orchestra. Georgette wipes her eyes and moves D. L. of C. Slim follows.)

GEORGETTE: I had hoped my crying days were just about over. I've cried a lot in my life since my Mama died. I'm gonna have to stop it.…Well, nothing like hearing things all at once. *(She looks at Margaret Rose sleeping.)* Bless her heart. Bless her sweet little heart. *(She turns to Slim.)* How am I gonna tell her, Mr. Slim? That's what I want to know. How in the world am I ever gonna get the heart to tell her? That's what I want to know. She wanted a daddy so. That's all she thought about and talked about. How am I gonna tell her he's run off from us——*(A pause. She sits on the steps.)* It's such a pretty night. Such a pretty night for such a thing to have happened. Well, I guess it's better she didn't have a daddy at all with Henry acting this way. *(A pause.)*

SLIM: *(Going to her.)* You and the little girl had better stay here tonight with us.

GEORGETTE: Thank you. That's very kind of you.

SLIM: Have you had anything to eat?

GEORGETTE: No.

SLIM: You better come in the house and let me get you something to eat.

GEORGETTE: No, thank you. I couldn't eat a bite. I think I'd better get to bed, I'm tired. I'm suddenly so tired. *(She gets up and starts to pick up Margaret Rose. Slim stops her.)*

SLIM: Here, let me carry her for you.

GEORGETTE: No. That's all right. I'm used to carrying her.

SLIM: No, let me. I'd like to carry her.

> *(He is about to pick her up when Henry Thomas comes in through hedge U. L. He has a handful of crushed flowers and is very drunk. He stands at the corner of the yard. Slim and Georgette see him. Georgette looks at Slim and he goes over to Henry.)*

HENRY: *(Chucking the flowers in every direction.)* They hid the whiskey bottle from me, and they thought I couldn't find it and I couldn't find it, but there's no law yet, thank God, in the State of Texas says a man can't buy another bottle of whiskey and another one and another…

> *(He looks up at Slim. Georgette picks up Margaret Rose, carries her up into the sun parlor and puts her down on the settee.)*

Where's my suitcase?

SLIM: I don't know, Henry.

HENRY: I lost my suitcase. I was going on a trip, but I lost my suitcase. *(He puts his hand on Slim's shoulder.)* Don't tell nobody, but I'm going on a trip, as soon as I find my suitcase.

> *(Moving D. L. Slim follows.)*

I'm going on a trip so I can get me some rest. Miss Kate Dawson wouldn't give me no rest. Mrs. Tillman wouldn't give me no rest. "Don't do that, Henry, don't do this, Henry."

SLIM: Come on with me, Henry.

HENRY: *(Starting toward the house.)* Where's my wife?

> *(Slim takes him gently by the arm.)*

SLIM: Come on, Henry.

HENRY: *(Pulling away to U. L. Slim follows.)* I want to see my wife and my baby girl. I've wronged her. I've wronged them both. I'm gonna get down on my knees and beg their forgiveness. I told them I wasn't going to be out for another week and I've been out for a month. After she went and worked her fingers to the bone to get me a pardon. What kind of a man would act like that? I'm just not worth killing.

(He starts again toward the house. Slim pushes him back. Henry begins to cry.)

I want to do right. I swear to my Maker I want to do right, but I'm weak. I'm just plain weak. I swore to my blessed wife if she would stand by me and get me out of the Pen, I would never forget it, but I'm weak. I was gonna desert her. I never intended gettin' in touch with her or the baby....

(Henry again starts to the house. Slim takes him by the arm.)

SLIM: Now, come on, Henry.

HENRY: *(Jerking his arm free.)* No. I'm not going. I'm not going any place. I'm not moving from here until I tell them the truth about me. I'm gonna tell them to go on back and forget all about me. I'll bring them nothing but misery and regret.

(He makes a dash for the house.)

Where are they?

(Slim has him by the arm again. He tries to lead him off to the gate.)

SLIM: I said I want you out of here.

HENRY: *(Screaming, as he pulls away and comes D. L. of C.)* Go on back to Tyler. Misery and regret. That's all I mean. Misery and regret.

(Georgette comes out and over to him.)

GEORGETTE: Henry.

HENRY: Misery and regret.

GEORGETTE: Henry.

(She takes hold of him. He pauses and looks up at her, then puts his arms around her and hides his face against her.)

Please go with Mr. Slim, Henry. Please go on, Henry. I don't want our little girl to see you this way. She might wake up with you hollering so.

(A pause. He is crying again.)

HENRY: Georgette...Can you forgive me?

(She takes his head in her hands and looks at him.)

GEORGETTE: We'll talk in the morning, Henry.

HENRY: I want to do right. I swear to my Maker I want to do right. *(He lets go of her.)* Please say you'll forgive me.

GEORGETTE: We'll talk it all over in the morning, Henry. You go on now.

(He stands there for a moment. No one speaks. The Mexican orchestra can be heard in the distance. Henry turns and goes slowly out through the gate. Slim follows him. Georgette stands for a moment, watching them go. Then she turns and walks up the steps into sun parlor and over to Margaret Rose asleep

on the settee. She bends over, takes her in her arms and carries her slowly into the house as the…)

CURTAIN FALLS

ACT III
Scene 1

Two days later, around ten-thirty in the morning.

  Miss Clara is sitting on the steps of the porch, working on a box of seedlings. She has a cloth and watering can. Slim is standing over by the yard chairs, punching holes in the straps of his suitcase which is on the arms of the R. yard chair. His jacket and map are on L. chair. Georgette comes out from the house with a pair of Margaret Rose's shoes. She places them on edge of sun parlor. In the sun parlor are some children's toys: a small toy bear, a skipping rope, a coloring book, as well as Miss Clara's embroidery, magazines, sewing box, knitting, etc.

GEORGETTE: Isn't it a pretty day?

SLIM: Yes, it is.

GEORGETTE: *(Coming out on the porch.)* What time did you say that bus left for Old Gulf, Mr. Slim?

SLIM: Twelve o'clock.

GEORGETTE: What time is it now?

SLIM: *(Looking at his watch.)* Ten-thirty-two.

GEORGETTE: Yessir. I think I'm gonna make that bus this morning.

SLIM: All right. Just whatever you want to do. I can ride you down when it's time to go.

GEORGETTE: Thank you. I'll go get my things together.

  (She starts in the house. He calls to her.)

SLIM: Miss Georgette…

GEORGETTE: Yes?

SLIM: I'm leaving today, too. I'm going down to the jail and say good-bye. Is there anything you want from downtown?

GEORGETTE: No, I don't think so.

  (Slim turns back to his suitcase.)

  Mr. Slim.

SLIM: Yes'm.

GEORGETTE: I wonder if I could ask you to do a favor for me.

SLIM: Why, certainly.

GEORGETTE: I wonder if you'd tell Henry for me we're leaving.

SLIM: All right. Anything special you want me to say to him?

GEORGETTE: No, sir. Just that I'm going and where I'm going.

(She goes back inside the house. Miss Clara waits until she's out of sight and then she turns to Slim.)

MISS CLARA: Now, I wonder why Henry hasn't let her come to see him at the jail?

SLIM: *(Turns to suitcase.)* I don't know. She says he never would let her visit him at the Pen either.

MISS CLARA: He saw Mrs. Tillman.

SLIM: He did?

MISS CLARA: Yessir. She was all set to hire a lawyer to see if he couldn't get him off, but Mr. Tillman put his foot down. *(A pause.)* I don't know, of course, why she would want to see him again. I wouldn't want to see him or hear from him ever again if he were mine. Have they sentenced him yet?

SLIM: No. Next week. But he knows he's got to go back to the Pen. Best he can hope for is a short sentence.

MISS CLARA: I wonder if she's told the little girl anything yet?

SLIM: I don't know.

(She gets up and gets a small trowel from toolbox.)

MISS CLARA: I think my flowers are going to look real pretty this year, don't you?

SLIM: Yes, I do.

MISS CLARA: I think it's nice the way people now are all taking an interest in their yards. Mrs. Tillman's yard looks like a regular flower garden. Of course, she's always had someone working in it full-time. A yard needs someone working in it all day long to get it to look its best.

SLIM: I know.

MISS CLARA: *(Walking over to him.)* Some day I'm gonna plant me all the fruit trees I want. I'm gonna plant me a pomegranate tree and a persimmon tree and a peach tree and a pear tree… *(A pause.)* Have you decided exactly when you're leaving?

SLIM: This afternoon after I see them off on the bus. *(A pause. Miss Clara looks at him.)*

MISS CLARA: You're in love with that girl, aren't you, Slim?

(A pause. He looks away.)

SLIM: Yes, Clara, I am.

MISS CLARA: Have you told her how you feel?

SLIM: No. I don't think I have the right to. She's still married to Henry and that's his little girl. And besides I don't know that she wants to hear it.

MISS CLARA: You don't think she'll try to go on with Henry now, do you?

SLIM: I don't know. I haven't felt I should ask her. And she hasn't wanted to tell me. There's a lot I want to ask her and a lot I want to tell her, but then I'm with her and I don't know how to talk to her about what I want to talk about, so we just discuss a place for her to go and find work.

(Sitter comes into the yard from D. R. Miss Clara goes and sits on steps and continues to work on her seedlings.)

SITTER: *(Coming to Clara.)* I guess you wondered what happened to us all day yesterday. I didn't put my foot out of the house, I was just prostrated on the bed all day. Just worn out by the other night. I'm still exhausted, heaven knows. Emotionally and otherwise.

(Sitting on L. end of steps. Mrs. Mavis comes in from D. R., goes across toward hedge U. L.)

Look at Mama. Isn't she a wonder? Fresh as daisy. Mama, where do you get all your energy from?

MRS. MAVIS: *(Stops L. of C.)* From livin' right. I live right, honey. I eat my greens. I get my exercise and I eat corn bread for breakfast every morning of my life. *(She goes out the gate and stands looking over at the graveyard.)*

SITTER: How are you all?

MISS CLARA: Pretty good.

SITTER: Too bad about Henry.

MISS CLARA: I know. *(Clara gets up and puts box of seedlings under the porch.)*

SITTER: Mama was right the other night. The Sheriff said he found the flowers on Miss Kate's grave just thrown in every direction. Isn't that spooky? I told Mama it's a wonder he hadn't killed her. Spying on him that way. She's gonna get killed one of these nights running around peeking. Where's Mrs. Thomas?

MISS CLARA: *(Looking at Slim.)* Packing her suitcase. She's leaving on the twelve o'clock bus.

(Slim turns away.)

SITTER: Is she? The poor thing.

SLIM: *(Picking up his suitcase.)* I've got to run downtown, Clara. Can I bring you anything?

MISS CLARA: *(Going over to him.)* I don't think so, Slim, thank you. I'll be over at Mrs. Tillman's, I expect, when you get back. She asked me to spend the day with her.

SLIM: All right.

(He goes out the gate and off U. R. Clara stands a moment looking after him, then goes and picks up and puts the map in his jacket pocket.)

SITTER: We went by Mrs. Tillman's before coming over here. She's terribly depressed. It's just pitiful. She feels so personally betrayed.

MRS. MAVIS: *(Coming back in the yard.)* I ate my corn bread this morning. I ate my corn bread yesterday morning.

SITTER: Sh, Mama. We know all about it. *(A pause.)* It's a pretty day. Isn't it a pretty day?

MISS CLARA: Uh. Huh. *(She goes and puts awl and trowel in the toolbox.)*

MRS. MAVIS: *(U. L. of C.)* Do you all remember the War?

SITTER: No and you don't either, Mama. You're not that old. Mama has been running around this morning talking about the Civil War like she had been there.

MRS. MAVIS: *(As she goes and sits in a yard chair.)* I was there. I remember the War like yesterday.

SITTER: You weren't there, Mama. Your mama was there, but you weren't there.

MRS. MAVIS: I was, too.

SITTER: How could you have been there when you weren't born?

MRS. MAVIS: Were you born?

SITTER: No, Mama. Good heavens.

MRS. MAVIS: Well, how do you know whether I was born or not?

SITTER: *(Getting up and going to her.)* Well, this is not gonna get us anywhere, Mama. Come on. I've got to get dinner on.

MRS. MAVIS: I don't want to go. You go.

SITTER: Mama, Miss Clara doesn't want to fool with you.

MISS CLARA: She won't bother me, Sitter. Let her stay if she wants.

SITTER: No. I'll just have to come for her later. Come on, Mama.

(Mrs. Mavis gets up.)

Tell Mrs. Thomas good-bye for me, Miss Clara.

MISS CLARA: All right.

(They start out of the yard toward gate.)

You come back later on.

SITTER: All right.

(They go out through the gate and off U. R. Georgette comes out into the sun parlor from house with her suitcase, handbag, and hats—one her own, one Margaret Rose's. Miss Clara calls to her.)

MISS CLARA: Finished your packing?

GEORGETTE: Yes, ma'm.

(She puts suitcase down beside chair L. Handbag and hats on chair. Miss Clara goes inside to sun parlor.)

MISS CLARA: Well, I'll say good-bye to you now, Mrs. Thomas. I'm spending the day with Mrs. Tillman and I've got to go in a few minutes.

GEORGETTE: I sure do thank you, Mrs. Breedlove, for all you've done for me and Margaret Rose. And I'm so sorry about all the trouble we caused everybody.

MISS CLARA: Well, heavens. It wasn't your fault. *(She puts cloth and water can on table.)*

GEORGETTE: I'm just so mortified by it all.

MISS CLARA: Well, you needn't be.

(A pause. During the following Clara gathers her sewing bag, embroidery, knitting, magazines, etc. Georgette gathers a small toy bear, color book, skipping rope and packs them in the suitcase.)

I understand you say you were going to Old Gulf?

GEORGETTE: Yes, ma'm. I've heard there's a boom on down there and plenty of jobs to be had.

MISS CLARA: *(By the rocker R.)* Of course, it's none of my business, Mrs. Thomas, but I don't understand why you don't go back to Tyler where you're known. It seems to me it would make everything so much easier.

GEORGETTE: *(At suitcase L.)* No, ma'm. It wouldn't. I would just hate to go back there. They'd ask so many questions. They all knew I was comin' here and why. An' then I wasn't able to find work back there before and I have to get work right away. We don't have a whole lot to last us.

MISS CLARA: Well, I don't blame you. I know how you feel. *(A pause.)* Have you told your little girl yet about Henry?

GEORGETTE: No, ma'm. I haven't. I'm a real coward about it. I tried all morning, but I haven't had the heart yet. I know I've got to. *(A pause.)* Mr. Slim's leaving today too, isn't he?

MISS CLARA: Yes, I think he's going this afternoon.

(Margaret Rose comes into the sun parlor from the house with a cry-baby doll.)

GEORGETTE: Margaret Rose, come and say good-bye to Miss Clara.

MISS CLARA: Good-bye, Margaret Rose.

MARGARET ROSE: Good-bye.

MISS CLARA: I've got to go on. Good-bye, Mrs. Thomas—Georgette. Good-bye. *(They shake hands.)*

GEORGETTE: I want to thank you again for all your kindness.

MISS CLARA: Well, I was glad to do anything I could. Send me a postcard and let me know how you make out.

GEORGETTE: Yes, ma'm.

(Miss Clara goes out the screen door, down the steps and out the yard and off D. L.)

MARGARET ROSE: Where is she going to?

GEORGETTE: To visit a lady friend of hers. Did you thank Mr. Slim for that baby-doll?

MARGARET ROSE: Yes, ma'm.

GEORGETTE: Margaret Rose…

MARGARET ROSE: Mama, tell me a story.

GEORGETTE: All right. Do you want a fairy story or a real one?

MARGARET ROSE: A real one.

(Georgette sits in rocker R. Margaret Rose on stool C. During the following Georgette changes Margaret Rose's shoes.)

GEORGETTE: All right. Once upon a time on a cotton farm outside of Lovelady, there lived a little girl with her mother and her daddy.

MARGARET ROSE: What was her name?

GEORGETTE: Who, honey?

MARGARET ROSE: The little girl's?

GEORGETTE: Georgette Price.

MARGARET ROSE: That was you, wasn't it?

GEORGETTE: Yes, ma'm. And that little girl had a dog named Bounce and a cat named Squirt. And she used to run through the fields with Bounce on one side and Squirt on the other. An' one day she begged her daddy to get her a pony, and he said he had too much to do to fool with any pony, but she begged and begged… *(She pauses. She holds Margaret Rose close to her.)* Margaret Rose, I'm going to have to talk to you about something. …

MARGARET ROSE: Yes'm…

GEORGETTE: You know we came here to get you a daddy?

MARGARET ROSE: Yes'm. He can't come today.

GEORGETTE: How did you know that?

MARGARET ROSE: I just knew you'd say that. But he can come tomorrow, can't he?

GEORGETTE: Well…I don't know yet…you see…

(Slim comes onto the porch from front of house U. R. He sees Margaret Rose and Georgette in the sun parlor. He goes down the porch to the screen door.)

SLIM: Margaret Rose, would you run out in the backyard for a minute? I want to talk to your mother.

MARGARET ROSE: Yessir.

(He holds the door open for her while she goes out to the porch and then down the steps and off to the backyard D. R. He goes back into the sun parlor.)

SLIM: I saw Henry. I told him you were leaving.

GEORGETTE: What did he say? *(She gets up and puts Margaret Rose's shoes in the suitcase.)*

SLIM: He asked what time and I said twelve and he said, well, I guess if I want to see her and my little girl it's my last chance for a while and I said I guess it was.

GEORGETTE: Yessir, but I don't want to take my little girl over to the jail, Mr. Slim. That's the one thing I can't do.

SLIM: He didn't ask that. He said he'd rather die than have either you or the little girl see him locked up. He said that's the reason he hadn't seen you before when you came to the jail yesterday. And that's why he'd never let you visit him in the Pen.

GEORGETTE: Yessir.

SLIM: *(Moving away to rocker.)* He asked the Sheriff if he would let him come out here to see you and your little girl.

GEORGETTE: Out here?

SLIM: Yes'm. The Sheriff said it was all right as far as he was concerned, and I said in that case he'd better hurry as you were leaving at twelve, so we put him in the car and brought him out. They're out in front now and I said I'd come on back and see how you felt about it.

(A pause. Georgette gets up and goes to the screen door, looking out.)

GEORGETTE: I don't know what to say. I haven't told Margaret Rose about her daddy yet. I was just trying to tell her when you came in. *(A pause—turns to him.)* What do you think I ought to do, Mr. Slim?

SLIM: I sure don't know how to advise you. Of course, having seen Henry and having talked to him I have to admit I feel kind of sorry for him. He looks so cussed and kind of down...

GEORGETTE: He does? *(She turns away and closes suitcase.)*

SLIM: Just whipped. Of course, you understand the Sheriff'll take the handcuffs off before he sees the little girl.

GEORGETTE: He will?

SLIM: Yes, ma'm.

GEORGETTE: Well, I guess I should in all fairness to him. He's never seen our little girl. *(A pause.)* All right. It'll be all right with me.

SLIM: Yes'm. I'll go and get Henry.

GEORGETTE: Yessir.

(He goes quickly out the door and up the porch and off U. R. calling: "Sheriff!" Georgette stands there a moment and then goes outside too. She stands on the steps thinking until she sees Henry approaching and then comes down the steps. The Sheriff brings Henry in through the gate. He walks away to the gate to one side and Henry goes over toward Georgette.)

HENRY: Hello, Georgette.

GEORGETTE: Hello, Henry.

HENRY: I sure thank you for letting me say hello to my little girl.

GEORGETTE: That's all right.

HENRY: And I want to tell you again how sorry I am for all the trouble I caused you.

GEORGETTE: That's all right, Henry. I guess we shouldn't have come on this way...without...but you see I thought I... (*A pause.*) Henry. What happened?
(*He has his head down. She sees he doesn't want to talk about it.*)
Don't you want to talk about it?

HENRY: No, not now, Georgette. I wouldn't bother you at all, but I didn't know when I'd get another chance to see the baby. I'm pretty sure I'll be sent back to the Pen.

GEORGETTE: I'm sorry, Henry. I won't tell her where you're going until later on. I'll just say you've come to meet her and you'll see her later.

HENRY: That's OK with me.

GEORGETTE: She didn't know you were in prison before either. She just thought you were away.

HENRY: OK I'm not going to say anything. Can I see her now?

GEORGETTE: Uh. Huh——(*She turns to go.*) Oh, one more thing. She's liable to ask you to sing "New San 'Tonia Rose."

HENRY: What is she gonna ask me to sing that for?

GEORGETTE: Well...you see I used to tell her about my first meeting you and how you were singing "New San 'Tonia Rose," with the string band....Do you remember, Henry?...

HENRY: Yep.

GEORGETTE: And I always promised her you'd sing it first thing when you met.
(*Slim comes in from U. R. to the gate.*)

HENRY: OK
(*A pause. They both seem embarrassed.*)

SLIM: I don't want to hurry you all, but if you want to make that twelve o'clock bus, Mrs. Thomas...

GEORGETTE: All right. I'll go get Margaret Rose.
(*She goes out the backyard and off D. R. The Sheriff goes and takes handcuffs off Henry and goes back and stands beside Slim who has come in just to the L. of gate. Henry walks away to D. L. Georgette and Margaret Rose come in from D. R. Margaret Rose gets very timid when she sees the men and makes her mother stop at the opposite end of the yard D. R. of C.*)
There's your daddy, honey. He can only stay a minute but he wants to say hello to you.

MARGARET ROSE: Yes'm.

GEORGETTE: *(Pointing to Henry.)* That's your daddy, honey. Henry, this is Margaret Rose.

HENRY: *(A step toward her.)* Hello, Margaret Rose.

MARGARET ROSE: Hello. *(She pulls her mother down to her level.)* Ask him to sing "New San 'Tonia Rose."

GEORGETTE: All right, honey. Henry, she wants to know if you'll sing "New San 'Tonia Rose."

HENRY: OK *(He walks toward them.)* Come here to me and I'll sing it to you.
(He stands there waiting for her to come. She starts toward him then hangs back.)

GEORGETTE: You go on and sing it, Henry, then I expect she'll come to you.

HENRY: O.K. *(He sings snatches from "New San Antonio Rose." He finishes singing, sits on arm of R. yard chair. He looks at Margaret Rose.)*

GEORGETTE: Wasn't that pretty honey?
(Margaret Rose doesn't answer.)
Aren't you gonna thank your daddy?

MARGARET ROSE: Thank you.

HENRY: *(Standing up.)* Will you come and shake hands with me now?
(She is still shy and looks at her mother.)

GEORGETTE: It's all right, honey. Go on and shake hands with your daddy.
(Henry comes toward her with his hand outstretched. Margaret Rose gets very shy and hangs back.)
Go shake hands with your daddy, honey.
(She buries her face against her mother's body, then she slowly walks toward him. Henry continues slowly coming toward them. When Henry gets up close to Margaret Rose, he suddenly makes a break and runs past her toward the backyard D. R. Georgette is horrified. She screams as if to stop him.)
Henry!

SLIM: *(Turns and sees him running. He calls after him.)* Henry! Henry, you crazy fool.
(He takes out after him with the Sheriff following. Henry is almost out when he trips and falls. Slim and the Sheriff grab him. Henry tries to get free but the Sheriff quickly handcuffs him and pulls him up to his feet. The Sheriff and Slim take him out of the yard. Margaret Rose and Georgette watch them lead him off through the gate and off U. R. Margaret Rose goes up to the gate and looks after them. Georgette sits on the steps and covers her face with her hands. She is crying.)

MARGARET ROSE: *(Coming back to the steps.)* Why are they taking my daddy away? *(Pause. She sits beside Georgette.)*

GEORGETTE: *(Wiping her eyes.)* Well, Margaret Rose, your daddy gets into trouble and…

MARGARET ROSE: What kind of trouble?

GEORGETTE: Oh, I don't know, honey. Just things he shouldn't do. He doesn't mean it, you see, but he does it. And then he has to be punished for it. ...

MARGARET ROSE: Will he ever stop getting into trouble?

GEORGETTE: I don't know, Margaret Rose.

MARGARET ROSE: Why don't you know?

GEORGETTE: Because nobody can know that, I reckon, but your daddy.

MARGARET ROSE: Aren't we gonna see him any more?

GEORGETTE: I'm afraid not for a long time.

MARGARET ROSE: Yes, ma'm. *(A pause. She embraces her mother.)* I'm going out to get baby-doll.

(Margaret Rose gets up and goes outside D. R. Georgette sits looking after her. Slim has come in through the gate. He stands for a moment watching. After a moment he comes down to her. Pause.)

GEORGETTE: What time is it, Mr. Slim?

SLIM: It's twelve.

GEORGETTE: When's the next bus for Old Gulf?

SLIM: Not until tomorrow.

GEORGETTE: *(Getting up and going up into sun parlor.)* Yes, sir. Well, we'd better go to the bus station and figure out where we're gonna go.

SLIM: *(Going up onto porch.)* Miss Georgette, do you know what you could do?

GEORGETTE: What's that?

SLIM: You and the little girl could drive down to the Valley with me. I've got plenty of room in my car and I'd like the company...

GEORGETTE: Oh, I wouldn't care to put you out any.

SLIM: You wouldn't put me out a bit. I hate to ride by myself.

GEORGETTE: Do you?

SLIM: Yes, ma'm.

GEORGETTE: *(Picking up suitcase, handbag, and hats.)* Well...

SLIM: *(Opening screen door.)* Please, come on and do that.

GEORGETTE: *(Coming out on the porch.)* Well...do you think I could get work down that way?

SLIM: Yes, ma'm. I know you can. There are a lot of towns down there close together. Nice clean towns I've heard. You could just take your pick. And they've got wonderful schools for the little girl and the best climate in the world. It's real dry.

(She puts suitcase and handbag down.)

GEORGETTE: Is that so?

SLIM: That's what they tell me. I think you'd like it down there.

GEORGETTE: I'm sure I would.

SLIM: Please say you'll come.

GEORGETTE: Well, OK If you're sure we wouldn't be putting you out any.

SLIM: Not a bit.

GEORGETTE: Well…OK

SLIM: Fine.

GEORGETTE: When would you like to leave?

SLIM: I'm ready any time. I just have to stop over at Mrs. Tillman's to tell Clara good-bye. I've got my suitcase in the car.

GEORGETTE: Well, I'll call Margaret Rose. *(She goes down the steps and toward R.)*

SLIM: *(Coming down R. of C.)* Miss Georgette…

GEORGETTE: *(Stops D. R.)* Yessir?

SLIM: I wanted to tell you. I thought I ought to tell you…I hope it won't change your mind or make any difference to you…

GEORGETTE: What's that, Mr. Slim?

SLIM: I love you, Miss Georgette. I fell in love with you the minute you walked into the yard the other day. I wasn't going to say anything, but now… *(A pause.)*

GEORGETTE: Yessir. *(A pause.)* I'm glad you told me. I told Margaret Rose last night that in my opinion you were the nicest man I'd ever met.

SLIM: You did?

GEORGETTE: Yessir. *(A pause. Georgette goes to the edge of the yard D. R. Calling.)* Margaret Rose…Margaret Rose… *(Margaret Rose comes in.)* We're about ready to go, honey.

MARGARET ROSE: Are we going to the ocean?

GEORGETTE: *(Leading her to C.)* No, sweetheart.

MARGARET ROSE: I thought you said…

GEORGETTE: I know, I know. *(Putting hat on Margaret Rose.)* We've changed. We're going to the Valley.

MARGARET ROSE: The Valley?

GEORGETTE: That's right.

MARGARET ROSE: What's there?

GEORGETTE: Lemon trees and orange trees and grapefruit trees and watermelon patches and cotton fields, lots of cotton fields. Acres and acres of cotton fields. *(She gets her handbag from porch.)*

SLIM: Are you ready?

GEORGETTE: I am. How about you, Margaret Rose?

MARGARET ROSE: Yes, ma'm.

(Georgette takes her by the hand.)

GEORGETTE: From Lovelady to Tyler, from Tyler to Harrison, from Harrison to the Valley. Margaret Rose, we sure do get around.

(Slim starts out gate with the suitcase. Georgette and Margaret Rose follow as the… Curtain falls.)

END OF PLAY

The Roads to Home

PRODUCTION

The Roads to Home was first presented by the Manhattan Punch Line Theatre, Inc., in association with Indian Falls Productions, at the Manhattan Punch Line Theatre, in New York City, on March 25, 1982. It was directed by Calvin Skaggs; the setting was by Oliver D'Arcy; costumes were by Edi Giguere; the lighting was by Richard Dorfman; the production stage manager was Ellen Sontag; and the general manager was Mark Richard. The cast, in order of appearance, was as follows:

Mabel Votaugh	Carol Fox
Vonnie Hayhurst	Rochelle Oliver
Annie Gayle Long	B. Hallie Foote
Mr. Long	Greg Zittel
Jack Votaugh	Jess Osuna
Eddie Hayhurst	Jon Berry
Dave Dushon	Ron Marr
Cecil Henry	James Paradise
Greene Hamilton	Tony Noll

SETTING

Act One: *A Nightingale*
Early April, 1924. Houston, Texas
The kitchen of Jack and Mabel Votaugh

Act Two: *The Dearest of Friends*
Early Fall, 1924. The living room of the Votaughs

Act Three: *Spring Dance*
Spring, 1928. Austin, Texas
A garden outside an auditorium.

THE ROADS
TO HOME

ACT ONE: A NIGHTINGALE

CHARACTERS
    Vonnie Hayhurst
    Mabel Votaugh
    Annie Gayle Long
    Mr. Long

Time: 1924, Early April
Place: Houston, Texas
The kitchen of Mabel and Jack Votaugh around seven in the morning. Mabel,
42, is at the window looking outside. After a moment, she comes back into the
room and goes to the stove and pours herself a cup of coffee. She stands, drink-
ing the coffee, thinking, when a neighbor, Vonnie Hayhurst, 40, comes in.

VONNIE: Morning, Mabel.
    (Mabel hasn't heard her enter and is so startled by the greeting that she almost
    drops the coffee cup.)
    Oh, I'm sorry I scared you. I thought you heard me come in.
MABEL: No. Heavens. I was lost in thought. I didn't hear anything. I was half
    expecting company and…
VONNIE: Oh, well, then if you're expecting company I'll go and come back
    another time.
MABEL: No. No. Don't go.
VONNIE: I'm not sensitive. I don't want to be in the way if you're expecting
    company. It's just that I saw Jack leave awhile ago for work, and I thought
    I'd come over to let you know I'm back from my trip before I started my
    housework.
MABEL: I'm glad you did. I've missed you while you were away.

VONNIE: Who is your company?

MABEL: Oh, God. *(She sighs.)* You know that sad little girl from Harrison that used to come over here all the time?

VONNIE: Oh, yes.

MABEL: Well, she's the one.

VONNIE: Oh. She lives on the other side of Houston now doesn't she?

MABEL: She does.

VONNIE: How does she come all the way over here?

MABEL: By street car.

VONNIE: It must take her forever.

MABEL: I suppose. She tells me she rides the streetcars day and night.

VONNIE: I thought she had stopped coming over here?

MABEL: She had. Then right after you left on your vacation she started coming over here again. She comes every day now. And she sits and she sits and she sits and she sits. Sometimes, she doesn't say a word. Sometimes, she talks just as normal as you and me and sometimes she just babbles, going a mile a minute. I don't know what her husband is thinking of, letting her roam around like this.

VONNIE: She has a husband?

MABEL: Oh, yes. Didn't you know that?

VONNIE: I guess I did, but I've just forgotten.

MABEL: And two sweet little children. And a mother and a brother. The brother is up north in school someplace. Some rich fancy school. They all come from the north originally, you know. I wrote my sister the other day and I asked her if she knew where the mother is. She is a sensible woman, even though she's had this miserable sad life, and I'm sure she doesn't know. …

VONNIE: *(Interrupting.)* Why was her life so sad?

MABEL: Whose?

VONNIE: The mother's.

MABEL: Oh, well. She was a Yankee, you see, and when they first moved to Harrison when she was a bride, they were very cooly received. Then they lost four children out of six, and she and her husband never were congenial, even though he made money every which way he turned. He had a store, he made money. He owned farms, he made money. He had a ranch, he made money. He was president of the bank. And then we had a series of crop failures and his best friend was a planter named Sledge, and Mr. Sledge had seven years of crop failures and he kept borrowing from the bank to keep going and one day Mr. Gayle, that was her father's name, without any warning, Mr. Sledge said, foreclosed on him and took all of his land and his plantation house. And that same afternoon Mr. Sledge came into town as Mr. Gayle came out of the bank with Annie and Mr. Sledge, they say, called his name, and Mr. Gayle walked over to him. He shot him, killing him, right in front of Annie. There was a trial, but Mr. Sledge pleaded temporary insanity and got free. We all felt sorry for Mrs. Gayle and her daughter and son, but they were left all kinds of money, and they traveled around a lot, up north mostly. Annie went to college someplace up there, and the next thing I heard she had married Mr. Long and was living in Houston. When Mama and Sissy came to visit me, we went calling on her. She didn't live far from me then. She said her mother traveled back and forth between Rhode Island and Houston. She showed us a picture of her husband and she said he was in business in Houston. The business of spending her money, Mama said later she'd heard. And she already had the two children. They were only a year apart and were still babies, but she had three in help, so she didn't seem burdened. The week after Mama and Sissy left she returned my call and then it started. She used to come every day. Sometimes before Jack left for work and she'd stay all day until Jack came home at night. Just talking about old times in Harrison, you know and all the people we knew back then, until Jack said I had to call her mother or her husband or somebody and tell them to keep her home, since he thought she was crazy. I said I didn't think she was crazy as much as upset, and I couldn't call them. But he did. He talked to the husband and he said he wasn't nice about it at all. But, anyway, she stopped her visits and the next we knew they had bought a palace of a house on the other side of Houston by the bayou, and we didn't hear another word from her until ten days ago when she appeared one morning, and said she had been riding the street car. I guess it was deceitful of me, but I didn't tell Jack about her coming back, but she stayed on last night until he came home, and he pitched a fit when he saw her. He marched right to the phone to call her husband, but he wasn't home, and he called again this morning before he left for work and he still wasn't home. But Jack said he will get hold of him if he had to call out there every five minutes, and I guess he did because she certainly hasn't come this morning. She is usually here by seven at the latest. How was your trip?

VONNIE: Oh, it was lovely. I hadn't seen my sister and her children for a year, and you know how children grow in a year. I just wouldn't have recognized the children at all. Sweet little things, you know. And the parties. Morning, noon and night. Coffee, teas and luncheons, bridge, dinner, picture show parties. I said Sister you all are wearing me out; I will have to go back to Houston for a rest. And I've gained too. All that rich food. Sister just begged me to stay another month. No, I better not, I told her, I don't want my husband to get too used to my not being around. That's how Celia Edwards lost her husband, you know.

MABEL: Who is Celia Edwards?

VONNIE: Oh, that's right I guess she had moved before you got here. She lived at the end of the block. She went away one summer to visit her family. She stayed for two months, and when she came home, she found her husband had taken up with someone else and wanted a divorce.

MABEL: Did she give it to him?

VONNIE: Yes she did.

(Annie Gayle comes in. Mabel glances at Vonnie.)

MABEL: Good morning, Annie. Have you met my next door neighbor, Mrs. Hayhurst?

(Annie looks at her.)

VONNIE: Good morning.

ANNIE: Is she from Harrison?

VONNIE: No, honey. I'm from Louisiana. Monroe Louisiana. I have never seen Harrison. Heard a lot about it though. It must be a lovely town from all I've heard. My husband works for the railroad just like Mabel's and we get passes and some Sunday I'm going to take a train ride into Harrison.

(Annie shapes a gun with her finger.)

ANNIE: *(Pointing at no one.)* Pow. Pow. Pow.

(Then she is silent and withdrawn. Mabel and Vonnie exchange glances.)

MABEL: How are your children?

(Annie doesn't answer.)

She has two lovely children. A beautiful girl and a handsome little boy. The little girl is name Esther and the boy Davis. Was Davis named after your husband?

(Again no answer from Annie.)

Let's see now. Esther is six and Davis is four and a half.

(Annie begins to vocalize, practicing scales, quietly at first. Then louder and louder. Vonnie and Mabel exchange glances and shake their heads in sadness. Annie stops vocalizing. She stands up, curtsies and then goes to the center of the room and sings. Very simply and beautifully and with deep feeling, "My Old Kentucky Home.")

She has such a sweet voice doesn't she? She sings just like a nightingale.

VONNIE: I don't know. I've never heard a nightingale sing. Have you?

MABEL: No. That's just an expression, you know.

VONNIE: I know that, but it just occurred to me I had never heard a nightingale. I had a cousin that sang some. They called her the Mockingbird of the South.

MABEL: Jenny Lind was known as the Swedish Nightingale.

VONNIE: Oh, yes. So she was.

ANNIE: Do either of you ladies sing alto?

VONNIE: No, heavens. I can't carry a tune.

ANNIE: Laura Vaughn sings alto. She lives in Dallas. I wrote her five times that I was coming to Dallas soon on a visit, so we could sing duets once again like we did when we were girls back in dear old Harrison.

MABEL: And they did, too. They sang beautiful duets together. Like two nightingales.

(Annie sits down.)

ANNIE: Do you remember that time back in dear old Harrison, when Randy Lewis and Marjorie Hancock and Elizabeth Vaughn gave a concert for charity. Elizabeth played the piano and Randy sang and Marjorie recited. Your turn will come next my Mama said. But we were gone by the next year. Gone from dear old Harrison. I hope sincerely to go back there one day to give that recital if Laura Vaughn will return too and sing a duet with me. I am practicing night and day for that event.

MABEL: Would you like a cup of coffee, Vonnie?

VONNIE: No, thank you.

MABEL: Annie?

(Annie doesn't answer. Again she shapes her hands as a gun and goes "Pow. Pow. Pow.")

VONNIE: *(Ignoring her.)* It's been a lovely spring, hasn't it?

MABEL: Too much rain though. Sissy says the cotton farmers in Harrison are about to lose their minds. Wet years, you know, are death on the cotton. My Papa used to always say, "I don't care how dry it gets, we'll always make some kind of a crop, but when it starts in raining you can just forget cotton and everything else.

VONNIE: Annie, what church are you affiliated with?

ANNIE: None.

VONNIE: None?

ANNIE: None.

VONNIE: *(To Mabel.)* What church is her family affiliated with?

MABEL: I don't know. They weren't churchgoers as I remember. What church were your sweet Mother and Father associated with, honey?

(Annie doesn't answer.)

I think they were Presbyterians or Episcopalian. They certainly weren't Catholics, I know that.

ANNIE: My husband, Mr. Long, is a Catholic. He's studying for the priesthood.

MABEL: No, you have that wrong, Annie. He's a married man. Married to you, sweetheart, a married man can't be a priest.

ANNIE: He's a priest and he says Mass every morning before breakfast. *(A pause.)* Harrison is not such a nice town after all, you know. My Mama never did care for it. She always said when I was growing up and saying how much I loved dear old Harrison and all my friends: Laura Vaughn, Cootsie Reynolds, Essie Hawkins and Callie Anne Knolt. No, this is not such a nice town. The streets are too muddy when it rains, like a bog hole, it rains all the time. Day and night. Rain. Rain. Rain. Rain. Watch out she used to say. We are all going to get web feet from the rain. Web feet. Quack. Quack. Quack. I am sorry I ever left Rhode Island she said. I regret the day. We would never have lost the children if we had stayed in Rhode Island. They have proper doctors there, and the swamps are drained and the rivers don't flood every other year, bringing typhoid and malaria, diphtheria and yellow fever. Go on back to Rhode Island, Papa said. No one is stopping you. Oh, you would like that, she said. A saloon every time you turn around, this is not a nice town. And it was not a nice town. Mama was right. It was certainly not a nice town. What's Mae Reeves and her husband doing driving out to the country every night not getting home until one or two in the morning? What's going on? He's embezzled the funds of his bank, Papa told her. He's been riding out in the country to try and talk people to keep their money on deposit and if he can't persuade them the bank will go under, for there is no money left in that bank now to withdraw. He gambled away some of it, loaned the rest foolishly to friends and now can't collect it. He's a bad banker, a corrupt and untrustworthy banker. They've closed the bank, and he's sent to the penitentiary. I've bought their house and we're moving in. I will not move in there, Mama said. I will not move into that tragic house. I will not. *(She stops talking as abruptly as she began. She begins to laugh softly. Then she opens her purse and takes out pictures of her children. She hands them to Vonnie and Mabel.)* Don't I have a sweet little brother and sister?

MABEL: That's not your brother and sister, honey. They're your children, Esther and Davis. *(To Vonnie.)* Aren't they lovely? *(To Annie.)* Where's your brother now? Still up North?

ANNIE: Harrison isn't such a nice town. Mama said she was glad that house

Papa made us move into burned down and we could move back to our other house. That was a fine enough house for her, Mama said.

MABEL: Oh, I remember that fire. It was terrible. We were awakened in the middle of the night. Mama sent her cook over to wake us up and we all sat on her front gallery and watched the flames...

ANNIE: Harrison is not such a nice town. Did you hear about the Baptist preacher? He ran off with Sis Gallagher's husband. Left her ashamed and mortified to face the town with two small children to raise.

MABEL: That's all forgotten, darling. Sis Gallagher's husband has come back to her now. It was sad. She had to leave Harrison. He stayed away for two years. Our dear Baptist church almost never recovered from that scandal.

ANNIE: Mr. Sledge murdered Papa, you know. He was his best friend and he murdered him. We were walking out of the bank...

MABEL: Now, honey. It's no use going over all that. Is it? Nothing can be done about that now.

ANNIE: I saw him, you know. I said, Papa he has a gun. I'm not scared of him, Papa said. He is a coward. And then he called out, Sledge you're a coward, you come one more step near me and I'll thrash you. Papa, please, I said, he has a gun. Papa... (She pauses.) I went to him lying on the pavement. Miss Rosa Daughtey came up to me and she said to pray like you've never prayed before. I don't know how to pray, I said. Get down on your knees, she said, and Jesus will tell you what to say. He's bleeding, I said. Call a doctor. Pray, she said. She held me and she began to pray out loud and Papa was bleeding and people come running from everywhere then. Dr. Green, Dr. Valls and Dr. Barclay. And they stood looking at him and Miss Rosa was praying and Dr. Barclay said you can stop your praying now Rosa, he's dead. And he was. He was dead. And someone called Mrs. Vaughn and she went to tell Mama, and when Mrs. Vaughn walked into our house, Mama said, Is there something wrong with Mr. Gayle? He's been shot, Mrs. Vaughn said. He was killed. (A pause.) Do you know my husband, Mr. Long? Papa never knew him. I had only been out with two gentlemen before Papa died. I met Mr. Long in Houston once when we had to come back to look after Papa's business interests. I love Houston. I love riding the street cars. I get up early in the morning, get on a street car, and ride out to visit one of my friends from Harrison. Inez Darst and her sister Mrs. Knott. Don't tell anybody back in Harrison, but they are terribly poor. Proud but poor. Inez cried and told me all her troubles last week. I wrote Mama and said to send them a hundred dollars at once. Mr. Long says I'm extravagant. He says he is not rich like my poor dead

Papa, and that my extravagance will ruin him. I hope not, Mr. Long, I said, I hope not. Did you all know that Laura Vaughn married Oliver Dawson? They live in Dallas. He works for the Post Office. Quite a come down some catty people say for a daughter of Henry Vaughn. I write Laura three times a day—so far she hasn't answered my letters. I hope she is happy. I surely hope she is happy. I want more than anything in this world to visit her and sing duets. *(She turns to Vonnie.)* What church are you affiliated with?

VONNIE: Baptist. *(She laughs and winks.)* Born one. Expect to die one.

ANNIE: Did you know that preacher that ran off with Sis Gallagher's husband?

VONNIE: No, fortunately.

ANNIE: Did you, Miss Mabel?

MABEL: Oh, yes. I knew him. Never liked him. I knew from the moment I saw him something was wrong. I told my son to keep away from him. And I told my husband, I said Jack, something is wrong with that man. That's your imagination, Mabel, he said, you're always imagining things. I do have a vivid imagination, you know. But even I couldn't imagine exactly what was wrong with him.

VONNIE: What kind of a preacher was he?

MABEL: I don't remember that. At the time I wasn't going to church a great deal. My feelings had been hurt. I had been faithfully playing the piano at the church services for more years than I can remember and there was a faction in the church headed by old Brother Payne who wanted to have a pipe organ installed, and the reason they wanted it because a woman with dyed hair named Ada Jackson, very rich, had just moved into town and she played the pipe organ. So old Brother Payne and the Paynites voted in the pipe organ, and Ada Jackson as the organist, saying, of course, that I could still play the piano, but not the organ. I can learn the organ, I said, but they said it would take too long and since I know when I'm not wanted I said, well, you can just get Ada Jackson to play the piano too, because I'll not put my foot back in that church and I didn't for several years. But then Mama and sister said I was setting a very poor example for my son, so I agreed to go back, although I still won't shake Brother Payne's or any of the Paynites hands. He's a snake, you know. He's always getting up and making long prayers about unifying the congregation. Oh, it's all very well, I said to myself, for you to talk about unifying. You have your pipe organ, which the church can't afford, and Ada Jackson with her dyed hair as the organist, while I sit here with my feelings hurt.

ANNIE: Miss Rosa Daughtey is a Methodist. She lives in Houston now. She used to come and see me all the time. She wanted me to come to her Sunday School class in the Methodist Church.

VONNIE: Which Methodist Church?

ANNIE: The one here in Houston.

VONNIE: I know that, honey. But which one. There are a number of Methodist churches in the city of Houston.

MABEL: First Methodist, I believe, Vonnie.

ANNIE: But she's not allowed to come to the house anymore because my husband, Mr. Long, caught her praying in the living room. She was on her knees praying for my poor dead Papa, and Mama and my Brother up North in military school and my sweet children Renee and Nathan.

MABEL: Honey, you mustn't get the names of your children confused. Your little girl is named Esther, remember? And your little boy is named Davis?

ANNIE: Then who are Renee and Nathan?

MABEL: I think they were the names of two of your Mama's children that died.

ANNIE: Maybe. Anyway, Mr. Long caught her praying and since he is a Catholic it made him furious.

MABEL: Catholics pray, honey.

VONNIE: Not like regular Christians. They have a funny way of praying.

MABEL: Anyway, I don't think Mr. Long is a Catholic.

VONNIE: What is he?

MABEL: I don't know, but he doesn't look like a Catholic to me.

ANNIE: He's a Catholic. A Catholic priest, and he said if there was any praying done at our house, he would do it. I said teach me to pray, Mr. Long. I want to know how to pray. I think if I'd been able to pray like Miss Rosa asked me to when my Daddy was shot, he'd be living instead of dead.

MABEL: You mustn't burden yourself with that, honey.

ANNIE: Do you ladies pray?

VONNIE: I do.

MABEL: Oh, yes.

ANNIE: Teach me to pray.

VONNIE: You can't teach something like that, honey. That's between you and God. Ask God to teach you. He will.

ANNIE: I have. But he hasn't.

MABEL: Do you know the Lord's Prayer?

ANNIE: No ma'am.

VONNIE: Well, then we'll teach that to you, honey.

ANNIE: Why?

MABEL: Because when you know that and someone says you should pray, you can just repeat that. Now—"Our Father which art in Heaven. Hallowed be thy name..."

ANNIE: Pow. Pow. Pow. Pow.

VONNIE: Now stop that. That's the devil trying to keep you from your Christian duty.

ANNIE: Pow. Pow. Pow. Pow.

MABEL: That old dyed red-haired organist, Ada Jackson, used to go over to the Baptist Church and practice day and night. I said to Jack she's just doing that to humiliate me. I don't think she's studying about you at all, he said. Oh, yes, I said. It's a vicious plot of the Paynites to humiliate me. Ride by there sometimes he said and see whose car is parked in front. Whose, I asked him. Mr. Lopez, he said. Mr. Lopez? What's he doing there? Figure it out for yourself, he said. Why that's scandalous, I said. The deacons should know about it. Who is going to tell them, he said. I am not. Are you?

VONNIE: What happened?

MABEL: Nothing as usual. The last I heard she was still practicing and he was still over there, listening, he says.

VONNIE: Is this lady organist a married woman?

MABEL: Oh, yes. And Mr. Lopez a married man. He's a deacon in the church besides.

VONNIE: A woman from a lovely family in Monroe is having an affair.

MABEL: Is she married?

VONNIE: Oh, yes.

MABEL: Is the man she's having an affair with married?

VONNIE: No. He's quite a bit younger than she is. He jerks soda in her husband's drugstore, and he has off the nights the husband works, and she goes for long walks out in the country, even though it's dark as pitch and then he rides out in his car to where she's walking and she gets in his car and they ride off together. I have a cousin that sits in his car uptown and every time he sees that soda jerk's car driving out of town, he follows him in his car. I said cousin you are going to get shot one of these days. The preacher preached a very strong sermon condemning adultery. She was there, and they said the preacher was looking right at her the whole time.

(There is a knock at the door. Mabel goes. She opens it. Mr. Long, 35, is there.)

LONG: Miss Mabel. Good morning.

MABEL: Good morning, Mr. Long. Won't you come in.

(He enters.)

This is my neighbor, Mrs. Hayhurst.

VONNIE: How do you do, Mr. Long.

LONG: Mrs. Hayhurst.

MABEL: We've been having such a nice visit with Annie…

LONG: Your husband left a message with my secretary at work. I just got it or I would have been here before. My secretary said he called me at home last night and this morning and he couldn't reach me. I don't know why. I was home both times.

VONNIE: Maybe he had the wrong number.

LONG: Maybe he did. Lehigh 8170?

MABEL: I don't remember but I'll write it down so he'll be sure and have it right the next time.

LONG: And I'm listed in the phone book.

MABEL: Where is Mrs. Gayle now? Still up north?

LONG: No. She's back South again.

MABEL: *(To Vonnie.)* Mrs. Gayle's Annie's mother.

VONNIE: Oh, yes.

MABEL: We were all friends back in Harrison. Is Mrs. Gayle here in Houston?

LONG: No, not at present.

MABEL: Well, tell her hello for me when you see her.

LONG: I will. *(He turns to his wife.)* Annie, are you ready?
    (She doesn't move.)
    Let's say good-bye to the ladies now, Annie.

ANNIE: Can I ride the streetcar home?

LONG: Sure.

VONNIE: What church are you affiliated with, Mr. Long?

LONG: None at present.

MABEL: Someone remarked that you were a Catholic.

LONG: They were mistaken. Let's say good-bye now, Annie. I have some important appointments today at the office.
    (Annie is silent and doesn't move.)

VONNIE: What line of work are you in, Mr. Long?

LONG: Produce.

ANNIE: My daddy owns a bank.

LONG: Did own a bank, Annie. He's dead, now. Remember? Annie sometimes gets a little confused. It was the birth of the second child that seemed to upset her.

ANNIE: Pow. Pow. Pow. Pow.

MABEL: Have you been to Harrison lately, Mr. Long?

LONG: No.

MABEL: How long since you've been there?

LONG: A year last fall. I went duck hunting with some friends. They have a hunting lodge on the coast.

VONNIE: I was telling your sweet little wife I've never seen Harrison. But my husband works for the railroad like Mabel's and we get passes of course, and some Sunday we're going to take a ride on the train into Harrison and look it over, so we'll know what you all are talking about. I'm from Monroe, Louisiana. I didn't think I could live any other place in the world. I've just come back from there. I had a months visit. It was just like I'd never been away. Have you ever been to Monroe?

LONG: No.

VONNIE: You've been to Louisiana, of course.

LONG: Yes ma'am I've been to Louisiana a number of times.

VONNIE: Some day you'll have to see Monroe. I just love it. We have quite a few Catholics there, you know. But, of course, there are a lot of Catholics all over Louisiana.

(Long looks at his watch.)

LONG: Now we have to go, Annie.

ANNIE: Pow. Pow. Pow. Pow.

LONG: Would you ladies be good enough to leave me alone with my wife for a few minutes?

MABEL: Certainly.

(She and Vonnie leave. He waits for a minute to be sure they're gone. He lowers his voice when he speaks so as not to be heard outside the room.)

LONG: Annie. I'm asking you to be reasonable now. *(A pause.)* Look at me please, Annie, and pay attention to me. I can't stay away from my job any longer. I'll lose my job if I do. You don't want that to happen. Do you? *(A pause.)* What am I going to do with you, Annie? You promised me faithfully you wouldn't go off from home anymore. I can't stay home and watch you. I have work to do.

ANNIE: Are you a preacher or a priest?

LONG: Annie, when you talk foolish like that I'm not going to answer you at all. You're just doing that to upset me, Annie. Come on now.

ANNIE: Don't touch me, or I'll scream. Where is my Mama?

LONG: Now you know where she is.

ANNIE: Get me my Mama.

LONG: She's not in Houston.

ANNIE: Where is she?

LONG: Now you know where she is. I told you five times this morning. I'm not going to repeat it again. *(He grabs her.)* Annie, come on. I cannot keep this up. Come on.

(She pulls away.)

Do you want to be locked up? Is that what you want? Do you want to be sent away to the asylum in Austin, because that's what we are surely going to have to do if you don't get hold of yourself.

ANNIE: I know two lovely boys in Austin.

LONG: I'm not talking about the University, Annie, I'm talking about the asylum.

ANNIE: That's what I'm talking about. There are two boys from Harrison there. Dave Dushon and Greene Hamilton. Greene is older than Dave. Dave is my brother's age. Greene is, I believe, a year or two older than I am. That would make him...Let's see. How old am I?

LONG: Annie, we are wasting time. I can't afford to stay away from work. I will lose my job.

ANNIE: How old am I?

LONG: You know very well how old you are. You just say these things to upset me. Well, I hope you're happy, because I am upset. I am very upset.

ANNIE: I'm sorry. I don't mean to upset you. I never mean to upset you. *(She cries.)* I am very nervous. I am frightened. I don't sleep well at nights. I am tired from lack of sleep. I am very tired.

LONG: I know. I know. *(A pause.)* But let's go home now and I'm sure you will be able to sleep.

ANNIE: I'm afraid to go home.

LONG: Now what are you afraid of?

ANNIE: I'm afraid of being killed like Papa.

LONG: Who would want to kill you?

ANNIE: You know?

LONG: No, I don't. I have no idea who could want to do that.

ANNIE: They want to poison me. I don't dare eat a thing prepared in that house for fear of being poisoned.

LONG: Now no one is trying to poison you. Now, Annie, we went over all that last night and I finally convinced you to eat your food and nothing happened did it?

ANNIE: No.

LONG: Don't you trust me?

ANNIE: Yes.

LONG: Do you like seeing me unhappy?

ANNIE: No. I don't like seeing anybody unhappy. That's why I like riding the streetcars. Everybody is so happy on the streetcars. They just laugh and have such a good time. Are you unhappy?

LONG: Yes.

ANNIE: Why?

LONG: Because you don't keep your promises to me. You don't stay home and rest so you can get well.

ANNIE: If I stay home will that make you happy?

LONG: Yes, it most certainly will.

ANNIE: Why?

LONG: Because I want to see you well.

ANNIE: Why?

LONG: Because you're my wife and I love you. Will you come with me now?

ANNIE: Yes, I will. Are you going to ride home with me on the streetcar?

LONG: No. I'll put you on your streetcar, but I'll have to take another. I have to go down to work, remember. *(Calling.)* Miss Mabel.

(Mabel and Vonnie come in.)

We're going. Thank you.

MABEL: That's quite all right. Can't I offer you a cup of coffee before you go?

LONG: No, thank you. I have to be getting back to work.

VONNIE: What do you do, Mr. Long?

LONG: I'm in produce.

VONNIE: Oh, yes. You told us.

MABEL: Annie, I've written something down for you.

ANNIE: What is it?

MABEL: It's the Lord's Prayer. Now you memorize it and when you feel yourself getting nervous you just say it.

VONNIE: I have three things I say in times of stress—The Lord's Prayer, The Ninety-First Psalm and the Twenty-Third Psalm.

ANNIE: I don't need prayer. Thank you. I need to be mature and self-reliant, a doctor told me., I need tenderness and mercy. *(A pause.)* My husband never knew my father. The other day on the streetcar, out by Montrose someplace, a man came up to me, a perfect stranger, and he said Mr. Sledge didn't kill your Father, your husband killed your Father. Mr. Long, I said. Yes, he said. He did not, I told him. He didn't even know my Father. He killed him, he said. No, I said. You are sadly mistaken. Mr. Sledge, my Father's best friend, killed him. He killed him in cold blood, in front of my very eyes. *(A pause.)* You go on back to work please, Mr. Long, and let me visit with these ladies a little longer.

LONG: You can't stay here, Annie, Mr. Jack doesn't want you here. He's very upset by your coming over here.

ANNIE: I know that. But I promise to leave before he gets here. I'll take the streetcar and go home and he'll never know I've been here.

LONG: Now you don't want to stay in a place where you're not welcome Annie. Besides these ladies, I'm sure, have work to do.

ANNIE: Can I go to Dallas tomorrow to see Laura Vaughn?

LONG: No…

ANNIE: Can I… (*But she doesn't finish her sentence. She turns to the two women.*) Will you come to see me, ladies?

MABEL: Yes, we will. And you come back to see us, sometimes…

ANNIE: Thank you.

(*Long and Annie leave.*)

MABEL: That's so sad, isn't it?

VONNIE: Oh, yes. Imagine her not knowing the Lord's Prayer.

MABEL: I'm sure she knows it, but she's just forgotten that she does. What are you doing today?

VONNIE: I thought I might take the streetcar and go downtown and see a matinee. There is a picture at the Kirby I think I'd like to see.

MABEL: What's the name of it?

VONNIE: I forget, but it's a sweet love story someone told me. I saw the sweetest picture, by the way, when I was in Monroe. I told Sister I just had to take an afternoon off from the parties and go and see a picture. So Sister said all right I'll give you a picture show party, and I said no, I'm going to be frank, I've had a number of lovely picture show parties, since I've been here, and although I appreciate all the attention you show me by giving me picture show parties, I didn't enjoy the parties at all, because the ladies always talk all the time the picture is going on, and just when something interesting is about to happen, one of you friends will say "How do you like Houston?" or "Do you play a lot of Bridge in Houston," or "How do you like living in a big city?" And then they all start giving their opinion about bridge, or Houston or cities, until like I told Sister we might as well just stayed at somebody's house and talked. So, Sister was understanding, and asked if I minded if she went along, and I said no, if she promised not to say a word and not to read the titles out loud, which is a bad habit Sister has, and she said she wouldn't.

MABEL: What was the name of the picture you saw?

VONNIE: You know I was trying to think of it last night to tell Eddie, and I couldn't remember it to save my life. Milton Sills and Alice Joyce were in it. They were in love with each other and then he had an accident and went blind. Sister was so overcome when he went blind I thought she would have to get up and leave. She said it was the saddest picture she had ever seen in her whole life, and I can't say I completely agree with her on that, but it was certainly sad.

MABEL: I think I'll go downtown too and do some shopping. Then I may stop by the Milby Hotel. There are usually some ladies from Harrison in there to use the rest rooms. I always enjoy talking to them. I get news of my friends that way.

VONNIE: Do you think they will put Annie away?

MABEL: I don't know. I just don't know. Mama says it's loneliness. Mama says as rich as they are, they ought to hire some nice refined widow from Harrison to come and stay with them to keep her company and help with the children.

VONNIE: Who stays with the children now, I wonder.

MABEL: Oh, I don't know. They have all kinds of help, but no one she can be congenial with. And she needs a nice white lady that wouldn't be expected to do any housework, but could just talk to her about all the things she likes to talk about, you know, things that happened when she was living back in Harrison. Now she and I weren't especially congenial back in Harrison. I knew her, of course, but we'd never think of visiting, because of the differences in our ages, but I tell you as upsetting as she is sometimes, I used to look forward to her visits, because we know all the same people back there.

VONNIE: My sister is coming here to see me next month.

MABEL: Is she? I look forward to meeting her.

VONNIE: I said don't expect me to entertain you the way you all entertain me. I said people just don't live that way in Houston, you know.

MABEL: I'm certainly giving a luncheon for her.

VONNIE: I felt sure you would. I told her I knew my friend Mabel will give you a luncheon, and I'll have a picture show party for her, of course, and let her talk all the way through it, if she wants to, and Eddie said he'd take us to supper at the San Jacinto Inn. Have you ever been there?

MABEL: No, heavens. Jack won't go anyplace.

VONNIE: Thank you for having Eddie over for supper while I was gone. He said you had such a good meal.

MABEL: Oh, we enjoyed having him.

VONNIE: I tried to have Jack for supper the last time you went to Harrison, but he wouldn't come.

MABEL: No, he won't go anyplace. It was the same in Harrison. He wouldn't even go to Church. Work, eat and sleep. That's all he knows. Mama said, when we were still living in Harrison, sometime I think you spend too much time over here at my house. I think you should stay home and visit with your husband. Well, why Mama, I said. He never talks. We just have Quaker meetings. Oh, you know Vonnie, he's a good man, but he's so quiet.

VONNIE: Eddie is certainly a talker. I used to wonder when I was in Monroe what he'd do when he came home at night without someone to talk to. He called me up once on the phone, and I knew it was because he was lonesome and didn't have anyone to talk to. I said do you want me to come home, I will if you want me to. No, he said, stay and get your visit out.

MABEL: He was home every night too. I could tell the minute he got there, because he always turned the lights on, all over the house.

VONNIE: Bless his heart. I said Eddie go over and visit with Mabel and Jack, if you're lonesome. Oh, they don't want to fool with me, he said, they've had me for a lovely dinner already.

(Annie comes back in.)

ANNIE: Excuse me.

MABEL: Why, Annie. I thought you were on your way home.

ANNIE: Yes ma'am. I started home. Mr. Long put me on the streetcar for home, and he took the streetcar for downtown. I had just gotten past the first stop when I looked around and saw I didn't have my children, so I said to the conductor stop this streetcar at once. Madam, he said, I can't stop it until the next corner. At once, I said, I have lost my children. I am in distress. Oh, I am so sorry, he said, and he stopped the streetcar and I got off and I went running back to the stop on the opposite side of the street to wait for the next car going to your house, but then I got frantic and I thought what will my two little children think of their mother going off and leaving them, so I ran back here every step of the way.

MABEL: Annie. Your children are not here.

ANNIE: Don't tell me that.

MABEL: No, honey. They must be back at your house.

ANNIE: No. I brought them here with me this morning. Don't you remember?

VONNIE: No, dear. You didn't bring them here. I was here, too, with Mabel when you came and there were no children with you. You had pictures of them, you remember. Which you showed us.

ANNIE: A little boy and a little girl.

VONNIE: Their pictures. But no children. None.

MABEL: Now, you stay here with Vonnie and I'll go call your house, and I bet you I'm going to find out your children are there waiting for you. *(She goes.)*

ANNIE: Isn't she sweet? She is the sweetest friend.

VONNIE: Where does your husband come from, honey?

ANNIE: Mr. Long?

VONNIE: Yes.

ANNIE: I don't know where he comes from. He never told me that.

VONNIE: Weren't you curious?

ANNIE: No.

VONNIE: Where do his mother and father live?

ANNIE: I don't know.

VONNIE: Didn't you ever ask?

ANNIE: No.

VONNIE: Have you ever met them?

ANNIE: Who?

VONNIE: Mr. Long's mother and father.

ANNIE: No. I wanted to be in the U.D.C. auxiliary you know, very badly. Every girl in town that I knew was, you know. Laura and Cootsie and Velma and Pauline. Miss Mabel's mother runs the U.D.C., and I said to my Mama I want to be in the U.D.C. auxiliary too with all my sweet friends. You can't, she said. Why, I said, because we were on the wrong side. When were we on the wrong side, I asked her. During the War she said. What War? The Civil War. What in the world does the U.D.C. auxiliary have to do with that, I said. Everything, she said. All of those girls of the auxiliary had fathers and grandfathers who fought for the Confederacy. That's why it's called the U.D.C. It stands for the United Daughters of the Confederacy.

(Mabel comes in.)

MABEL: They are there. I knew they were. They send their love to you. Vonnie, she has two precious children.

VONNIE: Yes, I know. I saw their pictures. Remember?

MABEL: The pictures don't do them justice. You have never seen two such beautiful children in your whole life.

VONNIE: Who do they look like, Annie or Mr. Long?

MABEL: A combination of both. No mistaking who the parents are. They are just precious.

ANNIE: I've got to go home now.

MABEL: Do you, honey. We've enjoyed your visit.

ANNIE: Thank you. I've been nervous. I wake up nervous, but I've got to go home now and see to my children. I have to fix supper for my children and Mr. Long. I haven't a thing in the house to eat. Anyway, I'll stop at the Piggly Wiggly now and stock up.

VONNIE: I like Westheimers myself.

ANNIE: I'm trying to remember that prayer.

MABEL: Just take this paper with you. See, I've written it all out for you. You take it with you on the streetcar and any time you need to remember it, take it out of your purse and read it over a number of times, and before you know it, you will have memorized it.

ANNIE: Thank you. If I don't get hold of myself they are going to send me away, you know.

VONNIE: Who?

ANNIE: Mr. Long, for one.

VONNIE: Where will they send you?

ANNIE: Up to Austin in the asylum. Mr. Long is beside himself he told Mama. Greene Hamilton and Dave Dushon are there Mama says and they are very happy there. They are both from lovely families. *(A pause.)* My children weren't home were they?

MABEL: Now Annie...

ANNIE: That's all right. I remember now, quite clearly. Mama took them to give me a rest, she said, because the responsibility is too much for me she feels at present. And I suppose it is. Anyway, I think sometimes I will never in this world see them again.

MABEL: Now, you know your Mother is going to let you see them again.

ANNIE: I suppose. Papa would, but they killed him. Mr. Sledge.

(She gets up. She leaves.)

VONNIE: Poor thing. Are her children at her house?

MABEL: No. A woman working there told me her mother took them away yesterday.

(Annie comes back in.)

ANNIE: Are you ladies going to have lunch in town today?

VONNIE: Yes, I think I will.

MABEL: I think so too.

ANNIE: And that's what I think I will do. Then I think I'll go to a matinee at the picture show.

VONNIE: There's a sweet picture at the Kirby. They say...

ANNIE: *(Singing.)* "The sun shines bright on my old Kentucky home." *(A pause. She looks at the ladies.)* I'm going to Kentucky you know. To the Derby—Mr. Long and Laura Vaughn and her husband and myself are all going up by rail. I look forward to it so. Laura Vaughn is my very best friend. *(She continues singing.)* "So weep no more my lady, weep no more today…"

AS THE LIGHT FADES

ACT TWO: THE DEAREST OF FRIENDS

CHARACTERS

Mabel Votaugh
Jack Votaugh
Vonnie Hayhurst
Eddie Hayhurst

Place: Houston, Texas
Time: Early fall, 1924
The living room of Jack and Mabel Votaugh's apartment. At rise Jack is in an easy chair with his eyes closed. Mabel comes in. She gets a crossword puzzle and she begins to work at it.

MABEL: Jack, what is a seven letter word beginning with 'K' that means…
(Jack begins snoring slightly. She looks over at him realizing he is asleep. She sighs, goes back to work on the puzzle. After a beat she goes to the window and looks out. Then she gets a deck of cards and begins a game of solitaire. Vonnie enters. Mabel gestures to her to be quiet and Vonnie tiptoes across the room to Mabel. Mabel, pointing and whispering.)
Jack is asleep.

VONNIE: I can see that.

MABEL: *(Whispering.)* Do you want to play some honeymoon bridge?

VONNIE: *(Whispering.)* All right.
(Mabel shuffles and deals the cards and they begin to play. They play in silence for a beat. Jack opens his eyes.)

JACK: Mabel.

MABEL: Yes.

JACK: What time is it?

MABEL: Eight o'clock. Vonnie is here.

JACK: Is Eddie with her?

MABEL: No.

JACK: Where is he?

MABEL: I don't know. *(To Vonnie.)* Where is he?

VONNIE: Still at work.

JACK: At eight o'clock at night? Isn't he still on the day run?

VONNIE: Yes, but he's been working two shifts lately.

JACK: Since when?

VONNIE: Since day before yesterday.

JACK: What's today?

MABEL: It's Thursday.

JACK: Thursday the what?

MABEL: The twelfth.

JACK: And tomorrow is the thirteenth then?

MABEL: Yes.

JACK: Friday the thirteenth.

MABEL: Yes. Thank God I'm not superstitious.

(He closes his eyes. Vonnie begins crying.)

JACK: Who is that crying?

MABEL: Vonnie.

JACK: Why is she crying?

MABEL: I don't know, Jack. Mercy—

JACK: Aren't you going to ask her. She may be sick.

MABEL: Are you sick Vonnie, honey?

(Vonnie shakes her head, "no," and then cries even louder. Jack sits up in his chair and stares at her. Mabel is sincerely distressed for her friend. She looks at Jack helplessly as if to say what can I do? Jack begins to vigorously pantomime that she do something. Mabel pantomimes back that she feels inadequate and helpless. Vonnie gets up and runs out of the room.)

JACK: What's wrong with her?

(Mabel doesn't answer him.)

Do you know?

MABEL: Yes.

JACK: Well, what is it?

MABEL: I can't tell you.

JACK: Why?

MABEL: Because I promised I wouldn't. Vonnie swore me to secrecy.

JACK: Is she going to come over here every night of our lives, start to cry and then run home?

MABEL: She's only done that four times.

JACK: Five.

MABEL: Four.

JACK: Five. Anyway I know what's wrong.

MABEL: What?

JACK: I can't say.

MABEL: Why?

JACK: I promised I wouldn't. *(He closes his eyes again.)* Anyway, we won't be bothered by that Gayle girl anymore.

MABEL: Why do you say that?

JACK: I know it. I ran into her husband coming home from work today. Her mother had her committed. They sent her to Austin. He said you get the best care in a state institution.

MABEL: Do you believe that?

JACK: That's what he said. He said the last few weeks had been quite a trial.

MABEL: In what way?

JACK: He didn't say.

MABEL: Who has the children?

JACK: Her mother.

MABEL: Where are they?

JACK: In Houston someplace.

MABEL: Poor little things.

> *(Jack closes his eyes.)*
>
> Jack. Jack.
>
> *(He opens his eyes.)*

JACK: Yes.

MABEL: What do you know that you can't tell me.

> *(He doesn't answer. He closes his eyes.)*
>
> Jack. Jack. What is it you know that you can't tell me.
>
> *(He begins to snore. She sighs. She takes up the crossword puzzle again. Then she puts it aside and starts another game of solitaire. Vonnie comes back in. She has stopped crying. She sits at the table.)*

JACK: Who is that?

MABEL: Vonnie.

JACK: Did she come back?

MABEL: Yes.

JACK: When?

MABEL: Just now.

> *(He opens his eyes and looks at Vonnie and then closes them again. Mabel, to Vonnie.)*
>
> Shall we continue our game?

VONNIE: Yes and I promise not to give way to my feelings again. I'm so ashamed.

MABEL: Well, don't worry about it. Over here you are among friends.

VONNIE: Dear friends. Dear, dear friends. I think friends are the most precious things on earth.

MABEL: And I agree.

VONNIE: Here I am far, far away from Monroe, Louisiana.

JACK: How far is it to Monroe, Louisiana from Houston?

MABEL: I thought you were asleep.

JACK: I was, but I woke up.

MABEL: Well, go on back to sleep.

JACK: How far is it from Monroe, Louisiana from here, Vonnie?

VONNIE: I don't know exactly. Maybe three hundred and fifty miles.

(Jack goes back to sleep. The women play cards. Jack begins to snore. Vonnie, whispering.)

Does Jack suspect anything?

MABEL: I don't know.

VONNIE: Does he ask any questions?

MABEL: Once in a while.

VONNIE: Like what?

MABEL: Like why is Vonnie so emotional.

VONNIE: I guess I am very emotional.

MABEL: Yes, you are.

VONNIE: I cry at the least thing.

MABEL: I know. I don't blame you.

VONNIE: I know you don't. You are such a dear, dear friend.

MABEL: I try to be.

VONNIE: I pray Jack never has to know.

MABEL: Well, I'll never tell him. You won't have to worry about that.

VONNIE: I'd die of mortification if he ever found out.

(They play cards.)

Is he asleep?

MABEL: Yes.

VONNIE: Sound asleep?

MABEL: Yes.

VONNIE: Do you think he'll wake up if we talk?

MABEL: Not if we keep our voices down low.

VONNIE: I didn't sleep at all again last night.

MABEL: You are going to ruin your health, if you don't start sleeping. Have you eaten today?

VONNIE: No.

MABEL: Let me fix you a sandwich. You have to eat.

VONNIE: No. I'd choke on it. Even the sight of food makes me nauseous.

MABEL: Oh Vonnie. Vonnie. Vonnie.

VONNIE: I blame myself really.

MABEL: Oh, my God. Don't say that. How can you possibly blame yourself.

VONNIE: I do. I do. I just do. I am being punished for something.

MABEL: What on earth for?

VONNIE: I don't know. I just am.

MABEL: That's a lot of nonsense and you know it.

VONNIE: If we only hadn't taken that trip to Harrison, but I'd heard so much about it from you and Annie Gayle.

MABEL: Jack ran into her husband today. They said they had to put her away.

VONNIE: Oh, where?

MABEL: She's in Austin.

VONNIE: Have you ever been to Austin?

MABEL: Four times. Three times to the U.D.C. convention when Mama was state president. I was living in Harrison then and I represented our J.E.B. Stuart chapter. And once to a Baptist convention...

VONNIE: Is it a nice town?

MABEL: I think so. The state capitol is there.

VONNIE: I know that. I learned that in school.

MABEL: And the Texas University.

VONNIE: Oh, yes.

MABEL: And the asylum where poor sweet Annie is. Her new home. God bless her.

VONNIE: I wonder if she can receive letters?

MABEL: I'm sure.

VONNIE: I'd like to write to her. I wonder what her address would be?

MABEL: I don't know. I'll get Jack to ask Mr. Long the next time he sees him. Maybe one day I'll get Jack to get a pass from the railroad and I'll go to Austin to visit her.

VONNIE: You better watch out riding on trains with your husband. You never know who your husband will meet.

MABEL: My husband won't meet anyone because he's a stick. I can't get him out of the house except to go to work. He'll never go to Austin with me. He'll never go anyplace.

VONNIE: I wish Eddie had never gone to Harrison with me that Sunday...

MABEL: Now, please it's done. Don't dwell on it. You'll get all upset again.

VONNIE: Oh, I know. But I can't help wondering what my life would be like if we'd stayed home and gone to church. But I was bound and determined he'd take me on the train to see Harrison, because I'd heard so much about it. And take me he did, so I've got no one to blame but myself. I had packed us a lovely lunch to have on the train, and we had just gotten into Sugarland when he said he was hungry and so we had our lunch and he said he was going up to the smoker for a cigar and I decided to have a little nap and when I woke up and saw him talking to this lady two seats ahead of us, and I got up to go to the rest room and when I came back he was in our seat and I said who was that lady you were talking to and he said, oh, just some lady who says she is from Harrison. He said he didn't catch her name, and I said do you think she knows Mabel and Jack and he said he didn't ask and he said he was going to take a nap and I started to go over and introduce myself and ask if she knew you all, but just as I was going I noticed she was taking a nap too, so I decided to read a magazine instead. And when we got to the station at Harrison, she got off the train right away and by the time *we* got off she was nowhere in sight. We had a lovely day too. We went to the Nation Hotel for dinner like you suggested.

MABEL: What did you have to eat?

VONNIE: I had the fried chicken and Eddie had roast chicken.

MABEL: Isn't the food good?

VONNIE: Delicious.

MABEL: Did you introduce yourselves to Mrs. Nation?

VONNIE: Oh, yes. I told you that.

MABEL: That's right. I guess you did.

VONNIE: Remember I told her we were friends of yours and she said what a lovely refined couple you were and that everyone in Harrison missed you and couldn't wait for you to move back.

MABEL: Wasn't that sweet of her to say so. Then what did you do?

VONNIE: Well, then we took the loveliest walk around town and out to look at the lovely old homes and then we went to the drugstore for ice cream and then it was time to take the train home. And who was on the train but that woman. I saw Eddie kind of looking at her and I thought to myself you better not go to sleep again, there is something suspicious about her.

(Jack wakes up.)

JACK: Mabel?

MABEL: What?

JACK: What time is it?

MABEL: Nine o'clock.

JACK: Wake me up at ten, so I can get ready for bed.

MABEL: Why don't you go to bed now?

JACK: It's too early to be in bed.

MABEL: Well, you're sound asleep, you might as well be in bed.

(He closes his eyes and goes back to sleep.)

How do you know that is the woman he is seeing.

VONNIE: He told me. He said he was seeing the woman he met on that Sunday on the train to Harrison. *(She begins to cry.)*

MABEL: Now, Vonnie you have to be brave and strong.

VONNIE: I know. I try. *(She cries again.)* Oh, Mabel. He asked me for a divorce.

MABEL: He what?

VONNIE: He asked me for a divorce.

MABEL: I don't believe you.

VONNIE: Well, he did.

MABEL: When?

VONNIE: This morning at breakfast.

MABEL: Oh, I can't believe it. I just cannot believe it.

VONNIE: May God strike me dead if it isn't true.

MABEL: Don't you give it to him. Don't you dare give it to him. Do you hear me?

VONNIE: Yes.

MABEL: Don't you dare give it to him.

VONNIE: Oh, I'm so humiliated. What if people back in Monroe found out my husband had asked me for a divorce. Oh, dear God. I can hardly face the day. I don't sleep at nights. I toss and turn.

MABEL: What about him?

VONNIE: Oh, he sleeps like a baby. He no sooner hits the pillow than he's asleep.

MABEL: The dirty dog. I'd kill Jack. I'd take a butcher knife and run it through his heart if he did something like that.

VONNIE: No you wouldn't either.

MABEL: Yes, I would.

VONNIE: Oh, no.

MABEL: I certainly would. I wouldn't care if they hung me for it.

VONNIE: No, you wouldn't either. You'd do just like I am doing. Sit here and cry.

MABEL: Oh, I guess I would. Did you ever find out the woman's name?

VONNIE: Yes, I did. He told me yesterday. Rachel…

MABEL: Rachel. Rachel what?

VONNIE: I don't know. That's all he said. Just Rachel.

MABEL: And she's from Harrison?

VONNIE: Oh, yes. Born and raised there. She works here in Houston, of course…

MABEL: Rachel? My God it is driving me crazy. I can't think who it can be. Rachel. Oh, my God. Yes. I bet it's Rachel Carson. *(She gets a phone book.)* Here. Rachel Carson. She lives in the Heights. Oh, the she devil.

(Eddie comes in.)

EDDIE: Do I have a wife over here?

VONNIE: Yes, you do.

EDDIE: Stay and visit as long as you like. I just wanted you to know I was home…

MABEL: Sit down and visit for awhile.

EDDIE: No, I can't. I'm tired. Jack is asleep?

MABEL: He's been asleep. Ever since supper.

(She goes over and shakes Jack.)

Jack, wake up. Eddie is here.

(He opens his eyes and sits up.)

EDDIE: You shouldn't have done that Mabel. Go on back to sleep, Jack.

JACK: No, I'm awake now. What time is it?

EDDIE: Nine thirty.

JACK: Just getting home from work?

EDDIE: Yes.

JACK: I wouldn't like to work at nights. I like my shift.

EDDIE: I still work in the day time.

JACK: Nights too.

EDDIE: Nights too.

JACK: Don't kill yourself.

EDDIE: Hard work never harmed anybody. Are you going home with me Vonnie, or will you stay for a while?

VONNIE: I'm going to stay.

EDDIE: Good night.

JACK: Good night. *(He goes.)*

VONNIE: Mabel tell Jack.

MABEL: Tell Jack what?

VONNIE: All about Eddie and how he's been behaving.

MABEL: I thought you didn't want him to know.

VONNIE: No, I've changed my mind. I want him to know. Jack, he's not working nights. How can he stand there and lie like that when he knows I know where he has been. Mabel, tell him.

JACK: I know all about it.

MABEL: What do you know all about?

JACK: What Eddie is up to.

VONNIE: How do you know?

JACK: Eddie told Cameron Russell about it, and Cameron told me.

VONNIE: Oh, I'm so humiliated. Who is Cameron Russell?

JACK: One of the men that works with us.

MABEL: The dirty dog.

JACK: Who's a dirty dog?

MABEL: Eddie.

JACK: Oh, I thought you meant Cameron Russell.

VONNIE: Was he shocked?

JACK: Sure.

VONNIE: Were you?

JACK: No. Nothing shocks me anymore.

MABEL: The dirty dog. Do you know who the woman is?

JACK: Yes.

MABEL: Who is it?

JACK: I don't think I'd better say.

MABEL: I know who it is, anyway. Rachel Carson.

JACK: You're wrong. It's Rachel, all right, but it's not Rachel Carson.

MABEL: What Rachel is it then?

JACK: I don't think I should say. I'm not really sure. It's all just hearsay. I might give the name of a completely innocent person.

MABEL: Oh, you make me sick.

VONNIE: I'm going home. Good night.

MABEL: Good night.

(*Jack has gone back to sleep.*)

Jack. Jack. What Rachel is it?

JACK: I'm not going to tell you so stop nagging me.

MABEL: All right, don't tell me, Mr. Closemouthed. I'll take the train tomorrow into Harrison and I'll stay there until I do find out. I'll get the name of every Rachel that ever lived there and has moved to Houston.

(*Vonnie comes back in.*)

VONNIE: I found out. It's Rachel Gibson.

MABEL: Rachel Gibson. Oh, my God. I can't believe it. Why she's a churchgoer and she's always acted so pious. How did you find out?

VONNIE: I asked Eddie and he told me. He said he loved her and couldn't live without her.

MABEL: He didn't.

VONNIE: Yes he did.

MABEL: Did you hear that Jack?

JACK: What?

MABEL: What Vonnie just said.

JACK: No.

MABEL: Rachel's last name is Gibson. And Eddie just told Vonnie he loved her and couldn't live without her.

JACK: Loved who?

MABEL: Rachel Gibson. Did you ever hear of anything like that?

JACK: Oh, he'll get over it.

VONNIE: Well, I'll never get over it. I'll go to my grave with the memory of all this.

MABEL: Rachel Gibson. I saw her at Munns shopping just last week. I called to her and she waved and said she couldn't visit as she had a lot to get done.

VONNIE: I wonder if she's in the phone book.

MABEL: Let's see. *(She gets the phone book and looks for her name.)* Yessir. Here she is.

VONNIE: Call her up.

MABEL: Call her up?

VONNIE: Yes.

MABEL: What for?

VONNIE: Just to see what she'll say.

MABEL: All right. *(She goes to the phone. She asks for a number.)* Hello. Rachel. This is Mabel. Mabel Votaugh. Your old friend from Harrison. Ever since I saw you the other day in Munns I've been meaning to call you. You what? Oh, I'm so sorry. *(She hangs up.)* I woke her up, she said. Out of a sound sleep. The sneaky thing. She sleeps and you don't.

VONNIE: What did she sound like?

MABEL: Oh, you know. Just ordinary...

VONNIE: Is she from a nice family?

MABEL: Nice enough. I've certainly never heard of any of them behaving like this before.

VONNIE: Is she older or younger than me?

MABEL: Younger.

VONNIE: How much?

MABEL: I'd say three years.

VONNIE: I'm going to call her up.

MABEL: What are you going to say to her?

VONNIE: I'm going to tell her flat out in no uncertain words to leave my husband alone. What's the number?

MABEL: Lehigh 1087.

(Vonnie gives the number to the operator. She puts the phone down.)

VONNIE: The line is busy. I bet I know who she's talking to.

MABEL: Who?

VONNIE: Eddie. *(She picks up the phone. She gives her own number. She puts the phone down.)* Yes. I knew it. Our line is busy too.

MABEL: How do you know he's talking to her?

VONNIE: I just knew it. He never talks on the phone.

MABEL: He called you in Monroe, you said.

VONNIE: Once in six weeks. Excuse me.

(She leaves. Mabel asks the operator for a telephone number.)

MABEL: Mr. Long. Jack said he met you on the street and you told him about Annie. I just want you to know how sorry I am. I was telling my friend Vonnie about it and she said she would like to write her and I would too, and in time pay her a visit. Oh, I see. Oh, all right. Yes. I understand.

(She hangs up. She looks over at Jack. He is asleep. She goes over to him. She shakes him. He opens his eyes.)

JACK: Is it ten o'clock?

MABEL: Not quite.

JACK: What did you wake me for?

MABEL: I talked to Mr. Long.

JACK: Who is that?

MABEL: Annie Gayle's husband.

JACK: Oh.

MABEL: He said they didn't want anyone writing Annie or going to see her at present.

JACK: Who was going to see her?

MABEL: I was thinking about it.

(Vonnie enters.)

Was he on the phone?

VONNIE: Not when I got there. He was getting ready for bed.

MABEL: Are you going to call her now?

VONNIE: Who?

MABEL: Rachel Gibson.

VONNIE: No.

MABEL: Why not?

VONNIE: Oh, I don't know. I just don't want to. I think it would demean me to do something like that. It would put me on her level.

MABEL: I agree.

VONNIE: Harlot.

MABEL: Jezebel. What we should do is write her pastor and tell him what is going on. In Harrison when Mr. Lewis, who was President of the Bank, was having an affair with that married lady, someone wrote his Minister and told him what was going on and the Minister called up Mr. Lewis and said he was coming over to pray with him.

VONNIE: And did he?

MABEL: Yes, he did.

VONNIE: And did it do any good?

MABEL: No. I'm afraid it didn't, but then some of the Bank Trustees heard about his behavior and went to him and told him if he didn't stop his carrying on he would have to resign as President of the Bank.

VONNIE: And then what happened?

MABEL: He had a nervous breakdown. I called Mr. Long about an address for Annie. He said they didn't want anyone getting in touch with her at present.

(Vonnie gets up.)

VONNIE: I'm going home.

MABEL: Are you tired?

VONNIE: Mortally.

MABEL: Maybe you'll sleep tonight.

VONNIE: I hope so, but I doubt it. Good night.

MABEL: Good night.

(Vonnie leaves. Mabel looks over at Jack.)

Jack.

JACK: Yes.

MABEL: How long have you known about Eddie and that woman?

JACK: Oh, a day or so.

MABEL: Poor Vonnie. It's gotten her down. She has no fight in her at all. I would fight, you know. If I even heard of your doing anything like that. I would take on you and the woman. Why I'd take a butcher knife and stab you in the heart. I told Vonnie I would, and I meant it too. Even if they hung me for it. Jack. Did you hear what I said? And I mean it too. Every word of it.

(He is asleep again. She looks over at him.)

Jack. Jack.

(He doesn't answer if he hears her, she sighs and looks out the window. He opens his eyes.)

JACK: What time is it now?

MABEL: Ten o'clock. One minute after.

(He gets up.)

JACK: I'm going to bed. Good night.

MABEL: Good night. What time are you getting up in the morning?

JACK: Five o'clock.

MABEL: Oh, my God that's so early.

JACK: You don't have to get up.

MABEL: I'll get up. I always like you to have a good breakfast.

JACK: I don't want you to get up. I want you to sleep. I can fix my own breakfast.

MABEL: Jack do you know what you can give me for Christmas?

JACK: What?

MABEL: You can get me a piano. I miss playing.

JACK: All right. *(He starts away again.)* Good night.

    (Vonnie comes in.)

VONNIE: Oh, I'm so glad you're not in bed. I don't have a single coke in my house. I hope you're not out.

MABEL: No, I have some.

VONNIE: Can you loan me three?

MABEL: Yes, I can. *(She goes.)*

JACK: Eddie in bed?

VONNIE: Sound asleep.

JACK: I'm going to bed too. Good night.

VONNIE: Good night.

    (He starts away.)

    Jack.

JACK: Yes?

VONNIE: Speak to Eddie. Tell him to come to his senses.

JACK: Oh, I can't do that, Vonnie. I can't get mixed up in that. That's between you and Eddie. But he'll get over it.

VONNIE: When?

JACK: Sooner or later.

VONNIE: You really think so?

JACK: Yes.

    (Mabel comes in with bottles of Coca-Cola.)

VONNIE: Jack thinks Eddie will get over this.

MABEL: I know I heard him say that before. Do you want a coke now?

VONNIE: Thank you.

    (Mabel opens a bottle and gives it to her. She opens one for herself.)

MABEL: Do you want one, Jack?

JACK: No. I'm going to bed. Good night. *(He leaves.)*

MABEL: Good night.

VONNIE: Good night.

    (Mabel has a swig of her coke.)

MABEL: Mama doesn't like me to drink these. She's always telling me about Mr. Newsame who drank so many cokes the lining of his stomach was eaten out.

VONNIE: Mercy.

    (Eddie comes in. He has his pajamas and a robe on.)

I thought you were asleep.

EDDIE: I had the light out, but I haven't slept. I'm out of cigarettes. Does Jack have any?

MABEL: I'll go see. *(She goes.)*

EDDIE: I want you to come back to the house with me.

VONNIE: Why?

EDDIE: I want to have another talk.

VONNIE: What about?

EDDIE: You know.

VONNIE: I'm not going to give you a divorce. I told you that.

EDDIE: Please.

VONNIE: I never will. Any way, Jack says you'll get over it.

EDDIE: What does Jack know about it.

VONNIE: I'm only repeating what he said.

(Jack comes out with Mabel. He is in pajamas and robe.)

JACK: Do you smoke *Camels* or *Chesterfields?*

EDDIE: *Chesterfields.*

JACK: I only have *Camels.*

EDDIE: They will do me until I can get to the store in the morning.

JACK: Take this whole pack.

EDDIE: What will you do?

JACK: I have two more.

EDDIE: I can't believe how I've been smoking. I've been smoking over two packs a day.

VONNIE: That's too much.

EDDIE: I guess so.

VONNIE: How much do you smoke, Jack?

JACK: I just don't smoke cigarettes. I smoke a pipe, too. And I'd chew tobacco if Mabel would let me. That's what I really enjoy.

MABEL: Well, you'll not do it. Not while you're married to me. If you are going to chew tobacco, you can just get yourself another wife.

VONNIE: Jack, I told Eddie what you said.

JACK: About what?

VONNIE: About his getting over…you know…

JACK: Well, I shouldn't have opened my mouth. None of it is any of my business. *(Eddie cries.)*

MABEL: Oh, Eddie. Poor thing.

EDDIE: I'm very confused. I've tried to live right all my life, to be good and do the right thing.

MABEL: Of course, you have.

VONNIE: Jack says you'll get over it.

JACK: Keep me out of it, Vonnie. I think this should be just between you and Eddie.

VONNIE: Well, if prayer does any good, he'll get over it. I pray night and day
that he does.

JACK: Can you see the clock from where you're sitting, Mabel?

MABEL: Yes. Ten twenty.

JACK: My god, that's the latest I've been up in I don't know when.

VONNIE: And God usually answers my prayers. So, I'm just going to keep on
praying and I know he won't let me down this time.

(They sit in silence.)

CURTAIN

ACT THREE: SPRING DANCE

CHARACTERS

Annie Gayle Long
Dave Dushon
Cecil Henry
Greene Hamilton

Place: Austin, Texas

Time: Spring, 1928

*A section of an enclosed garden adjoining a ballroom-auditorium where a
dance is being held. It is early evening of a mild spring night. The garden is a
simple one but well kept. There are a few flowers and flowering trees in bloom.*

*Annie Gayle is seated on a garden bench. Near her is Dave Dushon, in his
late twenties. An orchestra is heard in the ballroom, a small orchestra, playing
dance music.*

*Annie and Dave can see the ballroom and dancers from where they are
sitting. Only Annie from time to time looks in at the dancers. Dave stares up
at the night, or down at the ground, never at the dancers.*

ANNIE: It's a lovely night for a dance, isn't it? Everyone seems to be having such
a good time. I haven't danced in so long I bet I've forgotten how. Did you
ever like to dance? What good times we had at our dances at the Opera
House. Remember? *(See looks around at the garden.)* It's been a lovely
spring, hasn't it? Last night I woke up and I thought for sure I smelled

chinaberry blossoms which are my favorite spring flowers. This morning at breakfast I asked if anyone knew if there were chinaberry trees in our gardens here, and no one knew, so when I finished breakfast I went over all the grounds looking for chinaberry trees, but I couldn't find any. Any way, I no longer smell them. I smell cape jessamine and roses and magnolias but no chinaberry blossoms. *(She glances at the dancers.)* Greene is going to the dance. He is getting all dressed up for it. His mother sent him black patent leather dancing shoes to go with his dress suit. He seems very happy. *(A pause. She listens to the music.)* The orchestra isn't always in proper tempo, is it? I think a waltz should be a little more marked for the dancers. *(She looks back at the dancers, hums a little of the waltz as she watches. She points toward the dancers.)* Look. There's Greene. He's dancing. I can't quite tell who he's dancing with. I believe it is Mabelle what's her name from I forget where. The one who says she was born on a plantation called Sycamore. Oh, look. Greene is a very graceful dancer. Very, very graceful.
(The music ends. We hear couples clapping. She claps. Dave has not looked up once.)
I love to see people happy, don't you?
(Cecil, a man in his forties, comes in.)

CECIL: Annie, would you like to dance?

ANNIE: Thank you, but I can't. Thank you so very much for asking me, but I'm married, you know, and I have two children.

CECIL: I'm married, too. But there can be no harm in our dancing together. Lots of people out there that are dancing are married, but it doesn't prevent them from enjoying dancing.

ANNIE: I think I'd better not, thank you. My husband, I'm sure, would be very upset if I did.

CECIL: Oh, well, I wouldn't know about that. It all seems harmless to me, but you know your husband better than I do, certainly. *(A pause.)* May I sit and visit for a while?

ANNIE: Yes. Mr...

CECIL: Cecil, Henry...

ANNIE: Oh, yes, of course. My doctor says I'm not to apologize, but just frankly say at the present time I seem to forget names. And other things, too. But forgetting them is not as embarrassing as forgetting names. *(She turns to Dave.)* Mr. Cecil Henry. Mr. Dave Dushon. *(She looks back at Cecil.)* We came from the same town. Harrison. Forty miles from the Gulf of Mexico as the crow flies. I watched him grow up.

CECIL: I thought you lived in Houston?

ANNIE: I did. I lived in Houston after I married. I was born in Harrison. Where are you from, Mr. Henry?

CECIL: Please call me Cecil. Waco.

ANNIE: Do you have children?

CECIL: Four.

ANNIE: I have two.

CECIL: I'm to be released in another month they tell me.

ANNIE: I hope to be released soon, too. Dave is going away on a visit next month to Harrison. He'll stay for a month with his parents.

CECIL: *(To Dave.)* Then will you come back here?

ANNIE: Then he will come back here. He understands perfectly everything you say to him, but he doesn't care to talk.

(The three sit in silence. The music begins again.)

CECIL: My wife wants a divorce. I'm not going to give her one. I don't have to. I'm well. I'm cured. I'm getting out in a month. *(A pause.)* Do you think I should give her a divorce? After fifteen years of marriage? I've always been a good provider until I got sick. It's nobody's fault, you know, if you get sick.

ANNIE: No.

CECIL: Here's a letter from my wife asking for a divorce. Do you want to read it?

ANNIE: No.

CECIL: It would upset you?

ANNIE: Yes.

CECIL: You have a good husband?

ANNIE: Oh, yes.

CECIL: Loyal?

ANNIE: Yes.

CECIL: Are your children with him?

ANNIE: No. With my mother.

CECIL: My children are with my wife. She has poisoned their minds against me. They have not written me once. *(To Dave.)* Are you married?

ANNIE: No, he's not.

CECIL: How long has he been here?

ANNIE: Five years. Except for the month, usually in the summer, when he goes back to Harrison for a month's visit.

CECIL: Has he never married?

ANNIE: No.

CECIL: How old was he when he came here?

ANNIE: Eighteen. I was living in Houston at the time, but a friend wrote to tell me he had been brought here. I believe he was away at college and went home for the Christmas holidays when they noticed he had not spoken a single word all that vacation. And to my knowledge he hasn't talked since.

CECIL: How long have you been here?

ANNIE: Two years.

CECIL: Two years?

ANNIE: Yes.

(Dave takes a letter from his pocket and hands it to her.)

This is a letter from his mother. He knows I like to read them, because they're always full of news about my old friends in Harrison. No one from there writes me any longer. You see, all my close friends have married and moved away.

CECIL: Don't your mother and husband write you?

ANNIE: Yes. Every day. But they no longer live in Harrison, so they don't know what's going on there.

CECIL: How long have you been here?

ANNIE: Two years. *(A pause.)* Will you excuse me while I read the letter?

(She gets up and moves toward the light spilling out of the auditorium. While she reads, Cecil takes out his letter again and hands it to Dave.)

CECIL: Do you want to read my wife's letter?

(Dave makes no move to take the letter, so Cecil begins to read it himself. Greene Hamilton comes in. He has on an old-fashioned tux and he walks as if his shoes hurt him.)

GREENE: Annie?

(She looks up from the letter and sees him.)

How do I look?

ANNIE: You look very handsome.

GREENE: Thank you. I've been dancing.

ANNIE: I saw you. You're a very graceful dancer.

GREENE: Thank you. I had to stop. My new shoes were hurting my feet.

ANNIE: That's just because they are new. They'll stretch out in time and you'll get used to them.

CECIL: What size shoe do you wear? Wait a minute. Let me guess. I'd say eleven.

GREENE: Eleven and a half.

CECIL: Let me see your shoe and I'll see if you have the right size. I know my shoes. I used to work in a shoe store.

GREENE: I don't dare take them off. I'm afraid I can't get them back on. I had a rough time trying to get them on earlier.

CECIL: Are you married?

GREENE: No.

CECIL: How long have you been here?

GREENE: I don't remember, if I did remember I'd forget.

ANNIE: His father is a doctor. If I had lived in Harrison when I had my babies he would have delivered them. His Mother, Miss Molly, sent the shoes for the dance to go with his dress suit. Greene goes home next week.

CECIL: For how long?

GREENE: A month. Unless…

CECIL: Unless…

GREENE: You know. Something upsets me. Sometimes I get upset easily, not lately I haven't been upset.

CECIL: Maybe you're getting better.

GREENE: Maybe.

CECIL: I'm leaving for good in a month. I'm married and I have four children. My wife has just written me asking me for a divorce. It has upset me greatly. Here is the letter she wrote me. Would you care to read it?

(Greene takes it.)

How would you answer a letter like that? We've been married fifteen years. I was an excellent provider until I got sick.

(Cecil sees Greene holding the letter but not reading it.)

Did you read the letter?

GREENE: No.

CECIL: Why didn't you read it?

GREENE: Because it might upset me. I don't want to get upset. If I get upset, I won't be able to go home on a visit, although I always get upset anyway while I'm there.

CECIL: What upsets you?

GREENE: I don't know. I just get upset. I come from a very large family. My father is a doctor. My oldest brother is a doctor. My sister is a successful Houston businesswoman. I have two younger brothers both finding themselves. I'm the nervous one. *(He points to Annie.)* She's nervous too, and she cries a lot, but I don't cry. I'm just nervous.

ANNIE: I haven't cried all week. I've been very calm and happy all week.

GREENE: Yes, you have.

CECIL: I asked her to dance.

GREENE: She won't dance. She's married.

CECIL: I'm married, and I'm willing to dance. A lot of married people in there are dancing.

GREENE: I'm going to dance. *(He starts away.)*

CECIL: Excuse me. I think I will too.

(He follows Greene into building. Annie listens to the music. Dave falls asleep. Annie sees this.)

ANNIE: Don't go to sleep on me, Dave. Please, please, Dave.

(She shakes him. He wakes up.)

Let's talk. Did you read your Mother's letter? It was very interesting. Mr. Henry Vaughn died at sixty-eight. That came as a shock. Or was that in the letter? Maybe it was in another letter. Laura Vaughn is expecting her first child. She is my very best friend. But there is one thing in that letter that is not true, and you must write her at once and tell her. My husband,

Mr. Long, is not remarrying. That's quite impossible, because he is still married to me. Will you write and explain that to your Mother? And if you don't, please give me permission to write for you, for I'm sure she did not mean it unkindly, and I'm sure she would be the first to want such a story corrected. *(A pause.)* Dave, how long have you been here?

(A pause, as if she expected Dave to answer. He doesn't, of course.)

I told Cecil you have been here five years, and that would make you twenty-three—wouldn't it? *(Again she waits for an answer, before continuing.)* Oh, yes, because I remember distinctly you came here at eighteen. But what is confusing me, is that I just this instant remembered that yesterday was your birthday, and someone, maybe Greene, said that you were now twenty-eight. And if that is so, and you came here at eighteen, you have been here ten years instead of five. *(A pause.)* How long have I been here? I told Cecil two. Or is it four? Have I been here four years instead of two? If it's four my little girl was three when I left, so she would be five and he would be four. If... *(A pause.)* This is what makes me nervous, extremely nervous. I try to keep everything straight and clear. But then these doubts begin and I don't remember anything correctly. Not how long you have been here, or I have been here.

(Greene enters.)

Greene. Greene. Greene. *(She runs to him. She is trembling.)* Greene. Greene. Greene. Do you remember how long Dave has been here?

GREENE: Ten years?

ANNIE: How long have I been here?

GREENE: Four years.

ANNIE: Four years. *(A pause.)* You're sure?

GREENE: Yes.

ANNIE: Of course, that's right. Now I remember. It was raining when my Mother brought me here, and I asked at once to see the two of you, and I was told both of you were away visiting your parents. When you came back, they took me to see you, and I had to tell you who I was, because neither you nor Dave recognized me. Remember?

GREENE: Sometimes, I remember.

ANNIE: Sometimes I remember...I remember my little girl is seven and my little boy is six. I spent last Christmas with them. Of course, I did. I remember... *(A pause.)* I remember...Which Christmas was it? Was it this Christmas, or last? What year is this?

GREENE: 1926.

ANNIE: Did you know Mr. Harry Vaughn is dead?

GREENE: Yes.

ANNIE: Did he just die?

GREENE: No.

ANNIE: When?

GREENE: Last March.

ANNIE: Last March? A year ago?

GREENE: Yes.

ANNIE: And do you know if Laura Vaughn has had her baby?

GREENE: Yes.

ANNIE: When?

GREENE: Right after her father died. My father delivered the baby…

(Annie takes Dave's letter again and begins to read it.)

ANNIE: When was this letter written? *(A pause.)* When was it written? *(A pause.)* There is no date on it. *(A pause.)* I forget so much.

GREENE: And I forget…

ANNIE: But you know, I felt a certain suspicion even as I was reading the letter that I had heard this before. That's encouraging isn't it? You remember Dave in discussing the letter with you and it's news I was not sure if I had read about Mr. Henry Vaughn in this letter or another letter. It was in this letter, but still I felt, somehow I may have heard it before, so when you said to me Mr. Henry Vaughn has been dead a year. It wasn't a total surprise. That's encouraging isn't it? *(A pause.)* There is a lot I don't want to remember, of course. *(A pause.)* But I do remember all the same. *(A pause. She looks at them.)* Mr. Long and I are divorced. I remember that now. They told me at Christmas. Mama and brother told me when he didn't come to Christmas dinner. They sent the children for a walk with the nurse, and they told me. But which Christmas was it? Was it this Christmas, or last Christmas, or the one before? I remember, whichever Christmas it was, she told me we had been divorced for six months. My mother has the custody of the children. She is their legal guardian. She insisted on that, she said, before consenting to the divorce. *(A pause.)* Then I suppose it is true Mr. Long is marrying again, and there will be no need, Dave, to write your mother to correct the rumor, *(A pause.)* but if that is written last March then I suppose he is married already. *(A pause. To Greene.)* Mr. Long was my husband. I don't suppose you ever met him. I forget how long we were married. He was always, always, always, very kind to me and very patient…I met him in Houston. We had gone there to live after the death of my Father… *(A pause. The music begins again.)*

GREENE: Would you care to dance with me?

ANNIE: No, thank you kindly. I'm tired. I'll rest awhile and watch you dance.

(He starts away.)

Greene.

(He pauses.)

When do you leave?

GREENE: Tomorrow.

ANNIE: I thought in a week.

GREENE: No. Tomorrow.

ANNIE: Would you be kind enough to take this note with you. *(She opens her purse and takes out a folded note.)* And give it to your father and ask him please, in the name of charity and our old and dear friendship, to see that mother receives it. I don't think they allow her to receive the letters I've been sending from here, and it is imperative that she get this message from me...

GREENE: All right.

(She hands him the note. He puts it in his pocket.)

ANNIE: Thank you.

(Greene starts away.)

Greene.

(He pauses.)

When does Dave leave?

GREENE: Tomorrow.

ANNIE: Tomorrow? I thought in a month.

GREENE: No. Tomorrow.

ANNIE: Do you leave at the same time?

GREENE: I don't know. My parents come for me at seven.

ANNIE: In the morning?

GREENE: Yes. I don't know what time his parents will come for him. *(He starts away again.)*

ANNIE: Greene.

(He pauses.)

If I don't get to see you before you leave tell everyone in Harrison hello for me.

GREENE: I don't see anyone when I go to Harrison. Except for my mother and father.

ANNIE: What do you do when you are there?

GREENE: I sit on the porch and rock and rest so I won't get nervous. When people come up to the porch I go to my room and shut the door. *(He leaves.)*

ANNIE: Dave, I wonder if Laura Vaughn's baby was a boy or a girl? I must write and tell her how happy I am for her. She waited quite awhile before she was finally married. She went to Mexico on a two month trip, with her cousin Laura Weems, the year I was married. Laura Weems has never married. And some people think she never will. I surely hope you find a nice girl some day Dave, and when you're feeling better, you will marry and have children. I'd be lost without my children. *(A pause. She opens her purse and gets another note.)* I want you to take this note with you tomorrow and promise me you'll give it to your mother and ask her please to see that my mother gets it. I know that my mother has not been receiving my messages.

(Dave makes no move to take the note. She doesn't press it on him. Annie, reading the note.)

My dearest mother and brother: I want to come home and see my children. I know I shall be better and not be nervous if I can only do that. *(She looks at Dave.)* I miss my children. How long have I been gone?

(She folds the note up and puts it in her purse again. They sit in silence listening to the music. Cecil comes back in.)

CECIL: Your friend Greene won't be going home tomorrow after all.

ANNIE: Why?

CECIL: He got nervous, right on the dance floor. He was dancing with a young lady when the music stopped, but he wouldn't stop dancing and the young lady became hysterical and they had to separate them and take him back to his room.

ANNIE: Let's hope he will be all right by the morning. His mother and father will be here to get him at seven.

CECIL: Annie, would you care to dance?

ANNIE: No, thank you. I told you that before. I'm old-fashioned. I don't believe a married lady should dance with anyone but her husband.

CECIL: And I respect that. I would feel the same way if I were married.

ANNIE: I thought you were married.

CECIL: No.

ANNIE: Were you never married?

CECIL: Oh, yes. But my wife died some years ago. I think I get confused about time, so I don't remember exactly how many years ago. I do know I went home for the funeral. She had a very large one. She was very loved and respected in our town.

ANNIE: What town was that?

CECIL: Ennis. A little town in north east Texas.

ANNIE: Oh, yes… *(A pause.)* Ennis. Not Waco?

CECIL: No. I am not familiar with Waco. I have driven through it once or twice is all. Her death was very sudden. It came as a terrible shock to us all. She was known for her charity and good works.

ANNIE: Were there children?

CECIL: No…I'm sad to say. *(A pause.)* It's a nice dance. Isn't it?

ANNIE: Oh, yes.

CECIL: Everyone seems to be enjoying themselves.

ANNIE: Oh, yes. They seem to be.

CECIL: Do you mind if I sit here for a while and visit?

ANNIE: Certainly not.

(He sits. They listen to the music.)

Do you smell the chinaberry blossom?

CECIL: No. Do they have an odor?

ANNIE: Oh, yes. The loveliest most delicate fragrance. I thought for a moment I smelled them. I wasn't sure.

CECIL: I smell cape jessamine. *(A pause.)* I believe you said you were married?

ANNIE: Oh, yes.

CECIL: If you're married where is your wedding ring?

ANNIE: I lost it. My husband is replacing it next week. It's our anniversary.

CECIL: You were married in the spring?

ANNIE: April sixth.

CECIL: I was married in the winter.

(Greene comes in carrying his shoes.)

Are you calm again?

GREENE: Yes.

CECIL: I guess the dancing was too much of a strain. Why do you carry your shoes?

GREENE: My feet hurt.

CECIL: What size do you take? Eleven?

GREENE: Eleven and a half.

CECIL: Let me see your shoes.

(Greene hands them to him. Cecil examines them.)

They shouldn't be hurting you. It's eleven and a half. Maybe your foot has grown since the last time you had it measured. When do you leave for your visit home?

GREENE: I've been. I just got back yesterday.

CECIL: *(Pointing to Dave.)* When does your friend leave?

GREENE: He's been too. And he just returned yesterday.

CECIL: Did you have a good time?

GREENE: Oh, yes. Quiet. I didn't do much. I just sat on the front porch. They've paved the road in front of my house, and there are a lot of cars driving by now. *(To Annie.)* I gave your letter to my father and he gave it to your mother and she said to tell you she would see that you got home for a visit.

ANNIE: When?

GREENE: Soon.

ANNIE: Did she say how my children were?

GREENE: Yes. She said they were all well. She said they missed you and sent their love. *(The dance music begins again.)* If I could get my shoes on I'd go dance again. *(He tries, but he is unable to.)* But I can't. *(Annie covers her face with her hands.)*

CECIL: Annie is crying. Is she unhappy?

GREENE: Nervous.

CECIL: What can we do?

GREENE: She'll be all right.

CECIL: When is the next dance scheduled?

GREENE: In the fall.

CECIL: And then at Christmas.

GREENE: And then again in the spring.

CECIL: One year we had a Valentine's Dance. Remember?

GREENE: No.

CECIL: Do you remember, Annie?

ANNIE: Yes. My husband, Mr. Long, came down from Houston for it especial-ly. He brought me a lovely dress, white net with red Valentines stitched all over it. He said he was my Valentine and I was his. Forever. He wanted to come for the spring dance, but he couldn't get here—business.

CECIL: I'm sorry. It's a lovely dance though, isn't it?

ANNIE: Oh, yes. A very lovely dance. Once of the loveliest I do believe. Although I still feel Mr. Long will surprise me and come to the dance.

CECIL: That would be a lovely surprise.

ANNIE: Oh, yes. I've had many pleasant surprises like that in my life. Many.

(Greene gets his shoes on.)

GREENE: Now I can dance again. *(He leaves.)*

CECIL: Excuse me. *(He leaves. The music begins.)*

ANNIE: *(To Dave.)* Greene is dancing again and so is Cecil. *(A pause.)* Can you see them? *(A pause.)* Mr. Long is not coming, you know. I don't know why I said that, to keep up appearances, I suppose. But I know now, in my heart, he will never come again. And my children and my mother and my brother, have they all deserted me? Certainly not. I'll not permit thoughts like that, for then I'll despair and never get well and we want to get well don't we—for the sake of our loved ones and ourselves.

(Greene comes in.)

GREENE: May I intrude?

ANNIE: Certainly. You are always welcome. Isn't he Dave?

GREENE: Dave? Dave Dushon from Harrison?

ANNIE: Yes.

GREENE: And you are?

ANNIE: Annie, Annie Gayle Long.

GREENE: Oh, yes. And will you be staying for awhile?

ANNIE: Yes. I suppose I will—for awhile…

(The music is heard again. They listen. Curtain.)

END OF PLAY